Beyond Belief

True Story of Faith, Denial and Betrayal

Margôt Tesch

Copyright © 2016 by Margôt Tesch

All rights reserved.

No part of this book may be reproduced in any form or by any electronic or mechanical means including information storage and retrieval systems, without permission in writing from the author.

The only exception is by a reviewer, who may quote short excerpts in a review.

Publisher:
Margôt Tesch
1407 Spring Creek Road,
Cement Mills, Queensland, Australia

margottesch.com.au

National Library of Australia Cataloguing in Publication Entry

Creator: Tesch, Margôt, author.

Title: Beyond belief : true story of faith, denial and betrayal / Margot Tesch.

Edition: 2nd edition.

ISBN: 9780992467524 (paperback)

Subjects: Young women--Religious life--Australia.
  Women in fundamentalist churches--Queensland--Biography.
  Fundamentalist churches--Queensland.
  Hypocrisy--Religious aspects--Christianity.

Dewey Number: 289.95092

Why You should read this book ...

This book demonstrates the courage needed at times to be open to the truth, even when everything within you does not want to believe it. This story highlights the risk of our capacity to deny truth when we hold on to our beliefs too passionately. It may even help you to understand some of the choices you may have taken in your own life.

This narrative provides deep insights into the motivation people have in wanting to immerse themselves within an ideology, cult or religion. Perhaps you are or have been involved in one yourself, or know someone who is, or perhaps you enjoy reading well-written true stories. Either way, this book is for you.

Read on ...

Why I wrote this book ...

Life writing is one way to transport yourself back in time, to try to make sense of decisions made at a point in time. I wanted to understand why I had kept so many secrets, protecting powerful people, when their behaviours were in direct contradiction to the ideology I was embracing. It was important for me to do this with raw honesty. Why had I denied the truth when it was staring me in the face? How is this possible?

Such ideas intrigued me. I uncovered many truths about myself in the process of writing this work.

My approach to telling my story, written as a narrative in the first person, enables my readers to take this journey with me in a fast-paced easy-to-read style.

I've changed the names of characters, organizations and some of the places. Some of the characters have been blended and time-lines compressed to aid the story telling. However, I've worked hard to remain true to my memories, as trustworthy as they can be over time.

This work is a journey through the late 1970's and early 1980's.

Acknowledgments

I would like to thank Rachel Hoff, my editor, and my daughter, Zoë, for their feedback in creating this second edition.

Everyone's contribution helped make Beyond Belief, the experience of a lifetime – both in the living and in the telling.

Chapter One

Brisbane — October, 1976

I paused at the door. The service had already started. The music was loud and pounded my ear drums, like a rock band.

The crowd was large too, larger than I anticipated. This was not a small church.

Robert stopped and turned back when he realized I was no longer beside him. "C'mon," he said. "It's okay."

I wanted to go in, to follow him. But as I stood at the door it seemed as though I was standing on a threshold. *Was this the right thing to do?* Though I wouldn't admit it to Robert, I felt frightened.

Fear had been my friend until now … goading me, driving me to try new things, new experiences.

But could I still trust myself? Should I take this step?

"I'll come in a minute," I called to him but turned away from the door and sat down on a bench-seat outside nearby. I closed my eyes, trying to still my internal churn. Sweat soon broke out on the back of my neck, under my long hair. Usually I enjoyed sitting in the full sun, but today was particularly hot.

As I lifted my hair to allow some cool air underneath, it reminded me of another day ... another very hot day, two years earlier.

◊ ◊ ◊

November, 1974

It was hot. I lifted my hair to allow some cool air on the back of my neck.

Cat and I stood on the side of the highway with our thumbs out. We were just outside Brisbane on the way to the Gold Coast where Don had dropped us off, ready to start our adventure. We tried to sit on our large suitcases, but they were unsteady on the gravel. This was harder work than I imagined. Our suitcases were difficult to lug around. I hoped we didn't have to walk far with them.

It was the start of our new life. We'd broken away from our parental bonds. At seventeen, we were free agents to do as we pleased.

I shielded my eyes from the sun as I looked up to watch the oncoming traffic, hopeful to see someone slow down to give us a lift. My throat was dry, but we had nothing to drink. We hadn't thought about that. Cat held up our crude sign saying "Sydney" scrawled on the back of a cereal box. I worried the size of our suitcases might deter motorists.

Escaping to Sydney was my ticket to freedom. No oldies around to tell me what to do anymore and I would be amidst the excitement and adrenalin of the big city. I couldn't wait to see the infamous Kings Cross I'd heard so much about.

Heavy suitcases hadn't registered in my dream of a more exciting life.

"Do you think anyone will stop?" I asked.

"Maybe if we stick our legs out," Cat replied.

"Mm." I looked down. I had a good set of legs, but no one could see them under my long kaftan. I rehearsed hoisting it up to show them off but it didn't seem very practical. Having nothing on underneath meant I had to be careful swinging the flowing material around.

"Stand so they can see yours," I suggested. Cat's scant shorts were a better option. Her frayed cut-off jeans showed her slender legs nicely and her tight-fitting halter top complemented her perky breasts. Cat was very proud of her breasts and the way her nipples pointed upwards. She never missed an opportunity for maximum exposure. This gave us an advantage today and might be just what we needed to snag a lift.

I looked for something to shade my eyes from the hot sun. I fanned myself with a scrunched up flyer I'd found shoved in my crocheted shoulder bag. We both watched the road.

"I wonder what the time is and how long we'll have to wait here." I was thinking about my mother. I'd lied to her, telling her we were catching the train from Brisbane to Sydney. I'd tried to discourage her from coming to see me off at the station. But, just in case she wanted to surprise me, I'd told her the train left an hour later than it really did. A sharp pain made me catch my breath when I thought about lying to Mum. She would die if she knew we were standing on the side of the Pacific Highway flaunting ourselves, trying to hitch a ride.

The excitement of leaving home and beginning our adventure was waning a little in the hot sun. I wondered what we would do if no-one picked us up.

What if we have to spend the night here?

I looked around for a place to lie down. The shoulder of the road was stony and uninviting. I sighed.

Don's face popped into my mind as I thought about him waiting for us in Sydney. I remembered his goodbye kiss. It had been quick and hurried, just brushing my lips, before he set off in his little grey minivan. I had the address of Cat's older sister, Stella, in my diary where we would meet him again. Thinking of seeing him made me shiver with excitement. We were heading to the Big Smoke. Drugs were easier to get there. We were leaving behind the hick town of Brisbane and the anticipation made my face flush red.

A white sedan pulled onto the shoulder in front, surprising me. A guy in his twenties called out the window, waving us on. "C'mon! You wanna lift to Ballina?"

Cat and I looked at each other, eyes widening.

"Okay!" I yelled, relieved. We had a lift!

You'd have to say we dragged our suitcases more than carried them. I struggled to lift mine into the boot. It only just fitted, so we had to squeeze the other between us on the backseat. There wasn't much room, but we didn't care. We were out of the hot sun and on our way.

I was making my own choices. Where would it lead me?

◊ ◊ ◊

Robert sat beside me, disturbing my day dream.

I looked up at him. "I'm scared. I've done so many dumb things."

Robbie chuckled. "Well this is not a 'dumb' thing. This is a good thing to do. Just give it a try. See if you like it."

I sighed deeply. "Okay. Let's do it then."

We stood up and made our way back to the door. I looked inside.

The atmosphere was electric. The whole congregation was on its feet surging to the rhythm. The music drifted above us, seducing, surrounding … compelling.

I stepped over the threshold.

The service was in full swing now. As I took my seat, I felt it was happening around me. I was there, a witness, but not part of it somehow. There seemed a great deal to take in, which made it difficult to concentrate all the time. The atmosphere of the service seemed to ebb and flow and swirl around me. Something in its intensity made me reflective, caused me to drift back to moments in my past.

At some point the pastor started calling from the platform, commanding my attention. He said, "Won't you come? Won't you give your heart to Jesus? Won't you come?"

Something in his tone, in his earnestness, made my heart beat fast. I could hear it thumping in my ears.

A silent but persuasive drawing power seemed to pull at me. It was almost as though some force was willing me to walk to the front of the auditorium, to respond. I resisted, standing firm in my place towards the back, trying to make sense of it. My brother, Robert, lost in his own worship, was standing beside me. His eyes were closed, his face lifted upwards, smiling. His left arm was raised. He waved it from side to side as his body rocked to the rhythm of the music. His lips were moving in a silent, private prayer.

The pastor was calling again, calling for members of the congregation to respond. "Jesus said, 'Behold I stand at the door of your life and knock. If anyone hears my voice and opens the door, I will come into him.' I *will* come into him. Not *maybe*, not *if I feel like it*, but I *will* come into him."

My mind was racing, my heart drawn to respond. My knees seemed unsteady. A shiver went up my spine.

I saw someone nearby move out of their seat and walk towards the front.

"Thank you, sir. I see you coming. Thank you for responding to Christ tonight. He will change your life. Others of you, God is speaking to your heart right now. He is calling you. Won't you come?" He repeated his appeal as his eyes scanned the auditorium, his arm beckoning.

I had a sense that I was standing on a precipice, that this was a poignant point in my life, a decision time. I desperately needed to change. I wanted my life to be better. I wanted my life to *mean* something.

Uncertain, I closed my eyes trying to resist the pull. *Why am I feeling drawn? What is happening?*

Something about this pull reminded me of another pull I'd felt before, another poignant time. The noise in the auditorium faded and a vivid memory consumed.

◊ ◊ ◊

Sitting on my sleeping bag leaning against the wall and listening to Janis Joplin in Stella's tiny flat, I drew on my cigarette. I inhaled deeply, trying to let the music and the smoke still my churning stomach. Was I excited? Yes ... but also nervous. I closed my eyes and tried to imagine what my first hit would be like. What would that explosion in the brain feel like? I'd heard enough about it. Now it was time to experience it. Cat and I were trying to remain calm as we waited for Don to return with our first score.

We sat for a long time listening to the music, smoking cigarette after cigarette.

Finally Cat broke the silence. "How long is this going to take?" she said. "I want to find out what the hell's so good about this bloody heroin."

Waiting for Don's return was becoming unbearable. We were both on edge. Anxiety and apprehension caused questions to bounce around in my head. *Would he be okay? Would he get busted trying to score? Would he get ripped off?*

It was a relief when we heard Don's muffled footsteps down the hallway. Jumping up, I had the door open before he got there. A blast of musty stale air hit my nostrils as I peered down the dark corridor. I could feel my stomach tighten with a mixture of apprehension and excitement. Don was grinning when he reached us. I could see the gap in his two front teeth peeping through his thick red beard.

A rush of adrenalin made me feel dizzy as I watched him close the door and come into the room. He pulled out a small plastic bag and waved it in front of us. "This is your night girls."

"You got it!" screamed Cat with delight, giggling childishly.

The band around my stomach tightened a notch further. Suddenly the thought of Don sticking a needle in my vein made me take a sharp breath. Memories of needles at school jarred and made my knees feel weak. I sat down, swallowing hard. I had to believe in Don. He was experienced. I trusted him. He knew what he was doing even if he had been clean for a while. Spending time in jail had cured him of his addiction. Being caught busting into a chemist had made him determined to never get addicted again. I also knew deep down he didn't want me to do this. He also knew he couldn't stop me. Don was the perfect person to give me my first hit.

Cat and I huddled around the table watching as he pulled out the gear to get the hit ready. I looked down at my hands. They were trembling.

Don, carefully cradling the spoon, used the tip of the needle to dissolve the white powder. He held the spoon over his cigarette lighter until he was sure all the powder had dissolved. "Who's first?" he grinned as he reached for his belt.

Cat and I glanced nervously at each other. "You go," said Cat.

I didn't speak but nodded and stretched out my arm on the table.

"Are you sure about this?" Don said, pausing to look at me, giving me one last chance to opt out.

Nodding, I said, "Do it."

He examined my vein, feeling it with his finger. "Should be

okay. Let's give it a bit of help." He wrapped the belt around the top of my arm and tightened it.

"Ow!" It was tighter than I'd expected and was pinching.

"Sorry love." He eased it off a fraction but it still cut in. "Pump your hand. It'll help build up the blood."

I could feel my heart thumping in my ears again as I tried to brace myself for the worst bit … the needle. After carefully drawing up the heroin, Don held the syringe in front of his face and squirted some of the liquid out, checking for air bubbles.

"Okay love," he said inspecting my vein again. It was bulging. "Here we go …" I couldn't watch. I turned my head away and clenched my teeth, staring at Cat. Cat grimaced but didn't turn her eyes away. I felt the prick. I clenched my teeth harder but held still.

It was done. I'd had a hit. Don eased off the tension in the belt and rubbed my vein as he watched for my reaction. It was instantaneous, like an explosion in my head.

Now I understand why they call it a rush.

I stood up to move over to my bed and an unexpected wave of nausea overtook me. I was going to vomit! I stumbled to my sleeping bag and lay down, letting the stoned feeling overtake me. Thankfully, being horizontal seemed to ease the nausea and allowed me to give in to the feeling of euphoria spreading over my whole body. Nothing mattered anymore except to enjoy this one moment, to embrace it.

Don said something, his voice drifted over to me. I tried to sit up to hear him, but as soon as I did, a wave of nausea took hold again. I could feel vomit working its way up my throat. I lay back down instantly, letting the stoned feeling wash over me.

There was no further thought about this choice. There was only the knowing that this heroin would now be part of my life … this dreamland I'd stepped into.

◊ ◊ ◊

Rob must have brushed my arm. He returned me to the present, to this strange pull tugging at my heart.

I could hear the rustling of the congregation and realized they were finding their seats. The pastor had stopped calling for people to respond. I could see a small group standing at the front below the podium. The congregation fell into a hushed, expectant silence and the musicians held their instruments still. I could hear the odd cough around the auditorium as an eerie stillness settled.

My heart skipped a beat as I found my seat again. Had I missed an opportunity? Had the moment passed? Had I been offered a better way than the choices I'd taken so far? Am I too late?

I leaned back in the seat and closed my eyes. I could hear the blood rushing past my ears, thumping. I tried to still a rising sense of panic.

Chapter Two

The pastor started speaking again and I sensed yet another change in atmosphere, which made me pay attention. The music had started up again, quietly this time. Though the congregation remained seated, there was a sense of anticipation in the air.

"Won't you come? I know there is someone else here who Jesus is speaking to. There is at least one more that needs to respond. You need to acknowledge Christ tonight. This is very unusual, but the Holy Spirit is pressing me to do this. There is someone else here. Tonight is your night. Don't leave this auditorium without responding to him. He will change your life. He will change you on the inside." The pastor was appealing again, refusing to give up. His eyes willing, drawing, pleading as he scanned the congregation. It was as though he was looking for just one person.

An eerie feeling gripped my chest. Was he speaking to me? Could he possibly be talking about me?

A hush settled on the congregation. Expectancy was thick in the air. It was as though everyone in the room held their breath.

Something had to give. I could hear my heart beating in my temples. I knew my life was on a downward spiral and I wanted desperately to turn it around — somehow. Maybe, just maybe, this was it. Maybe God could change me — make my life better and help me turn it around somehow. Living in the drug scene, despite its initial enticement, had accumulated memories I'd rather forget. It had drawn me into a social circle filled with betrayal, lies and deceit.

Moving back to Brisbane had helped somewhat, but ... where was my life heading? *I need to stop my life spiraling out of control!*

I took a deep breath and stood up. If God was real, maybe he could change me. I kept my head down as I squeezed past the people sitting next to me and made my way to the aisle and out to the front of the auditorium.

A tension in the air eased, the congregation breathed again.

"Thank you for responding young lady. Yes, God has been calling you and waiting for you to respond to him. I knew there was someone else. Well done for your courage." I didn't know if anyone else had moved. I kept my head down watching my feet as I walked towards the front at a slow but steady pace. My eyes were smarting as tears stung.

Somehow I made it to the front and stood behind the other people already there. The atmosphere was strange, weird. I felt lightheaded. It was as though I was surrounded by some sort of presence, an aura. It seemed very bright. It was a pleasant feeling though overwhelming. I closed my eyes and turned my heart and mind towards God, focusing on my decision. I wanted to forget about the people around me. I wanted to be in my own intimate place.

The pastor stopped calling for anyone else to respond. The musicians were quiet again. He looked over the small crowd that was now in front of him. The congregation behind waited patiently for what was about to happen next.

The pastor talked directly to us. "I want to thank each and every one of you for having the courage to respond to God tonight. You will never regret this decision. It will change your life. I'm going to say a prayer and I want you to repeat the words I say. So listen carefully, close your eyes and follow me."

"Dear Lord Jesus,"

"Dear Lord Jesus," we chorused.

"I confess my sins tonight, right now."

We repeated.

"I ask you to forgive me for all the wrong things I've done in my life."

I could feel tears welling up inside me. I had trouble containing them. It was as though all the sadness gathered so far in my lifetime was welling up and wanted to spill out like water, overflowing.

We continued repeating each line after him though I had to drop my voice as it trembled with emotion.

"I open the door of my heart and I ask you to come in and live with me."

"I acknowledge that you are the Son of God and that you died for my sins."

"I accept you as my Lord and Savior, right now."

As I repeated each line and thought about the words, it was as though guilt was draining out of me. My inner being was overcome with a wonderful sense of relief, a sense of peace. For some inexplicable reason, I felt as though I was going to be okay now. My life was not ruined. God loved me and was going to help me from now on. I wanted to kneel down and sob, but was too self-conscious. Instead, a few tears slipped out and streamed down my face. I couldn't stop them.

The refrain had come to an end. I could still feel the tears on my face. Stealing a few furtive glances around me, I saw other wet cheeks.

"Now I want you to follow John Fieldman over there. Give them a wave, John. John is going to take you downstairs briefly and give you some things you can take home to help you. You are starting your Christian walk tonight. John and some other folk will tell you what you need to do next. It won't take long, then you can go back to your seats. You will never regret this night. Welcome to the Kingdom of God. Everyone, give them a clap as they leave."

Applause pealed out across the auditorium and, as if on cue, the music picked up its beat at the same time.

John, a tall slender man with flowing blonde hair, had a Bible tucked under one arm. He led us down some stairs behind the podium, his face beaming. Behind us now, I could hear singing, clapping and the sound of shoes tapping on the floor. It sounded like the congregation was dancing. I resisted the urge to look back and followed the young man in front. The door closed behind us and I found myself in a musty, dimly lit room. The magic of the auditorium seemed suddenly eerily distant.

Have I made the right decision? What am I doing here?

A young woman approached me as I stood looking around a little bewildered. She took me by the hand, smiling. "Hi. My name's Carol. I'm so glad you gave your life to Jesus tonight. Come and sit over here with me and we can have a little chat."

We sat down on the floor. My head still felt a little light, but Carol's warm enthusiasm helped to dispel my momentary hesitation and feeling of disorientation. She gave me some tissues and I managed to regain some composure.

"Here is our new Christian pack. It's got lots of information for you. And there's this too." Carol handed me an envelope full of papers and she pulled out a form.

"You don't have to fill this out, but if you do, someone will come and visit you to see how you're going." As we sat cross-legged on the floor, Carol talked about the youth group and the exciting events they organized. "Here's our latest newsletter," she said, pulling out another sheet. "We have the best fun; I can't tell you how good it is. You have to come along. It's a great place to make new friends."

"Okay," I said, feeling uncertain.

"How did you come to be here tonight?"

"Oh, well … my brother asked me to come. He's been coming here for a while. I came with him."

"Okay. What's his name?"

"Robert, Robert White."

"Robbie? Really? You're his sister. That's great!" It was obvious from Carol's enthusiasm that she liked Robert very much.

We talked further. I liked her. She was friendly. Chatting with her was helping me find some confidence in my decision. I could feel myself relaxing a little. I didn't know what it meant to be a Christian. I wondered what I was supposed to do now.

"Where do you live, Megan?"

"Um, ah, I live with my boyfriend Don. We've got a flat in New Farm."

Carol pulled her head back suddenly. Though she kept smiling at me, I felt a subtle change in her composure. "Hey Megan, how about you fill out that form? You won't regret it. I promise. It will help to have someone come and visit you. It really will."

"Oh, okay. I guess."

"While you're doing that, I'm going off for a bit. I want you to meet someone," she said as she got up and moved away.

I looked around the room. It was buzzing with conversations. Holding the form Carol had given me in one hand and the pen in the other, I hesitated. *Do I want to fill it out?* Faced with yet another decision, I felt weary.

Noticing a post nearby, I moved over so that I could lean against it. Tilting my head back, I closed my eyes, wondering at my situation. I didn't know what it meant ... to call myself a Christian. Another memory jostled for my attention.

It was getting close to midnight as I followed Stella the few blocks from our little flat up to the Cross. She was on her way to work and had invited me to come with her. She'd probably only given me the invitation because I'd pressed her with so many questions. But when I'd quizzed her, she had seemed genuinely proud that she found it quite easy to pull tricks. This, of course, fascinated me further. It was like looking at life from a completely new ... and strange ... perspective.

I was now living with a prostitute with job satisfaction. *Huh?*

This was a long way from my childhood growing up in suburban Chelmer, Brisbane, but my insatiable appetite to learn new things and understand life drove my inquisitiveness, as usual.

Prostitutes weren't evil. They were people, like everyone else, trying to earn a living. Here I was following one to her "beat".

Stella kept turning back to make sure I was close behind her. "It's not far," she said. "I've got a spot on the next street."

"Okay," I said, puffing a bit from the walk up the hill.

Finally Stella stopped and turned around. "Here it is." She looked down at her loose fitting short kaftan. Stella was a big girl and her choice of outfit had been considered. Her black bra, completely visible through the sheer white material gave exposure to what she considered her best asset. The kaftan was short and though her legs where pale and a little chunky, her platform shoes helped to create a pleasant presentation.

Fluffing up her blonde wavy hair, she laughed nervously. "Well, this is it." She looked up the street at the oncoming traffic. Though there were some people walking on the footpath, it was relatively quiet for the Cross. Things didn't get pumping here until well after midnight. "You stand over there," she said.

"Okay. I feel a bit weird."

She pulled a funny face and her smile dropped. "I do too to be honest." She chewed on one of her fingernails. "But I have to fucking do it. I need the cash so I can score later. I'm already itching." She started scratching under one arm.

A horn tooted and she turned around immediately with a plastic smile. "Hey honey," she called.

The car pulled in to the curb and a man wound down his window. He pulled a cigarette out of his mouth but he didn't speak to Stella. He didn't even look at her. Instead he nodded in my direction. "Her," he said.

I gulped air, shocked. I realized that by association, by being here, I was considered a prostitute too. *My God!*

Stella's face dropped. "She's not working. It's me or nothin'."

The man looked her up and down. In a moment the window was up and the car gone.

Stella's face was smitten momentarily, then she brightened almost as quickly. "It's the Greeks that like me. They love a bit of meat on a girl," she said, shaking a lump of her generous stomach in her hands. "The Greeks and the Italians."

It was an awkward moment. "Stella, I think I better go."

"Yeah, me too. Ya better go. It's not all roses, but it's not all bad either. I can make this work."

"Of course you can."

"You be right getting home?"

"Sure."

I turned and walked off at pace, not looking back. But as I hurried away, I couldn't help wondering if this was where I might be heading. The thought burdened me. It made me wonder whether it might be time to go back to Brisbane and … get out of here.

I opened my eyes, feeling sick again. In retrospect, perhaps being called a Christian was not such a bad thing. I picked up the pen and started filling out the form.

Before I'd finished, Carol returned with another woman.

"Hi Megan. This is Andrea Dawkins. I wanted you to meet her. She's our youth leader and would like to talk to you for a minute. I'll leave you to chat. It was great meeting you. Hope to see you at the next youth meeting. We're going to the beach for the day. Get Robbie to bring you along. See ya!"

"Bye. Thanks."

Carol left and Andrea took her place on the floor next to me.

"Hi Megan." She took my hand and smiled warmly, looking straight into my eyes. "I'm glad you made the decision to invite Jesus into your life tonight."

Shrugging, I said, "Thanks".

"Carol told me you're living with your boyfriend."

"Yeah, Don. We've been together for a couple of years. We've got a flat in New Farm."

"Is he a Christian?"

"Ha! Not likely! No, Don's no Christian. He wasn't interested in coming with me tonight."

"You know Megan, God is very clear about people living together when they aren't married. You have made such a great choice tonight and you know, you need to go all the way. I've found the best thing is to not hesitate when you commit your life to Christ. You have to jump in boots and all."

I looked at her a bit puzzled, unsure where she was going.

"Megan, you need to go home tonight, pack up your things and move out."

I gasped and looked at her wide-eyed. "Move out tonight?" I could feel the tears starting again. This was too much.

"You know God will reward you for your obedience to him. There's no grey with God. It's black and white. Living with someone when you aren't married isn't right. I think it would be the best for you to make this decision right here and now. Go all the way and follow God."

I couldn't stop the tears. I looked down, trying to comprehend what she was asking me to do. I wanted to do the right thing and get my life in order. I had made the decision to follow God's way, but this seemed a much higher price than I anticipated.

"Will you do it?" she was looking deeply into my eyes, appealing to me, urging me.

"I don't know," I replied.

Andrea continued to talk, working hard to persuade me to move out tonight. The tears wouldn't stop flowing when I thought about leaving Don so abruptly, so dramatically, but eventually her emphatic coaxing became too much.

I succumbed. I agreed to go home that night with my brother Robert who was still living with Mum.

Andrea was ecstatic. "Good on you," she said, glowing. "God will reward you and you will have an amazing walk with him. Making a decision like this will enable him to do so much in your life. He'll be able to help you change dramatically because of your courage. This is such an important night for you. I admire you already."

She hugged me and walked back with me to find Robert in the auditorium.

Robert grinned, beaming joy and excitement. "I knew you were ready! I knew you were ready! I knew if I could get you to come with me, something would happen and it has." He wrapped his arms around me in a bear-like hug.

◊ ◊ ◊

Mum pulled out the fold-up bed and put it up in the lounge room for me. She seemed pleased to have me home, pleased at my decision to become a Christian. I still didn't know what that really meant. I felt exhausted. So much had happened so quickly, I needed time to work things through in my head.

Finally alone, the tears flowed again. I cried into my pillow. I thought about Don at home. He would be wondering where I was and why I hadn't come in. The evening had been touching, moving, life changing, yet so very hard, all at the same time.

I cried some more before falling into a restless sleep, tossing and turning.

Chapter Three

It was a sultry summer evening as we sped up the highway towards Gympie. We had both wound down our windows in the hope that the warm air would cool us a little as it raced through the car, trying to find a way out. I knew my hair would be a mass of knots by the time we arrived, despite my ponytail.

I was nervous but excited at the same time. This would be my first youth camp. I'd heard so much about them, but that didn't stop me being apprehensive.

"Amazing things happen when you go to youth camp." "Your life will be changed," I'd been told. "Miracles can happen." "It's so much fun."

I was glad Robert was with me and that he had promised to look after me.

The changes in my life had been steady and sure since my big decision four months earlier. I'd begun to get to know a few people. I hoped I'd make some new friends over the weekend. Becoming a Christian had given my life purpose – a reason for existing. It made me feel warm inside knowing that

God loved me and cared about me. I wanted to love him back and show him how good I could be.

Robert was quiet as I drove, gazing out the window. He left me to my thoughts.

I missed Don. Leaving him had been the hardest thing I'd had to do so far. I hadn't been able to do it at first. But after a few weeks, I'd had a revelation, an epiphany. I realized the best thing I could do for *Don* was to leave him so I'd made a pact with God. I was willing to give Don up so that God could reach him. Once Don became a Christian, we could be together again. In the meantime, I just had to wait and pray.

We hadn't fought as I packed my things to leave. Don had been quiet but not angry. He'd helped me put everything in my little blue Volkswagen and kissed and hugged me goodbye.

"I love you," I had said as I got in the car. I could feel the tears welling up now as I remembered him calling, "Bye, love. See ya," as he stood on the footpath waving goodbye. I'd cried all the way as I drove home to Mum's feeling my heart would break in two.

I'm doing the right thing, I had persuaded myself. *This is the best thing for Don.*

All I could do now was pray.

My heart was aching, thinking of him now. The wound was still fresh and deep. In an attempt to dissipate the agony threatening to consume me, I did the only thing I could. I started praying for him as we drove along.

"Are you alright?" Rob said peering at me in the dim light of the dashboard.

"Yeah, but I'm a bit nervous. You won't leave me alone, will you? I'll feel like a jerk standing around by myself. I don't really know anyone."

"You'll be fine."

◊ ◊ ◊

It was dark when we arrived at Araluen, the church's retreat. I was glad Rob was with me. It was intimidating arriving somewhere you had never been before and where you hardly knew anyone. I'd never mixed with people like this, Christians. It made me nervous. I wasn't sure what to expect or what people would expect of me.

We pulled into the car park and the sound of vibrant voices drifted through the car window.

"Grab your bag and I'll show you where the girl's dorm is," Robert said, giving me an encouraging smile as he pulled his own gear out of the boot.

"Okay," I replied tentatively, my eyes scanning the surroundings. We were parked between two large buildings, which I guessed were dormitories. The air smelt fresh. It had cooled a little as the night closed in. I heard some music start up in the distance.

"C'mon," Robert urged. "The meeting's already getting started. Just throw your gear on a bed." I followed him as he pointed to one of the long wooden buildings. "That's the girls' dorm. I can't go in there. Go find yourself a bed anywhere. I'll meet you back here in a few minutes." His excitement was obvious. I could tell he didn't want to miss out on anything going on at the meeting hall.

I climbed the steps and walked inside. It was a large dorm with rows and rows of triple bunk beds. Gear and sleeping bags were strewn around, on the beds and on the floor. It was a big mess. I could hear some muffled voices at the far end of the room, and giggling.

Throwing my bag haphazardly on a spare bunk, I retreated to wait for Robert. I could see the toilet block under the stairs so I decided to go down and take a peep. It was a chance to have a look at the facilities while I waited. I hoped I might be able to straighten my crazy, wind-blown hair.

"Hello," said a girl as I paused at the door to the shower block.

"Hi," I said moving to fix my hair in the mirror.

"We're going up to the meeting. Do you wanna come? What's your name? I'm Debbie," she said smiling. She was waiting for someone in one of the cubicles. She seemed friendly enough.

"I'm Megan," I replied a little shyly. "I'm waiting for my brother Robert."

"Oh! So *you're* Robbie's sister. I heard you were coming. It's great to meet you." She came over and took my hand warmly. "It's great you've started coming to church."

The toilet flushed and the door to the cubicle opened. Another Debbie stepped out. "This's my sister Melissa," said Debbie.

"Are you twins?" I couldn't help asking as they looked exactly alike.

"Triplets actually. C'mon, the meeting's started. We don't want to miss it." Debbie grabbed my hand as she rushed out the door with Melissa close on her heels.

I could hardly refuse. Debbie obviously knew where she was going and wanted me to come with her. I followed them as they headed towards another building. I looked behind now and again for Robert, but I didn't see him.

Oh well, I'm sure he'll find me.

"This's the mess hall," said Debbie as we walked through a large room full of tables with a buffet servery and kitchen to our left. "The meeting room is through here." The music had lulled a little and I could hear Andrea's voice over the microphone as we walked through the open double doorway into a large room.

There were a few musicians playing in a semi-circle on a crude platform. Andrea, the youth leader who I had met on my first night at church, stood in front. Her face seemed alive as she smiled and talked into the microphone. Fifty or sixty young people were already scattered around the room. Most were standing, facing the front. It struck me that everyone seemed to be smiling. There was something else, too, that I couldn't help noticing as I walked into the room. *What is it that I can see on their faces? Anticipation, that's what it is, anticipation.* There was no doubt that the people in this room expected something exciting to happen tonight. The feeling was infectious.

Debbie and Melissa found their sister, Sandra, and made me sit with them. They all looked exactly alike and I wondered how I was going to tell them apart. In fact, I already had them mixed up. Their thick strawberry blonde hair was no help, even though one of them had it pulled into a rough ponytail. I didn't know which one she was. Regardless, their eagerness and excitement were compelling.

As I surveyed the scene, I couldn't help thinking what a change this was for my life. It seemed such a stark contrast to the darkness, the sadness, the lies, and betrayals endemic in the drug scene. Taking drugs had been fun at first, but the scene around it had been a bitter disappointment. The friends I'd made valued using drugs and getting stoned above everything else in their life. Somebody was always getting ripped off. I remembered opening the door late one night to a friend who stumbled inside clutching a stab wound.

But that was all behind me now and while I didn't feel comfortable in this new environment, I was committed to giving it a go. I hoped, now, that I might be able to do something meaningful. I wanted to be part of this place, this excitement, this sense of shared purpose. I needed to get to know these people, so that I could get more involved. Who knows, maybe I'd even find someone I could trust … a *real* friend. It would be refreshing not to have to worry about watching my back all the time.

More young people were coming in through the doors, meeting up with friends and finding seats.

Andrea was working hard to get everyone's attention. "It's great to see you all here tonight. Come in and find a seat. Let's get this meeting started. It's going to be a fabulous weekend. God is here. He's going to do some special things over the next couple of days. He's going to do some special things in *you*. So come in with your heart open. Be ready for something. Be ready for anything. Be ready for God to touch you."

The atmosphere was charged. I couldn't help feeling swept along.

The musicians started up again with gusto – a couple of guitars with drums. I recognized the chorus leader, John Fieldman, as the one who led me downstairs on my first night at church. Reading the words projected on the wall. I tried to join in the song.

"I've found a new way of living
I've found a new life divine
I've got the fruit of the spirit
I'm abiding, abiding in the vine ..."

The triplets beside me were waving to people they knew between jumping up and down in time to the music.

John's flowing blonde hair waved in the air as he jumped to the music. His smile was infectious and his eyes glittered under the lights.

This was more fun than any church service I'd ever been in before. Breathing deeply, I tried to soak up the atmosphere, imbibe it. The music wasn't boring and sedate; it was loud and alive. More people were making their way through the door, which added to the energy.

As Andrea took the microphone again, I noticed how striking she was. Her face was thin, yet attractive. Her rather long, Italian-like nose gave her face strength, definition. Her wavy short brown hair softened and framed her face. She carried her slim figure with a confidence and elegance I admired as she too, moved to the music. I liked her. I wanted to listen to what she had to say.

As Andrea moved the meeting into its next phase, the musicians stilled and we took our seats. It took a few moments for the room to quieten enough to be able to hear what she was saying.

Andrea was talking about commitment. She was talking about something she called "stickability". She spoke convincingly and with passion. Walking back and forth across the platform, her eyes scanned the group making contact with many. At times, I felt as though she was talking directly to me.

She spoke in earnest. She wanted her youth group to count, to be worth something. She wanted them to have the courage to press through difficulties and to be fully committed. She wanted her youth group to be a significant part of the larger church, New Start Centre. She wanted her team to play a major role in the church's vision to change Australia.

"God has a purpose for you, for us. He has so much to do. He needs to be able to rely on you — even when the going gets tough. I know it isn't always easy being a Christian. But you need stickability and determination to stick at what God has intended for you and your life."

The group was silent. Everyone was listening, hanging on every word. I felt something stirring inside me. Stickability. It sounded like something I wanted to have in my life. I wanted to be someone God could rely on. I'd made some poor choices in the past, but I wanted to put that behind me, move forward.

"Being a Christian can be hard," Andrea continued. "You've chosen this path but it isn't always going to be easy. Sometimes God requires us to give up things. Sometimes we might have to give up a lot - things that might get in the way of serving God to the very best of our ability. Things that can stop us from giving our best — things that can distract us." Andrea paused. She had everyone's attention but she said nothing further, waiting for her words to sink in before continuing.

"You might need to give up your time. You might need to give up your hard-earned cash. If you want to see the Kingdom of God grow in Australia and you want to be part of it, you will have to make sacrifices."

Andrea paused again, giving us all a chance to ponder the impact of her words.

"It might be that you even give up the idea of marriage and having a relationship." She paused again. There was a heavy stillness in the air. The room was silent, pregnant with anticipation.

I had the strong impression that Andrea had already taken this step. Andrea had given up her desire to find a husband, to create a family, in order to serve God to the best of her ability. She was willing to give everything to God and now she wanted us to follow her example. She was asking us to give God the same degree of dedication.

It was a big ask, but there was no doubt that her words were challenging me and that her example gave me something to aspire to. Listening to her, watching her, made me feel I wanted to do my best; to give my all.

"I sense tonight that many of you want to go to the next level; that you've made a decision to follow Christ. You've made some changes in your life, serious changes, but tonight you want to take it further. You want to tell God that you mean business. You want to tell God that you are willing to pay whatever price he might ask of you, whatever that might be."

Andrea paused again as she signaled to the musicians to

start up. The music was soft and pensive as she stepped off the platform and walked across the front of the room. Then she made her way up the aisle. She didn't say anything but her eyes scanned the group, imploring. She was giving everyone time to think, but challenging us with her eyes and her manner, her aura.

"Think about it sincerely. Is this you? Do you want to go to the next level?" She continued to walk up and down, looking at us, challenging us, exhorting us.

"If this is you, then I'd like you to come down the front now. Join me. Say to God, 'Yes, I'm willing.' Put your life on the line — do it tonight, now."

She moved back onto the platform. John took a microphone and followed the musicians, singing softly in the background. Some people stirred in their seats. One of the triplets stood up and pushed past me saying, "Excuse me. I'm going out there right now." She marched confidently, definitely down the aisle and stood right in front of Andrea.

Andrea looked down at her and smiled. "Good on you," she said, nodding her head in approval.

This encouraged others to follow. Many moved out to the front, mostly girls, but some of the guys too.

I felt stirred to respond but I held back. But as I hesitated, it seemed to me that if I was going to give this new life I'd chosen a serious go, it had to be "boots and all". I didn't want to be a half-baked type of Christian.

Finally, I turned in my seat and squeezed past the other two triplets and walked out to join the others at the front. Before I knew it, I was crying. I'm not sure why, but the tears rolled silently down my cheeks, uninvited. I wanted to be as committed as Andrea. I wanted to be strong like her. I didn't know if I could be that strong — but I was willing to try.

Chapter Four

I pulled up outside the old Queenslander and turned off the ignition. The yard was unkempt, but a curtain flapping though an open window gave me hope that my friends Cat and Stella would be home. It was a bit nerve wracking, wanting to invite them to church.

I opened the car door, eyeing the front stairs. Suddenly, I couldn't move. Something about those stairs, the look and style of the house, demanded my attention. It was exactly like my grandmother's … where we lived when I was very little.

The sight of it spun me out and had a strange effect. It yanked a long-buried memory. I could see myself sitting on the bottom step as a small child, alone, abandoned …

◊ ◊ ◊

Cradling my cropped brown hair in my hands, my chest heaved as I gasped for air in despair. I was only four. What should I do alone? My eyes squeezed shut, I could feel my cheeks tighten with a curtain of tears gone dry. I had been discarded. Why had I been forsaken?

Where was my mother? Why had she left me, here, alone … now? I'd searched the rambling old Queenslander, looked from room to room, even under the beds. I'd checked downstairs, in the laundry, but I had not found her. Bewildered, I'd discovered an empty space under the house where she usually left her bicycle. It was gone … missing.

She was gone. My mother was gone.

I wished my three brothers were still here, but they must have left for school. I imagined them happily trotting off, holding hands, as they traversed the few blocks to school, secure in each other's protection. But I was all alone.

Would Mother ever return or had she left like my father? I'd waited a long time for him to come back. I hadn't wanted him to leave. He's never coming back, they said. Surely they were wrong. Now that my mother had left, would he come back for me?

No one came to the sound of my cries.

So I sat, alone, sobbing, feeling a terrible weight pressing on my chest … a weight I feared might never leave. It would crush me until all the air in my lungs was squeezed out. I was sure of it. It would kill me. Perhaps that would be best.

"What's the matter?" Mother said as she wobbled up the driveway on her bicycle.

I couldn't speak. My chest still shuddered. My mother had returned, but the weight that gripped my chest was not willing to let go.

"Why are you crying?" she asked again.

"You … left … me."

"I took Robbie to school; that's all. Scott and Michael are walking together. They're big enough now. I can't take you and Robbie at once. I had to take him first. I came back for you … as soon as I could."

"You … left … me," I said again between gulps of air.

Mother peered at me quizzically, one leg holding the bike upright as she frowned, looking confused. I blinked hopefully through swollen eyes, but feared she was about to scold me. "Megan, I would never leave you … ever."

"Never?" I took one big gulp of air as I waited to hear her voice again.

"Never. I don't understand why you have got yourself into such a state. C'mon, that's enough. Get yourself up and wash your face. I'll be up in a minute. Kindy can't start till we get there … the Mums'll be waiting for me."

My mother had dismounted now and leaned the bike gently against the rail of the stairs.

I did as I was bid. I got ready to go with her to work, swallowing my terror, burying it beneath my mother's remonstrations.

It was just another day after all.

Shaking a little from the poignant memory, I managed to climb the eerily familiar stairs. My mother never had left me alone again. But my father never came back. He couldn't now, having taken his own life when I was nine.

But that didn't matter anymore. I had a new and bigger family than ever now … NSC. It was time to push such memories away and see my old friends and hopefully persuade them to join this family too.

At the top of the stairs I knocked and, pressing my ear against the door, I listened for movement in the house. Dull footsteps finally indicated someone was coming. I heard the door latch turn and it was open. Stella stood in front of me.

"G'day mate!" she said, her face beaming in her pleasure and surprise to see me. "Come in. Haven't seen you for ages. How are you? It's good to see you."

"I'm good. I'm good." I replied nodding as I stepped inside. "Is Cat home?"

"Yep. She's out the back. We're taking care of a little possum."

I followed her down the hallway through the center of the untidy old Queenslander, no longer reminded of my grandmother's house.

This place had that hippy feel about it with a piece of muslin draped over the couch and the smell of sandalwood and patchouli oil hanging thick in the air. The house had a quaint but cluttered feeling. Stella, being a hoarder, collected bric-a-brac such as old teapots and unusual pots and pans. She had placed them around the room in a semi-orderly fashion.

I dropped myself rather heavily into a chair in the back sunroom. I'd put on quite a bit of weight lately. I guess it was a byproduct of giving up drinking, drugs and cigarettes. I was glad neither of the girls commented on my weight gain.

"Hello." Cat smiled up at me as she lit a cigarette without getting up. She held one hand protectively over a hessian sack next to her chair which wriggled from time to time. The possum made no noise.

Checking out their pupils as we struck up a conversation, I felt comfortable they looked reasonably normal. I'd heard they were on the methadone program now — a government-run drug addiction management program. It was supposed to help them get clean, but all it seemed to do was enable them to get stoned every day for free. I guess it helped them avoid the criminal element of the drug scene and, of course, it meant Stella no longer needed to work as a prostitute. Thankfully, that world was behind her.

"What's new?" I asked Cat.

"Nothin' much," she shrugged as she replied.

"How's Peter?" Peter was the latest in a string of

boyfriends. I'd only met him once briefly and hadn't found him very inspiring. But Cat seemed to like him and I guessed he was good company.

"He's good, really good. We're planning to buy a boat," she announced rather proudly.

"Wow. That *is* exciting, a boat. What're you going to do with that?" I asked.

"Go out on the bay and stuff," she replied vaguely.

We chatted and caught up on news. But I'd come there for a specific purpose and was just waiting for the right moment to broach the subject.

"Are you still going to that church? What's it called? I can't remember," Cat asked me.

"New Start Center but we call it NSC or the 'Center' for short. Yeah, I sure am. I've been going there for a while now - nearly a year. It's great. I love it. It's really made a difference to me." This was the perfect opportunity to steer the conversation to exactly where I wanted it.

"Yeah, you said that last time you visited too."

"I think it even more now. Have you thought about coming along? I know I've asked before, but I think you'd enjoy it. I'd love to show you what it's like. It's not like any other church you've been to before. Seriously, it's different."

Cat looked pensive, but unconvinced and pursed her lips thoughtfully as she reached for another cigarette.

Stella listened as she ironed what looked like a nurse's uniform in the corner of the room. "Hey Catty, you might enjoy it."

I was surprised to get her support. "Stella ... you could come too. Why don't you both come?"

"Ha ha," Stella laughed out loud. "Never thought of myself as a church-goer. Not sure that's the place for me. Lot of hypocrites I reckon. Hey, do you want to hear something funny?"

"What?" I asked.

"I know a minister who's screwing his secretary!"

"True?" I was shocked. "That's terrible!"

"Hypocrites. That's why I don't want to go to church. They're a bunch of hypocrites, I reckon."

We talked on for a bit longer. I was emphatic. I really wanted them to come. I'd asked Cat a few times already, with no success so far. I had to try again. "C'mon. Why not come along once, so you can see what it's like? I know you'll love it. It's so different. If you don't like it, I won't bother you again. But it's made such a difference to me. I haven't looked back, not once. You never know. It might make a difference for you too."

Cat looked at Stella, weakening, "I'll go if Stella goes too."

I looked up at Stella to gauge her reaction. She seemed thoughtful. It thrilled me that she might even consider it. Cat looked at me and shrugged, dragging on her cigarette again. No one spoke.

Stella sighed, pushing the iron back and forth, checking now and again for wrinkles. Her frown was the only clue that she was still thinking.

"C'mon Stella, just for me, just this once."

"Hmmm. You know, alright. I might just do it ... just once, for you. No harm, I guess, in going along for a visit."

Though surprised at her compromise, I was thrilled. I could only assume that she thought going to church could be a good influence for Cat. As Cat and I had followed Stella into the drug scene, I wondered whether Stella ever felt guilty about that. Maybe she thought it was time to be a better influence. Perhaps she had been able to see what a difference being a Christian had made in my life. Perhaps she thought there was hope for Cat to get involved as well. I could only hope.

But, whatever her reason, I was glad of her support.

"Fantastic!" I was ecstatic. "Sunday night is the best time to come — more of the youth go then. This Sunday night then? I'll pick you up and take you."

Cat and Stella exchanged glances. Stella tipped her head to the right a little, thinking. "Should be okay, I guess. What time?"

"I'll pick you up around five. It starts at six."

"What do we wear?" Cat asked, frowning.

"Just wear jeans and a nice top. It's pretty casual, not like old-fashioned church. You can pretty much wear what you like."

It was agreed. They were coming. This could be a turning point for them, for both of them. It was difficult to contain my excitement.

I'd better start praying.

Chapter Five

The music had already started when we arrived.

Cat and Stella looked around the primitive but large converted warehouse. It was obvious this was not what they had imagined.

"It's different, isn't it? I told you. Kevin Williams, our pastor, started this place and doesn't believe in old stone churches. He believes they're dead and living in the past and aren't relevant today. He's started this new type of church. One that's alive. You're gonna love it. C'mon, let's go and find a seat."

The rows of seats in the auditorium were almost full to capacity.

"How many people are here? I never imagined so many," Stella asked. Cat looked around, wide-eyed.

"I dunno. Getting close to a thousand I think these days. It's growing all the time. Amazing, hey? We might have to get a new building soon."

Stella and Cat looked awkward, tentative, like fish out of water. I was glad they had stuck to their agreement to come.

Though they hadn't been ready when I came to pick them up, they had moved pretty quickly with my persuasion and encouragement.

Now, here we were. It was the first time I had brought a visitor to church. I felt proud. I was no longer the newcomer myself. I was inviting other newcomers.

It was important for them to experience the atmosphere of this place, to feel the hope that I felt. I wanted them to realize that their lives could change for the better. My deepest wish was that they too would come to realize that they had a purpose in life and a reason for being.

The worship and musical part of the service was well underway as we slipped into some empty seats up the back. Stella had been insistent that we sit as close as possible to the door. I suspected she wanted to be able to make a quick exit if she needed to. The congregation was responding to the music: clapping, singing, jumping up and down.

The youth loved Sunday nights and made up most of the congregation, which helped to build a greater sense of excitement. John was leading the singing, which was always a bit louder than the morning service with the tempo also raised a few notches. The music charged the atmosphere.

I looked at Stella and Cat. They looked far from excited and opted to sit down even though everyone else was standing. They were observers, watching what was going on, trying to take it in.

I couldn't wipe the smile off my face. I put my Bible on the chair next to me and stood up to join in the singing, proud of my visitors. I could see some of my friends in front. Robert must have been looking out for us. He waved, grinning.

I leaned down every now and again to explain to Stella and Cat what was happening and to tell them who was who. They nodded and listened and watched, incredulous.

The service proceeded as normal. John, bringing the

worship part of the service to a close, announced that the pastor, Kevin Williams, was away. I felt more than a little disappointed. It was Kevin's preaching that I had responded to on my very first visit to NSC. I had wanted Stella and Cat to hear him too.

I sat down in my seat trying to shrug off the disappointment. They were here at least. I had to believe that something would still happen; that Stella and Cat would be touched somehow, Kevin here or not.

We watched the platform to see what would happen next and my disappointment dissipated somewhat when I saw Andrea take the microphone. As our youth leader, she was always preaching and taking services for the youth, but she rarely led the service in the big church. Even though she wasn't much older than me, she was a good speaker and never failed to motivate and challenge. Maybe Stella and Cat would be moved by her too.

"This is going to be good," I whispered to the girls, explaining who Andrea was. Stella was peering at the platform. She looked a bit funny, quizzical, like something was troubling her. She stood up to get a better look.

"What's the matter?" I asked.

Andrea had begun talking.

Stella was watching her intently, listening to her. Then she turned and looked at me. "Um, I don't know how to say this."

"What?" I asked, intrigued.

Stella's face seemed drawn and pale, "That's her."

"What do you mean?"

"Well, you know I told you that I knew of a minister who was screwing his secretary."

"Yeah …," I responded, puzzled, confused. She had told me that story. I couldn't see what point there was in bringing that up here and now.

"That's her. She's the one. She's the secretary."

I looked at Andrea. I looked at Stella. Cat sat forward in her seat, peering at the platform.

"No!" I didn't believe it.

"That's her. I've seen her. I'm telling you that's her alright. She's the one that's having it off with her boss."

I looked at Andrea talking intently to the congregation as she always did with sincerity and devotion. I was dumbfounded, shocked, disbelieving. My ears were ringing. It was as though a bomb had gone off.

I was trying to take it in, process what she was saying. Yes, Andrea was Kevin's secretary. I knew her office was just outside Kevin's office. I also knew that she walked around her office praying that God would tell her when Kevin needed a cup of coffee. She was totally devoted to Kevin and to her role in the church, both as his secretary and the youth leader. I'd also seen Kevin's wife around. Even though she didn't seem involved in running the church, she was there, every Sunday, every meeting.

*Kevin and Andrea having an affair? Kevin's got three kids at school for goodness sake! He's an **old** man!*

My mind was spinning, my thoughts racing. Stella had talked about this "minister" and his "secretary". Stella had always seemed rather amused by the story, rather than shocked. In fact, when I thought about it, Stella had seemed to find the whole story quite *funny*.

The possibility of *my* pastor and *my* youth leader having an affair didn't seem very funny to me at all!

I pulled Stella's arm and made her look directly at me. "Are you *absolutely* certain?"

"Mate, there's *no* doubt in my mind. That's *her*!"

I turned to look at Andrea on the platform once more, my body trembling. The ringing in my ears was getting louder and seemed to be muffling all other sounds around me.

A vision of Andrea counselling me on my first night at NSC

flashed into my mind. I replayed her words in my head. I could see her face imploring me, unhesitatingly, to leave Don immediately — straight away, that night. I could see her persuading me, telling me that God would reward my obedience. I'd believed her. I'd believed that great things would be in store for me if I had the courage to act as she had advised, immediately.

Andrea was speaking into the microphone with her usual level of passion and authority. I sat back in my chair, stunned.

Andrea Dawkins is a complete hypocrite. She is pretending to be something to everyone in this room. She is pretending to be something she isn't. This church and this so called Christian life is a complete sham. It was clear that Andrea was not living what she was preaching and neither was Kevin Williams.

I stood up, resolved. Such hypocrisy demanded action. "I'm going up there to grab that microphone and tell everybody. This is shocking. Everyone here needs to know the truth, Stella. This is terrible."

Stella grabbed my arm, panicked. "No, love, don't do that. You can't do that. Calm down. I shouldn't have said anything. Calm down. What good's that going to do?" Stella was distressed, imploring and no longer amused at all.

I was breathing heavily like I had been in a running race. I knew I was in shock. I couldn't listen to what Andrea was saying. The meeting was progressing, but I wasn't part of it. I was an observer now, like Stella and Cat. But I wasn't even observing. My mind was racing. I felt confused, mixed up, *angry*.

This can't be right. It just doesn't make sense. It doesn't add up.

I needed to get out of there. I needed to go somewhere, anywhere. I needed to go somewhere I could breathe ... and think.

Chapter Six

Church hadn't finished as we left. Andrea was still on the platform preaching as I led the way out with Stella hot on my heels and Cat lagging behind. I didn't know whether Robert saw us leave.

We headed out to the car without looking back. "Let's get something to eat," I suggested.

"Good idea," said Stella.

"Yeah, I'm hungry too," said Cat.

We drove across the Grey Street Bridge to Petrie Terrace just outside of the city. It wasn't far from the church warehouse at West End. I knew of only one 24-hour take-away hamburger shop in Brisbane. It was just what we needed.

I managed to get a parking spot right outside. Brisbane was pretty quiet this time of night on a Sunday.

We ordered some burgers before getting into serious talk again. My head was still spinning. It was hard to come to grips with the information Stella had shared with me. I wanted to, needed to, find out more.

Being takeaway only there were no tables or chairs, so we sat on the gutter outside waiting for our order.

"Stella, how do you know Andrea is that secretary?" I asked, looking her straight in the eye, probing. "Tell me more."

"Well mate, you know our grandmother lives in West End. She's got a granny flat underneath the house that she rents out. At the moment she's renting it to Andrea. I've seen her a few times when I've been over visiting Gran."

I listened intently, not wanting to miss any details.

"Yeah, she gets good money for the rent," Cat added.

"Once Gran got me to knock on her door and ask her for the rent when it was due. Andrea didn't open the door. A man did and he was standing there without a shirt on. He introduced himself, but I can't remember his name. He was pretty tall with dark hair and I know he was a lot older than Andrea. Gran told me he comes to visit Andrea pretty regularly. Gran knows he's her boss because Andrea introduced him once. Sorry I can't remember his name, but Gran knows that Andrea is his secretary and he is the minister."

"Okay," I said, nodding, trying to take it in but not wanting to believe it. "But that doesn't mean they're having an affair. I admit it's a bit odd that he'd be there without a shirt on, but maybe you're jumping to conclusions. Maybe he was doing some work around the flat for her or something."

Stella gave me a knowing smile shaking her head again. "There's no doubt, mate. I've been visiting Gran when they've been at it. Sometimes Gran gets me to stay overnight to keep her company. I've heard them screwing. The whole house rocks. It's unbelievable. You can hear the banging and it's so loud you just can't ignore it."

"What? You're joking!" I said, shocked. If it had been about someone else I would have laughed, but thinking about Kevin and Andrea in this way was unimaginable. The double standards, the hypocrisy, it was all so deeply troubling and confusing.

Stella threw her head back, laughing. "Mate. This is how bad it is. When it starts up, we put a cup and saucer on the table and wait to see how long it will take before it jiggles off! They really go for it. There's no doubt about it, love. They're both into it."

I grabbed my forehead. My head hurt. Kevin and Andrea had offered me so much hope. They had set such a standard for me to aspire to and now I'd found out that all this time they'd been living a totally different standard.

"It upsets Gran a bit, to tell you the truth, but she doesn't know what to do about it. She's happy to get the rent and Andrea keeps the place clean. So she puts up with it — even has a bit of a laugh about it sometimes."

Cat, enjoying watching the drama unfolding, nodded in agreement but didn't add anything.

The woman behind the counter yelled at us, trying to get our attention. Our orders were ready. We picked them up and walked back to the car and got in. I hadn't realized how cold it was until now. I was shivering and needed to warm up. We sat in the car with all the windows up. I didn't worry about the windows steaming up. At least we were warm.

"What're you going to do now?" Stella asked me.

"I don't know," I confessed. "It just makes me so unbelievably mad! I don't know what I'm going to do. I need to think about it and pray about it … or something!" I groaned. A great heaviness was resting on my shoulders and pressing on my chest. It was sickening. I bit into my burger but realized I wasn't very hungry after all. I wrapped it up again.

"Well I suppose I should take you home."

"Yeah, I think I've had enough for one night," said Cat

through a mouthful of burger.

We didn't talk as I drove them home. I didn't want to talk about church at all. It seemed irrelevant. I had wanted so much for this evening. I'd believed this could be a turning point for Cat and maybe even Stella. I had thought it might change their lives; influence them for the better. But instead we had a mess, and it seemed like such a mountain of a mess. It was too big for me, but here I was right in the middle of it.

This was going to affect so many people's lives. NSC was a big church and growing all the time. This was big.

How many others had made such drastic changes in their lives because of Andrea and Kevin's influence? How huge and devastating was this betrayal?

As I drove home, I pondered what I should do. I needed to talk to someone. I felt the only thing I could do was to talk to Robert but it would have to be tonight. I couldn't bear to sleep on this.

The goodbyes were somber as I dropped Stella and Cat home.

"Are you going to be alright?" Stella asked me. "I'm worried about you, mate. I think you need to forget about it. Maybe you should find a different church to go to or something. I don't think you should go around telling everybody though. I just don't see how that would help."

I looked at her, hearing her, but not really taking it in. "I can't just forget about it Stella. It's wrong. It's sooooo wrong. It makes me feel sick in the stomach. Anyway, I'm going home now. I'm sorry it all turned out so bad. I don't really know what to say." I shrugged. As I gave them a hug goodbye I couldn't stop a tear squeezing out. Embarrassed, I waved and jumped into the car.

What do you say in a circumstance like this? Just what the hell do you say —?

◊ ◊ ◊

My head was spinning as I sat in the car outside home. So many thoughts and feelings were racing around inside me. Things felt out of control and I didn't like this feeling. Just when I'd begun to feel my life was *in* control, this had to happen. I didn't want to think about it. It was too exhausting but I couldn't hide from it.

I pushed open the car door and went inside. It was a relief to find Robert already home.

"What happened?" he asked. "I went looking for you after the meeting but I couldn't find you."

I spoke in a hushed tone so as not to disturb Mum, who was in bed asleep, "Rob, I've got some terrible news and I don't know what to do. I need your advice. I'm going to make a cup of coffee. Let's talk in your room so we don't disturb Mum."

He looked puzzled, but sensed my urgency. "Alright, okay … let's talk."

Robert lived in the flat downstairs. It used to be our rumpus room when we were kids, but Mum had converted it into a flat with a bathroom and makeshift kitchen. Robert lived down there, so he could come and go and do his own thing.

I made coffees and we took them downstairs where we could talk more freely. We both got comfortable on a couple of big cushions. He didn't have a lot of furniture.

Sipping my coffee, I told him everything Stella had told me. I told him about Kevin with no shirt on and the banging they heard when *'they were at it'* and how they waited for the crockery to jiggle off the table.

Robert, who usually kept his feelings pretty much to himself, could not contain his shock. He kept saying, "Really? Is that right?" over and over again. I'd told him everything. It was out now; I'd shared it. It felt better to have shared it with someone.

"What now? What the f—," I was tempted to swear because I felt so exasperated, but I had worked so hard on myself lately to *not* swear. I took a deep breath and managed to stop myself. Instead, I said, "What the *hell* do we do now? My instinct is to tell everyone; to tell everyone the truth. We've been lied to, deceived. All the things they've told us are fake. They're pretending. They're complete hypocrites. I believed it all. I really did."

"Now, hold on just a minute. I'm sure there is some sort of explanation. We need to find out more, I think. God's bigger than all of this. Let's not limit God in the middle of everything."

We sat silently for a few minutes, both lost in our thoughts, both feeling the weight of it all. I could feel it pressing on my chest again, making it hard to breathe at times. I had to shift my position on the cushion to let some air into my lungs. The extra padding around my tummy didn't help either.

"What does the Bible tell us to do? What does the Scripture say?" He looked into the distance, not focusing on anything in particular as he racked his brains to remember what he had been taught. "Mmmm," he said. "I have an idea."

I looked across at him, hopefully. He was right to put things into a bigger perspective. I believed in an Almighty God, a Supreme Being. Kevin and Andrea were tiny dots compared to him. I felt a little relieved, a little comforted. Maybe my world wasn't totally falling apart. I sighed deeply and continued to listen to Rob's reasoning.

"I think the Bible says that when there's an accusation made against someone, you should confront the person being accused. You need to give them a chance to speak, to hear their side of events. I think that's what we should do. We shouldn't say anything to anybody else though. I think that'd be like gossiping. We should go straight to Andrea and tell her what Stella said. See what she says about it. Confront her.

What do you think?"

"Mmmm." I let his words sink in. "That doesn't sound like a bad idea." I tried to imagine what I might say to Andrea.

Robert went on, "I don't think we should be angry and accusing though. I think we should go and talk to her, tell her what Stella said and see what she says. If we're angry, it means we've judged her. I don't think we're supposed to judge her. We need to give her a chance to explain, to say her piece."

"Okay. So we should try and make an appointment for tomorrow. What if she's busy? Does she even work on Mondays? I couldn't stand to wait. I *have* to talk to her tomorrow."

"I don't know. We have to tell her we need to speak to her urgently. Do you want me to do it?"

"No Rob. I think I need to do it. But you come with me, 'cause I don't know what to say or how to say it."

"It's agreed then. We better get some sleep. It's pretty late."

We both looked at the clock. He was right; it was nearly 2:00 am.

We stood up and gave each other a hug. I grabbed the coffee cups and headed upstairs to my room. We had made a decision. We had a plan. We had a course of action to take. It helped with the pain in my chest.

Somehow I managed to push it all out of my mind enough to drift into a fitful night's sleep.

Chapter Seven

We sat in the reception area of the church offices waiting to see Andrea. Dianne was managing the reception desk and answering phones. I had seen her around at youth group events. I hadn't known she worked in the church offices and didn't know her name until now. She had a neat little badge pinned to her chest above her left pocket. She seemed suited to manning reception with her neat blonde hair and welcoming smile.

I felt a little envious of her, working for NSC.

She must get to see a lot of comings and goings, a lot of excitement.

I envied her being in the midst of the Center. Or did I? My mind turned to what I would say to Andrea when we got to see her. I chewed my lip and tapped my foot with nervous anticipation.

The reception desk was serviceable but obviously secondhand. The seats we were sitting on must have been acquired from somewhere or other; no doubt for free as they didn't match. Kevin Williams didn't believe in fancy offices and church buildings. He wanted to invest in God's Kingdom - its people. He had dedicated his life to building something for God. He wanted to make a difference in Australia and the world. His priorities were reflected in the furnishings of this modest office setting.

Andrea had agreed to meet us at four o'clock, which worked out well as it meant Robert and I could get there after work by simply leaving a bit earlier than usual.

Robert seemed to be enjoying watching the bustle in the busy reception but checked his watch every now and then. It was just after four.

"I still don't know what I'm going to say," I said.

"Just say what Stella told you."

I took a deep breath, leaned my head back on the wall, closed my eyes and tried rehearsing something in my mind. Nothing came.

"Megan," called Andrea loudly as she pulled open a door on our left. I nearly jumped out of my skin.

"Sorry, I didn't mean to startle you. Hi Robbie. I didn't know you'd be here too. Come on in, both of you." Andrea motioned us to follow her. "This is my little office." She looked relaxed and her eyes had their usual sparkle.

I picked up my crocheted bag and tried to breathe evenly to calm my thoughts. Robert followed.

Andrea's office was very small. There was just enough room for two visitors' chairs opposite her desk. An electric typewriter to her left was set ready with some paper. Andrea was dressed modestly but business-like. Her desk reflected her sense of order. It was clear except for a neat pile of papers near her typewriter.

We squeezed into the seats in front of her desk and both looked at Andrea, waiting for her lead.

She had a pen in her hand which she clicked nervously. "Well, this is a bit unexpected. I'm intrigued. What can I do for you both?"

I took a deep breath, "Well … it's kinda hard to know how to start."

Andrea looked puzzled at my hesitation. She leaned back in her chair. "Give it a go. C'mon, tell me what's on your mind."

A smile played on her face as she encouraged us to reveal our agenda. I hadn't talked this closely with her since the first night I had come to NSC when she had talked to me in the back room, told me to leave Don. Being in such a big youth group, you didn't always get a chance to talk this closely with the leadership. Normally, I would have felt quite privileged to be here, but not today.

I pushed these thoughts out of my mind and decided it best to begin at the start.

"Well, Andrea, I managed to convince a couple of my old friends to come to church last night. I used to be good friends with them in my old life. I wanted them to get to know about God like I have. It's taken me a while to convince them, but last night they finally came along."

"That's great Megan. Good for you. That's really good news."

"Well, their names are Cat and Stella Ogilvey." I paused, waiting for some sort of reaction or response. There was none. Andrea just looked at me with a soft, encouraging look.

"Yes?"

"Stella says she knows you."

"Really? Stella Ogilvey —" Andrea looked away thinking. There seemed to be a hint of recognition.

"She said you rent a granny flat from her grandmother in West End."

"Oh yes, Ogilvey. I thought it sounded familiar. Yes, Gladys Ogilvey owns the house. It's a lovely old place and close to the church offices. I moved in there not long ago."

I watched her face intently, looking for a reaction,

something. But she just maintained a mildly interested look. I'm sure Robert was watching just as closely, but I didn't look at him.

"Stella told me you were having an affair with Kevin Williams." There, it was out. I had said it, rather matter-of-factly, but I had said it. I waited, watching her every expression, her every move.

Andrea held my gaze without flinching, though her eyes widened imperceptibly. Then she jolted forward. The movement took me by surprise and for a second it seemed as though a spring had thrown her forward, out of her seat.

"What? What did you say? Stella said what?" Andrea appeared genuinely shocked, disbelieving and uncertain.

"Stella told me you are having an affair with Kevin," I repeated, evenly.

"Megan, that's absolutely ridiculous. I would never do that. I'm shocked that she would … that anyone would … think that about me. That's horrible." Andrea sat down again and leaned back in the chair. It creaked with the sudden movement. Her hand was around her throat, her eyes like saucers and her nose flared. It was an unmistakable look of horror. Then she looked directly at me, leaning forward, a little angry this time.

"Why on earth would Stella think that?" She was more demanding now. "What did she tell you?"

It was out now. No point stopping. I needed to bring out all the sordid details.

"She told me she came to get the rent off you one day and Kevin answered the door. He didn't have a shirt on." I paused again, watching her response.

Andrea stared at me, frowning. She thought for a moment and then said, "Well, Kevin did help me move in. We were so busy it was difficult to get time off, so he gave me a hand to make it as quick as possible. He needed me around here as we were organizing a conference. There's so much going on in the church. We're expanding in so many ways all at once. Perhaps Stella saw him around that time. But I don't ever remember Kevin answering the door for me. That would be unusual. What she's told you doesn't make any sense. She's mistaken."

I had to keep going. I had to get it all out.

"Stella said she and her grandmother have heard you having sex. She said it rocks the whole house. They can hear the banging." I heard Robert shift in his seat but he didn't say anything. He had nothing to add.

Andrea stood up, aghast. Her chair banged into the wall with a thud that made the wall shudder. The air seemed to hang heavy, still.

"Oh Megan, I can't believe she said that! This is absolute nonsense. What on earth is this girl saying and why is she saying it? I'm shocked that she would say these terrible things about me when I don't even know her. That is so ugly and so not true and so not me." She gnawed on her thumbnail, obviously distressed. She seemed at a loss to know what to do next. Blood had drained from her face.

I looked at Robert. I wanted to see how he was reacting. He looked at me and shrugged almost imperceptibly. We both turned back to Andrea, watching. We waited.

She walked backwards and forwards behind her desk, pacing. There wasn't much room, so she could only take a couple of steps at a time before she had to turn around. We waited quietly, continuing to watch, trying to make sense of her responses.

Andrea tried to compose herself a little. She turned to us and sat back down in her chair. She looked me straight in the eye and then turned to Robert and looked him straight in the eye. She seemed to be speaking in earnest, as though she had nothing to hide. "You have to believe me, both of you. This isn't true. Stella is mistaken. You know me. You both know me. I would never do something like this, never."

I didn't know what to say. Believing Andrea meant not believing Stella. I'd known Stella for a long time. There was no doubt about her checkered past, but I could see no reason why she would make up a lie such as this. Neither Robert nor I said anything further. The accusation was out there, hanging in the air. Andrea seemed to be wholeheartedly rejecting it. I wasn't sure what that meant, nor how I should react next.

We sat looking at her.

"Banging? What on earth is she talking about? The only thing I can think of is the possums. They're terrible. They make such a noise at night. They live in the big fig tree next to the house and they climb around in the roof and make an awful noise. It keeps me awake at night. That girl is so terribly … horribly … mistaken."

Andrea was imploring us with her eyes now. "You know me, both of you know me. I'm one hundred percent for Jesus. I've dedicated my life to him. That's all that's important to me; serving Jesus and doing what's right for him."

A new idea seemed to dawn on her and horrify her even more. She leaned across the table and took my hand. "Megan, the devil hates what we're doing here. He would do anything he could to destroy it. What our church is doing has never been done before in Australia. We've grown so quickly. I know with all my heart that God has placed a special mantle over Kevin. God has a special job for him to do. He's going to lead a revival in Australia. The devil wants to stop it; destroy it if he can."

She looked at Robert, making sure that he was listening too, taking it in.

"A story like this would destroy us. If people believed such a lie it would be devastating to what Kevin has built so far; to the work that has been done. We can't let that happen. *You* can't let that happen."

She stood up again. "This is so serious. Wait here a minute. I'm going to have a chat with Kevin. I think he's in his office."

She pulled the sliding door open to the right of her chair and I caught a glimpse of Kevin sitting at a large desk talking on the phone. Andrea slid the door shut behind her. We could hear muffled voices.

"She's right," said Robert. "It could ruin the church if this got out."

"But why would Stella make up something like this? It doesn't make sense. It really doesn't make sense."

"I'm sure Stella believes what she's told you. But she must be mistaken. We must be very careful not to talk to anyone about this. Did you tell anyone else?"

"No, I only spoke to you. You know that already," I answered, annoyed at his capitulation.

"Are you sure?"

"Yes, I'm sure," I said, getting angry.

"Okay, okay, then."

The door slid open again and Kevin entered Andrea's office. I'd never been this close to him, nor had I ever had a conversation with him. He was the charismatic pastor on the platform inspiring, informing and teaching me. Now I was meeting him in the flesh for the first time. I have to admit, it was a little intimidating, especially under these circumstances.

He was smiling, charming. He leaned over and shook my hand. "Kevin Williams," he said, introducing himself. "Hello Robert. How are you?"

"I'm good," said Robert, standing up as he shook his hand.

"Andrea has told me you heard some crazy rumors." He didn't give us a chance to say anything. "Andrea is shocked and a little upset at the vicious nature of the rumors." Kevin apparently had nothing to deny. He only seemed a little concerned that Andrea had taken the rumor so personally. I wondered if he had faced these sorts of accusations before. He was confident, sure of himself, unhesitating.

"You know what the Bible says about rumors. I know you don't want to be part of any vicious scaremongering, but when you are in my position you have to be extremely cautious. Even the most ridiculous stories and rumors can be very damaging. The devil is always trying to disrupt God's plans. But God is greater and he has a plan for this church and I know neither of you would want to stand in the way of those plans."

Robert and I both stared at him. Kevin's presence filled the room. His confidence and assuredness was seductive, compelling.

There wasn't anything to add; there wasn't anything else to say. Kevin had addressed the situation emphatically and without hesitation. There seemed no doubt of his innocence. How could his ease and confidence be questioned? I felt consumed, surrounded by his presence. It made me realize this rumor had to be shut down and shut down now.

"Would you like me to pray with you?"

How could we say no? Before we had any chance to reply he had his head bowed and his hand was resting on mine. A tingling sensation went up my arm, emanating from his touch.

We obliged by closing our eyes, submitting to his request.

"God, I ask you to bless these two special people right here, right now. I ask you to give them the strength and courage to be a part of your plan for their lives and to be a part of your plan for this church. I know you have a very special purpose for each of them. God, permeate them now with your special wisdom." He was silent for a moment, but didn't move. The air was thick and a heaviness seemed to envelop me. It was a pervading sensation that left me no room for doubt. *God was in the room.*

Suddenly, I realized that Stella must be mistaken, so

horribly, horribly mistaken. The idea that Kevin and Andrea were having an affair was preposterous. It simply was *not* possible.

Chapter Eight

I walked round and round in circles behind the stage rehearsing the words in my head. I was nervous, excited too, but more nervous. Despite the early summer sun, I was trembling. Every now and then I peeped around the scaffolding that supported the temporary structure to see how many passers-by had stopped to listen. I couldn't really see though, without making it obvious.

"You'll be alright," said Steve. Stephen Green was one of the leaders who supported Andrea and I had always found him to be friendly even though I didn't know him very well. He was standing at the bottom of the stairs holding the running sheet for the morning's speakers and various planned items. He must have noticed how nervous I looked.

"Do you know how many people've stopped?" I wasn't sure whether knowing how many people might be listening to me share my testimony would help my nerves or not, but it was a relief to make some conversation anyway.

"There're a few people gathering. You know how it is. The music always draws a bit of a crowd. We'll get some more morning shoppers yet. It's still pretty early for a Saturday, you know."

I simply nodded. I knew King George Square would be buzzing with Saturday morning shoppers before long. Anyway, it didn't matter how many people were listening. I had to put that out of my mind and simply concentrate on what I planned to say.

Chatting with Steve was a welcome distraction.

"How long have you been part of the street witnessing team?" he asked.

"I did my training a couple of months ago. I've been out quite a few times on Friday night, but this is a bit different," I replied, tilting my head towards the structure.

"Yeah, I imagine chatting with people face-to-face is a lot different from standing on a platform preaching at an outreach like this. But I'm sure you'll be fine, just fine."

"I hope so."

"Well I think it takes guts to be in the street witnessing team. How do you find it?"

"Well, actually ... I like it. It was a bit scary at first, but it's been good to be part of the team. I didn't realize it, but it's been a great way to get to know people. Andrea puts us in pairs – someone experienced with someone new. Sometimes it's tough though, trying to talk to people who don't really want to talk to you."

"Good on you for giving it a go. That takes a lot of guts. I don't know how you do it, to be honest."

"Well you never know, I might actually say something one day that could help change someone's life for the better. You never know. Have you ever done it?"

"Me? Yeah, I got involved for a little while, but I found I can't do everything. I had to make a choice between things."

"The part I like best is mucking around after we've been out witnessing ... when we have supper." I looked around again.

"Last week Peter and John were having races with a couple of trolleys. Those guys are hilarious. It was so much fun. I couldn't stop laughing. I didn't know you could have so much fun without drinking."

Steve was smiling, listening, nodding.

"Sometimes my face gets sore from laughing so much."

"What're you going to do today, up there, now?"

"Andrea asked me to give my testimony; tell the story of how I became a Christian."

"Oh good," he said, looking down at his sheet. "You're on next you know."

That sent the nerves in my stomach into a spin again. Chatting with Steve had made me forget for a minute that I had to get up on that platform and speak to a bunch of strangers.

I concentrated on taking deep breaths to try to slow my heart rate. Fortunately it was warm but not oppressively hot like it would be in a few weeks when summer took hold. I was grateful for the gentle breeze blowing. It was cooling against my nervous perspiration.

The musicians had started playing one of their more up-beat choruses. The acoustic guitar added a folk-like quality to the sound. I moved to the corner of the stage where I had a better view of the front. The music had attracted quite a few people, as Steve had predicted.

As the song finished, the music lulled and I could hear someone speaking. The sound was a bit muffled from the back of the stage. I couldn't listen anyway; I was too nervous and my mind was going over and over again what I was going to say.

Just take your time, don't rush it. Speak slowly.

I could hear John Fieldman start up another song. He was good at creating energy and building momentum and excitement. He certainly had plenty of practice at youth events

… jumping around, his long blonde hair waving. He was working particularly hard today.

Steve called to me again, "Megan, this is it. Are you ready?"

"As ready as I'll ever be, I guess," I replied as I walked towards him.

"Wait here until John calls you up," he said. We stood at the bottom of the makeshift stairs that provided access to the back of the platform. Steve stood with me as we both watched John on the stage, waiting for his signal.

"Just go for it, Megan, when you get up there. You'll be great," he said.

Finishing the song, John motioned me to come onto the platform. I climbed the stairs tentatively with my palm cards in my right hand. John signaled to the musicians to stop before introducing me.

"Megan White is going to share something with you now. I'd like to introduce Megan. Megan has been on an interesting journey and would like to share it with you."

He put the microphone back on the stand and adjusted it for my height. He winked and nodded before moving to the back of the stage.

Take it slowly; breathe.

I looked around the front of the platform and was surprised to see how many people had gathered. There was a small crowd of about forty people looking expectantly at me, waiting for me to start.

Oh well, here goes.

"I would like to tell you this morning that my life has changed dramatically. I'm a different person today from the one I was about twelve months ago. In fact, looking back, I think I was living at the top of a great precipice. I could have easily fallen over. I think I came very close to falling over and if I *had* fallen, I don't think I would ever have been able to get back up again. But God had a different plan for my life. I'm so glad about that because he has completely changed me." I paused and looked around at the people listening to me. To my surprise none of them moved. They stayed still, watching, waiting and listening. Encouraged, I continued.

"A couple of years ago, I hitchhiked to Sydney with my girlfriend. We went down to Sydney because we wanted to be in the middle of the drug scene. I wanted to try everything I could and unfortunately, I did. When you get involved in the drug scene one problem is that you need money, lots of money. And when you need lots of money, you start to think of ways to get it. Sometimes you even think about illegal ways, like stealing it. You want to get it any way you can. You get desperate."

I took a deep breath and reminded myself to talk slowly, not to rush what I wanted to say. I looked around at everyone looking at me. I kept going.

"When you get involved in drugs, it's hard to stop. You keep going, doing more and more, using more and more. Your life spirals out of control. *My* life was out of control." I said, holding my hand on my chest.

I paused and looked around again, posing my next question directly at the people listening, "Have you ever felt *your* life was out of control? Felt that you really needed to change something, but you couldn't? Have you ever felt like you were on a merry-go-round and you couldn't get off?"

I paused again before continuing. "I was on that merry-go-round. I was going round and round, spinning; until one night I made a decision. I made a decision that changed my life. It turned my life around and I was able to get off that merry-go-round. I gave my heart to Jesus Christ and I asked him to change me. I can stand here today and tell you that he *did* change my life. I'm no longer involved in the drug scene at all. In fact, I'm a different person now. I can recommend it to you. I haven't looked back for one moment."

I didn't know what else to say and was too nervous to look at my palm cards, so I turned to John. He moved to the front of the platform, talking as he pulled the microphone off the stand again, "Thank you Megan. Thank you for sharing that with us. Yes, Jesus has changed her life. He can change your life too." He motioned to the musicians to start up the next song as I moved off the stage towards the stairs, trembling all over. I had done it. I had given my testimony. It felt good, but at the same time it was a relief it was over.

◊ ◊ ◊

The atmosphere was abuzz as I walked into the auditorium. I'd arrived early in case help was needed before the service. Now that I was on the Youth Committee, I was responsible for helping organize these events. It was expected that I arrive early to help with whatever needed doing. I was happy to help, but didn't always know what I was supposed to do.

"Hey Megan, great testimony this morning," Debbie, one of the triplets, greeted me as I walked in. "You were really good."

I was surprised. I'd gone over my few words in my head again and again since this morning, reliving the experience. I hadn't said half the things I had intended, but it was nice to get some positive feedback.

"Thanks," I said.

"Do you think it will be a good meeting tonight? Will you sit with me?" Debbie asked, bubbly and enthusiastic as usual. It was impossible not to like her. Like me, she was serious about being involved at NSC. I felt she showed lots of courage at times and was always willing to try new things. It seemed to me she wanted to go all the way in her walk with God.

The street-witnessing team had invited everyone they had met in King George Square this morning to the meeting. I didn't know how many flyers had been handed out, but we hoped a lot of people would turn up to this special youth outreach. I put my Bible down on a seat near Debbie and walked up to the front to see how I could help. Andrea was talking intently to John. They both turned and smiled as I walked up.

"Ah, here's the new preacher," John Fieldman teased, eyes mischievous. "No seriously, you were really good this morning — preacher in the making. I was proud to be on the stage with you." He gave me a friendly punch on the shoulder. I could feel a blush creeping up my neck and face. I looked down, embarrassed.

"Hey Megan, have you thought about going to Bible College?" Andrea asked me.

"Well yeah, actually I have been giving it a bit of thought," I replied. Kevin had been promoting it on Sundays, trying to get people interested. This year was the first time that NSC had run the college and Robert had been first in line to get involved. He seemed to be enjoying it though I missed him being around.

"Good. Think about it some more. I really think you should do it."

Wow, Andrea thinks I should go to Bible College. It was just the sort of encouragement I needed. I had been thinking about it, but was still wondering if it was the right thing for me to do. It was a big decision.

"Now tonight, Megan, I want you to stand at the door and welcome people." Andrea was getting down to business. "Look out for anyone who has come for the first time; especially if they were in the Square this morning. I want you to make them feel welcome and comfortable. Show them where to sit, be friendly, and look after them. Can you do that for me?"

"Sure," I replied. "I'll give it a go."

I grabbed Debbie and pulled her along with me. We took up our post at the door. Other members of the youth group had started arriving. Debbie and I practiced our greetings, welcoming them with great gusto and ceremony; shaking their hands.

I was a little unprepared when Kevin Williams turned up at the door. He was to be our speaker tonight.

"Hello Megan. I hear you are our next budding young preacher," he smiled as he took my hand and shook it rather vigorously, completely ignoring Debbie. I was shocked and wondered what he had heard. I didn't know what to say and I could feel that blush creeping up my neck again.

"Good on you for sharing your testimony this morning. I heard you really got people's attention," Kevin said.

"Thanks," was all I could muster, with an awkward shrug. Though embarrassed, I was thrilled to get this feedback and recognition from Kevin. I still couldn't believe that my little talk was very good but couldn't help but feel complimented by all the attention and encouragement I'd received since this morning. I really seemed to have made an impression. It made me wonder if maybe I could be a preacher one day. The idea excited me. Maybe that was God's plan and purpose for my life.

Perhaps I should go to Bible College.

As Kevin walked off to find Andrea, my mind was racing and I felt I was walking on air, my head inflated. It was hard to absorb so many compliments in one day, especially from Kevin Williams, and still keep my feet on the ground!

Thinking of myself as a preacher pulled me up suddenly. It spun me back briefly in time to two years earlier. I remembered sitting around chatting with Stella and Don one night over a few beers. We were planning a robbery. We were talking about robbing a payroll Stella had inside information about. She knew where they stashed the cash and it wasn't very secure. The only reason we never actually executed the plan was because someone else beat us to it.

The thought of me considering being a preacher seemed a lifetime away from those days. It seemed surreal, but here, now, I was contemplating just that. I was seriously considering going to Bible College and being trained for full-time ministry.

It was exciting to think that I might actually take the platform and have the opportunity to influence other people's lives the way I had been influenced. It was inspiring to contemplate.

My life had gone from being out of control - drugs, alcohol, mixed up relationships, the wrong side of the law - to being in control - no drugs, no alcohol, and no sex, not even swearing. Now things had gone even further and I could see a future for myself in being able to influence others to change. It had all happened pretty fast. In fact, it was a little over a year ago that I had first started coming to church. It made me marvel at the dramatic change in such a relatively short time.

Chapter Nine

"Hey Megan, you got a minute?" Andrea called to me across the room as I helped to set up chairs for the next meeting.

"Sure." As I approached Andrea, I couldn't help thinking about the first youth camp I'd attended with Robert. I had been so nervous back then, not knowing anybody. It was a stark contrast to how I felt now, at this youth camp. Now I was part of the youth leadership team and devoted my time to making other newcomers feel welcome. At least I could still remember how I'd felt at first. I guess that helped me to be more empathetic.

"What's up?"

Andrea had been consulting with John, but they both looked up as I approached. "Ah, Megan, come here and sit down for a minute. I've got a special job for you."

"Really? Okay."

John pulled out a chair which I took, wondering what was coming next. I sat on my hands and kicked my feet in rhythm, waiting to hear what Andrea wanted to say.

"Mmm Megan, I need someone I can rely on to do this. I think you're just the person. See that girl over there?" Andrea indicated a young woman standing at the back of the room, pointing her out as discretely as possible. She didn't want the girl to know we were talking about her.

"Do you mean the girl with the two long pony-tails?"

Andrea nodded without looking around. "Yeah, that's the one I mean. Her name's Jane, Jane McIntyre."

I moved my chair around so that I could see Jane without having to turn my head. I hoped it looked a little less obvious that we were talking about her. Jane was standing with a couple of other young people though she looked a little aloof, uncomfortable. She was listening more than talking. Her long dark hair was pulled rather abruptly into two pony-tails perched high up on her head, over her ears. It was more a style you would expect to find on a very small child and I couldn't help wondering at her choice to wear her hair that way. She wore a large dress that I guessed was intended to hide her rather bulging waist line. Jane was a big girl.

"Jane's come here from Sydney recently. She got into a bit of trouble in her church down there. Um, I don't want to go into the details. I don't think that's necessary, but I've spoken to her youth leader on the phone. He thought it might be good for Jane to have a change of scenery. I've agreed to take her in up here and try to give her a bit of a new start for a while. She's pretty shy."

I watched Jane thoughtfully, wondering what mischief she might have been involved in that would make her youth leader want to send her away. It provoked a lot of questions … questions I didn't think Andrea would be likely to answer.

"Okay. Sounds a bit mysterious … and a bit interesting." I continued to watch Jane as Andrea spoke. She twirled one of her pony-tails around her finger nervously.

"Megan, I'd like you to take her under your wing. It's a bit of a project for you. I want you to help Jane make some friends, help her to fit in here at NSC. Do you think you could do that for me?"

"Um, I guess. Sort of introduce her to a few people you mean?"

"Yeah, sit with her at the meetings, at lunch, whatever, you know. Try to make her feel welcome. She's very shy probably partly because she has a hearing problem. I want to give her the best opportunity we can. Oh, and I don't just mean while we're here at camp. I mean around youth meetings in general. Do you get what I mean?"

"Okay. Alright, I guess I can give it a go. I can try but is she seriously deaf?"

"No, she can hear … just not very well. I think she has learned to lip read."

It was hard not to stare. "Sure, I'll do what I can."

"Good girl. C'mon then, let's go and I'll introduce you to her right now." Andrea stood up and grabbed my hand, pulling me along behind her. I'd never done anything like this before; looked after someone. I felt a little apprehensive. *What if I don't even like her?*

Jane and the girls she was talking to looked a little surprised as Andrea approached with me in tow.

"Hi guys, how's it going?" Andrea asked.

"Good Andrea," one of them responded. I could tell they felt intimidated being this close to Andrea.

"Excellent. Hey, I'm glad you guys are making Jane feel welcome. Jane, I wanted you to meet Megan."

"Hi Jane, nice to meet you." It was awkward. I didn't know if I should shake her hand, give her a hug or what. We stood in a circle a little stiffly, looking at each other.

"Anyway guys, I've got to get a few things ready for the meeting. I'll catch up with you later." Andrea was gone.

"Andrea said you came up from Sydney?" It was the only

thing I could think to say. Jane's eyes caught mine and she swung her shoulders from side to side, embarrassed. But her eyes struck me by surprise. They were large, black, like marbles. She had beautiful long eyelashes that had been carefully stroked with mascara. Seeing Jane close up, I realized how carefully groomed she was. I warmed to her a little.

"Yes, I'm from Sydney. I don't know many people … no one really."

"You were going to church there?"

We managed to strike up a conversation, even if a little clumsily. I was glad when we could hear the meeting getting started behind us as talking to Jane had been hard work. She didn't seem to want to say too much.

"Come and sit with me, Jane. Over here."

Finding some seats seemed a welcome diversion.

The Iron Man race was about to start. The gutsy competitors were lined up on the starting line, loosening their limbs. They were dressed in old clothes and sneakers as the first leg of the race meant crossing the dam. They would be wading through mud. How I wished I was brave enough to join them! But I was too worried about embarrassing myself. It would still be fun to watch though.

Remembering my responsibility, I glanced around looking for Jane and finally found her at the back of the spectator group. She wouldn't have a very good view from there. Over the weekend, I'd been faithful to my commitment to Andrea. I'd made sure that Jane was either with me or had some good company.

"C'mon Jane. Come down the front with me." I grabbed her hand and pretty much dragged her along behind me. I sensed her reluctance, but she yielded and followed me through the crowd. We found a good spot at the front with a great view of the dam and the starting line.

"Hey look, there's Debbie. Can you believe she's going in it! I think she's the only girl. Wow." Debbie was trying to pull her thick hair into a pony tail as she hopped nervously from one leg to the other.

Jane said nothing in response but followed my gaze. Jane's hair, no longer caught in child-like pony tails, tumbled around her face. It acted as a veneer, a shield for her to hide behind. As usual, she looked a little uncomfortable but she was enjoying taking in the scene, as we all were.

"Man that girl has got guts! Wonder how she'll go?" I said.

Peter Cartwright, the champion trolley racer, stood to one side of the competitors with a starting gun. He was trying to get everyone to be quiet so that he could get the race underway. Someone let out a loud whistle which had the desired effect and, once the crowd had lulled, Peter was able to get the race started.

"On your marks, get set, GO!" He fired the starter gun into the air and the competitors sprang to life charging into the dam. It must have been cold. Some yelled with the shock as the water reached their chests, but they were cheered on by the spectators yelling and laughing. I could only imagine the sensation of mud squishing in their shoes and the horror of the unknown on the dam floor as they charged across.

"C'mon Jane, let's go around and watch the next bit." I grabbed Jane's arm again, ready to race around the dam to watch the next component of the race but Jane resisted, firmly this time. I turned to see her face resolute.

"You go Megan. I'll catch up."

"C'mon. I want to see them eat the cold pies. They have to wash them down with a hot coke. Yuk! Can't imagine doing that."

"I know, but um, Megan. I can't run. You go. I'll be fine." I let go of her arm, finally understanding her reluctance to take off at a sprint.

Realizing that running was something that Jane just wasn't going to do, I conceded. "Nah, it's okay. I'll walk with you. C'mon."

Taking a steadier pace, we followed the spectators to the next point, chatting as we moved. As we neared the competitors, we could see them out of the water trying to eat their cold meat pies. Jane distracted me. "Hey Megan, do you know that guy over there, the tall one with the blonde hair?"

I strained to see who she was talking about. "Sure, that's Chris. I'm not sure of his last name though. He's a pretty big guy."

"I think he's cute."

Surprised at her personal comment, I searched her face and smiled. Jane smiled back. "Do you think he's cute?"

I looked at Chris again. "He's alright, I guess," I said grinning, both surprised and pleased that she was sharing such an intimacy. "We'll have to keep an eye on him."

"That'd be fun," Jane giggled, stroking her fingers through her hair, eyes mischievous.

The competitors were struggling to swallow their pies in a hurry. The rules dictated they had to present their mouths, empty, before being cleared to run the next leg. The pressure was on. I could see John Fieldman's stomach convulsing as he tried to swallow the last mouthful. His face had paled as he struggled to swallow; he was straining not to vomit it back up again. I wondered whether it would disqualify him if he did.

The crowd was cheering, laughing and urging them on. Debbie had done well crossing the dam, but was dropping behind now. She seemed less able to abandon any sense of propriety eating her pie and was taking bites that were too small to keep her seriously in the competition.

"C'mon Debbie! You can do it!" I yelled in support. Turning to Jane to share the moment, I realized she only had eyes for Chris and was watching his every move.

Some had finished their pies and coke and were off at a pace. I knew Jane wouldn't want to follow, so we stood watching the last pie eaters re-join the race.

"So, how do you know Chris?" I asked.

Jane's eyes flickered momentarily with excitement. I had stumbled upon her favorite subject. "I don't really know him. Well I kind of do. I've been watching him."

"Yeah, but does he know you? Have you talked to him?"

"Um, no … no way. I'm too shy to talk to him."

"Are you joking? You have to at least *talk* to him to really get to know him. I'm sure we can arrange that."

"Would you? That sounds scary. I'm not sure I'm ready for that."

"Oh well, we'll just see what happens."

The race had moved away and we had been left behind. A loud cheer went up from the other side of the hill and I gathered a winner had been declared. We didn't move to follow.

"Wonder who won and I wonder how Debbie went. We'll find her later. Let's go get ready for lunch. They're setting up the mudslide for this afternoon. Can't wait for that! It's going to be great."

"Mud slide? Mmmm, heard about that."

"You going on it?"

"Me, no way, not me. I'll just watch."

"Okay, if you want, but there's no way I'm missing out on that. That's what I've been waiting for. Can't wait. Let's go and see how the mud pit's going."

"Nah, I'm heading up. I'll see you later."

"Okay. See you at lunch." I watched Jane as she walked away. Perhaps looking after her wasn't going to be as bad as I first thought.

Who knows, maybe we might even become friends.

I couldn't help feeling surprised that Jane had opened up to me already. I had made quicker progress than I expected.

Chapter Ten

9 Months Later - August, 1978

I kept breathing out through my mouth, enjoying the vapour created in the chilled morning air. I dug my hands deeper into the pockets of my jacket and, as usual, my fingers slipped through the familiar hole in the seam. I walked back and forth along the bridge close to the entrance to Araluen.

Once I got to the bridge, I usually enjoyed my early morning vigil. I had to admit, though, getting to the bridge was hard work some mornings but today hadn't been too bad. Being Friday it had been easier to rouse myself from sleep and get moving for the day.

I'd come to enjoy this time of the day. It was quiet. I could hear the odd clang of pots coming from the kitchen as the cook prepared breakfast. No one else was around. Most of the other Bible College students preferred to sleep until the last minute. I wondered whether it was because I was now living in such a close-knit community that I enjoyed this peaceful morning solitude.

I agreed with Kevin Williams that Araluen provided an

excellent environment for study. The separation from the hustle and bustle of the city was conducive to learning. But the tensions and pressures of living so close together presented another set of challenges at times.

Today I didn't feel like praying. I usually prayed for Don. I thought about him and missed him as usual. I wondered whether he would ever become a Christian now that he had moved back to Sydney and I never saw him. His letters came less often. I didn't feel like praying for Don this morning.

Instead, my thoughts turned to the day ahead as I strolled back and forth with an easy rhythm. Friday was my favorite day at Bible College. Kevin Williams lectured on Fridays, on 'Moving in the Spirit'. Kevin's responsibilities in our growing church were pressing and made it hard for him to meet his lecture commitments at times. But when he did get here, it was well worth it.

As I walked, I reflected on last week's lecture. Kevin had talked of his intimate relationship with God, even described personal conversations. It had been mesmerizing. Kevin's passion for these dialogues with God was evident on his face. An intensity had settled on the room like a cloak as he had talked. The way Kevin reconstructed his conversations with God reflected his deep, intimate relationship. I wondered why God had singled out Kevin in such a way and wished that God would talk to me in the same way. The class had been enraptured, hanging on every word. Such sessions reinforced our sense of awe, both of God and Kevin, our pastor.

Kevin's lectures often seemed timeless. It was always a shock to walk out of our primitive lecture room, one of several converted old army barracks. As you walked through that door, you were taken from being immersed in the mysteries of the spiritual world back to the harsh realities of our closed community and shared accommodation.

I wondered how today's lecture would be as I paced to and

fro on the little bridge, listening to the sounds of the campground coming to life. Araluen, the church retreat, had become a haven for many struggling souls. In Kevin's usual compassionate approach, he had allowed a number of careworn folk and their families to set up tents or caravans while they got back on their feet.

The morning dew was glistening as the first rays of the sun peeped through the foliage of the surrounding eucalyptus trees. I felt excited. If Kevin made it to the lecture today, it would be a good one.

◊ ◊ ◊

I felt as impatient as everyone else as we sat in the lecture room awaiting Kevin's arrival. The irritation showed in the other students: Peter was tapping his ruler on the desk like a drum and humming a new chorus he had recently learnt; Alan kept straining to look out the door to see if Kevin was coming. He was late.

I sighed and turned around in my seat to talk to Sandy sitting behind me. Sharing a room with her had brought us close together. Though there was the occasional tension between us, mostly I was glad of her company and friendship. You needed a good ally in a live-in Bible College such as this. It had been disappointing that Jane hadn't wanted to register with me. She had been adamant she didn't want to pursue life in the ministry. I missed her.

"I hope he comes today," I said.

"Yeah, me too. No one really compares, do they?" Sandy replied. "I think he was going to build more on last week's lecture about the secrets of waiting on the spirit. I've been waiting all week to hear more."

"Me too. He gave us a lot to think about."

We could hear the crackle of stones as a car swung into the

car park. We all jumped out of our seats and moved to the window to get a better look, our seats scraping the bare wooden floor. Two men in short-sleeved safari suits got out of the car. Kevin wasn't one of them.

There were a few audible groans of disappointment as we turned away and moved back to our seats.

I looked at Sandy and shrugged, saying, "I wonder what and who now?"

Sandy pursed her lips, her anger evident in her frown. We arranged our pads and pens and pulled out our Bibles. Everyone was looking serious and studious by the time the two men reached the lecture room door.

We looked up as they walked in. One of them looked familiar, but I didn't know his name. The other man I had never seen before. He had wavy grey hair pulled back behind his ears and a rather pointy nose. He had a funny habit of licking his bottom lip. He seemed a little uncomfortable. They brought a strange atmosphere into the room, a tension. The room was quiet. I put down my pen and leaned back in my chair. This looked interesting and definitely out of the ordinary.

The more familiar man spoke first. "Good morning students. I'm Arthur Carson, one of the senior pastors at NSC. I've met some of you before but not all. How are you doing?"

"Good morning," some of the students mumbled.

I sat quietly, watching and waiting for the stranger's introduction. He had a couple of books under his arm. He looked like he might have come prepared to lecture. I felt rather frustrated by this. I had saved my money and paid all my fees for Bible College upfront – no mean feat on a junior stenographer's wage. I'd paid for this opportunity and Kevin Williams was meant to teach us on a weekly basis. I understood that missing the odd week was probably unavoidable in such a large church, but Kevin's absences had become more and more frequent over the last couple of months. I felt cheated, ripped off.

Arthur shut the door and sat on the edge of one of the tables at the front of the room. He didn't seem to be in a hurry. "How are you all enjoying Bible College?" he asked.

"It's good when Kevin gets here," I responded quickly, glad for an opportunity to release some frustration.

Arthur smiled knowingly. "Yes, I'm sure you feel that way. Kevin's a very enthusiastic teacher and I know he loves coming up here and sharing the things he knows with you. He hates it when he has to miss a lecture. He has taken a great deal of personal pride in overseeing your development and watches your progress here at college very closely."

No one said anything. There was a heavy silence in the room with everyone sitting and listening. All eyes were on Arthur, though each of us stole glances at the other man from time to time. He still hadn't been introduced. He had moved behind Arthur but remained on his feet. His hands were behind his back and he stood almost as though he was at attention. He was giving Arthur room to speak. He seemed very interested in something on his shoes, or something on the floor that had taken his fancy. He didn't look at us.

"I've got some news for you Bible College students. It's very important news and I'm asking you to treat what I am about to tell you with the strictest confidence. There is to be an important announcement in church this Sunday. We chose to tell you all first, though, today."

He slid off the table and moved around the front as he spoke.

"This Bible College and you students in particular, are crucial to the future of New Start Centre. As you know, NSC is spearheading a move of God across Australia. You're going to be a part of that move. When you leave here in a few months' time, many of you will take on various leadership roles. The church needs you."

He was speaking earnestly, looking at each of us as he spoke, making eye contact. "That's why you're hearing this news now. I've come here especially to give you some hard news as well as to introduce you to Phillip Hannigan."

Phillip looked up a little surprised when he heard his name. He smiled and nodded to us.

I shifted in my seat. This was all quite puzzling. I swiveled around to catch Sandy's eye. She returned a bewildered look and shrugged her shoulders. She had no idea what was coming either. I turned back to Arthur, wondering what was coming next.

"Kevin won't be able to fulfill his lecturing commitment today. In fact, he won't be able to fulfill his lecturing commitment for the rest of this year. I know personally that he is very torn that he has had to break this commitment. But he has no choice."

Arthur paused, letting the shock of the news sink in before he continued. There were gasps and groans across the room as we reacted. I could hear other students moving in their seats. I'm sure they shared my own sentiment – a sense of being cheated. Something terrible must have happened to Kevin. He had been in a car accident once before and broken his arm. I wondered what could have happened this time.

No one said anything or asked the obvious question, *why*. We waited for Arthur to continue.

"The church board has decided that Kevin should stand down from his responsibilities as Head Pastor of NSC for a period of six months." Arthur paused again and waited for our reactions to subside and quiet down. He wanted everyone's full attention before he continued.

"It has come to the attention of the Church leadership that Kevin has been involved in an inappropriate relationship; a relationship he shouldn't have been involved in … one that's not beneficial to the church or the work of God. That relationship has ended. Kevin has repented. He's humbled himself before God and before the church board and has agreed to do whatever they decide. What is of utmost importance to Kevin, as you would expect, is to see the work of God continue and he'll do whatever he can to protect what has been achieved so far. He's deeply sorry for the poor choices he has made."

No one knew what to say. I gripped the table with my hands so hard my knuckles went white. I sat rigid in my chair. I didn't look at anyone except Arthur Carson. I was numb, shocked. My breathing deepened and slowed. Each breath was taken with thoughtful purpose as I gnawed on my bottom lip. I didn't move in my seat. I waited, frozen. My brain wasn't functioning properly. The only thought that managed to crystalize in my head was - *Those slimy, two-faced bastards.*

Phillip Hannigan shuffled his feet uncomfortably. He had a funny grin on his face. His tongue kept darting in and out, licking his bottom lip. He reminded me of a lizard. He made no eye contact with any of us. He looked at Arthur and waited for him to continue.

I sat and watched, my eyes moving from one to the other, as Arthur still held the floor. I wanted to know more.

"Now, I know this comes as a shock. But you have to remember that we are all human. We all struggle with different issues in our lives. We all have to work to get on top of them. Kevin is no different. What is most important in all of this is that the work of God proceeds. We can't stop or slow down. The Holy Spirit is on the move and we need to move with him. *You* are a critical part of that movement."

Peter took advantage of Arthur's dramatic pause and asked boldly, "Who was he having the relationship with?"

Peter had asked what we all wanted to know. His question

relieved some unseen pressure in the room. Many of the students moved in their seats again, waiting for Arthur's response.

Arthur pulled his hand across his mouth and rubbed his chin thoughtfully. He took a deep breath and sat down on the table again and asked, "How many of you are involved in the youth group?"

Most of the students in the room put up their hands.

"Hmm, that's what I thought," Arthur responded. He took another deep breath. Phillip shifted on his feet again.

"Unfortunately, he was having a relationship with … Andrea."

There were audible cries from the room. I remained frozen, immovable.

Those slimy, two-faced bastards! The words were screaming in my head, reverberating, sending a tremor throughout my body.

It was difficult to take in what I was hearing and yet … not a shock at all. I felt something stirring deep inside me. It was anger … anger rising from the very pit of my stomach, from the depths of my being; anger and … a sense of shame. Thoughts were swirling around in my mind. It was hard to fixate on them. I felt confused. Had I been a part of this deception? Had I unwittingly, innocently, unknowingly *helped* them?

The internal tremor had reached my hands. They were shaking. I didn't want to speak because I knew my voice would waver. My mind went blank. I couldn't think about anything. All I could feel was this raw anger, gnawing away inside, rising bit by bit like an internal tidal wave.

Suddenly, I felt terrified. What was happening to me? I wanted to run out the door. I wanted to run and run and run – run to anywhere. It didn't matter where; anywhere, just away from here and this room, hearing this news.

I wanted to get out ... yet I also wanted to stay. I wanted to hear more. I needed to hear more. What did this mean? What did this all mean to *me*?

My Christian life seemed to flash before my eyes - the night I had made the big decision - I could see Andrea's face as she leaned towards me telling me I needed to move out of the house where I was living with Don that night, immediately. I remember the night Stella and Cat came to church and made outrageous accusations; the day Rob and I went to Andrea's office and confronted her; Kevin's persuasive prayer that dwarfed me and diminished our accusations.

I must get out of this room ... now!

Chapter Eleven

Somehow I managed to block out my emotions and feelings. Somehow I managed to replace the anger with an icy cold feeling. It was numbing, but allowed me to get control, to stay the need to run for the moment. I looked at Arthur, who was still speaking, and forced myself to focus my attention on him. The numb feeling helped me tune my ears to his voice again.

"There's no arguing that this is a setback for the church, but we need to work together to minimize that setback as much as possible. And it mustn't affect *your* devotion to the Lord or your dedication to serving him. You have a few months of college left. You need to settle down and continue to focus on your studies. In many ways you are lucky to be here, at Araluen, away from the mainstream church. You'll be shielded to some extent from much of the turmoil."

"What about Andrea?" Peter asked. "Who's going to run the youth group now? Who's going to run the church?"

"Andrea is leaving Brisbane. She's travelling to Adelaide as we speak. A wonderful church down there has agreed to take her under their wing and help her get back on her feet. As for the youth group … well a decision about that hasn't been finalized as yet. A new youth leader will be appointed as soon as possible. I've taken over the general running of the church for the time being."

My eyes darted around to room to gauge the reaction of the other students. It was a double blow. We had just lost our youth leader as well as our pastor in one fell swoop. Everyone moved uncomfortably in their seats.

"Kevin will still be around. He isn't going anywhere. But he won't be on the platform at church for at least six months. Chuck Bronson, a very well-known pastor from America, has agreed to counsel and help him work through his issues. Everything will be reviewed in six months' time. Look, I know this's a shock for all of you. But to be honest, things will pretty much continue to tick along as they have done until now. Kevin will work through this and so will all of us. You need to remain true to your relationship to the Lord and your commitment to the church. All will be fine. All the holes will be filled. Don't worry about that."

"What about Kevin's lectures?" Peter asked.

"Good question. We have that covered … more than covered." Arthur stood up. "Come around, Phillip, and let me introduce you."

"Sure." Phillip came and stood beside Arthur.

Arthur put his arm around him. He obviously knew him well and had a great affection for him. "Phil joining our team is a tremendous bonus for NSC. I still can't believe it's happened this way. It makes it obvious that even with all this turmoil, God is still in control. Phil comes with great credentials. He's been working in the ministry in New Zealand for many, many years and has an international reputation as a speaker. He's focused much of his study on future events predicted in the Bible, particularly the Book of

Revelation. He loves the Word and has devoted his life to studying it. He is well qualified and totally committed to taking over as principal for this Bible College. You're going to love him."

He finally gave Phillip the floor.

"Hello, hello, students. I have to tell you that God works in mysterious ways. I know you've had some difficult news this morning, but I want you to realize that God really is in control. The fact that I'm here is quite a miracle. God spoke to me only a few short weeks ago about making a dramatic move. It was very clear to me that he wanted me to move into a teaching role. I've been pastoring my own church in Christchurch for ten years or so now – great bunch of people. It hadn't occurred to me to move on. But then I got this clear message and direction from God. It was confirmed a couple of times independently, quite miraculous really, so me and my family have been preparing for a move and a big change. Then I got the call from Arthur and it all fell into place and here I am. I marvel at God and the way he works. I'm excited to be here, truly I am. I'm excited to have this opportunity to teach you."

He sat down on the desk at the front and looked around the room before continuing.

"Listen students, this morning's been difficult. How about we take a short break, get a cup of coffee and reconvene in say …" he looked at his watch, "fifteen minutes? Then we can get down to business."

Everyone started shuffling their books and papers.

At last I could leave. Not caring that my chair scraped on the wooden floor, I stood up and walked out the door without speaking to anyone or looking at anyone. I wanted to be alone. I headed for my favorite spot, my retreat at the bridge.

◊ ◊ ◊

I didn't know how I felt as I walked backwards and forwards across the bridge.

Am I angry? Am I mad? I must be angry. I must be!

I didn't feel angry though.

Then I thought of Andrea and how she had lied to me and the anger welled up. My mouth suddenly, involuntarily, seemed to fill with saliva at the thought of her name. I spat on the ground in disgust. She had blatantly lied to me and what was worse, I had believed her, believed Kevin.

Should I walk away from all this?

But even now, even in the midst all of this turmoil, I knew deep down I couldn't deny that my life had changed so much for the better since I had become a Christian. *Was it all a sham? God seems so real to me!*

I sat down on the edge of the bridge and dangled my legs over the side, looking down at the trickle of water in the gully below. I didn't want to lose God and Jesus from my life. Knowing them had given me purpose and a reason for living. Somehow I had to find a way to rise above this. Had my experience been based solely on Kevin and Andrea? If it was, it shouldn't have been. I had made a decision to follow a supreme being. Sure, Kevin and Andrea had helped me make that decision, but I ultimately wanted to please God, not them.

Somehow, I knew that I had to forgive them. But I wasn't ready for that. Not now, not today.

I sighed deeply and turned inwardly to ask God for help.

I looked up as I heard a car swing into the driveway. I jumped up as the bridge was narrow and I needed to move to a safer spot to let the vehicle pass. The car pulled to a stop next to me and the driver wound down his window. "G'day," he said, smiling.

"Hi," I said. I'd seen him around. He was tall and kept his dark hair cropped very short like someone in the marines. I'd heard he was an alcoholic and was trying to quit.

"I'm Ray. You alright?"

"Hi Ray. Yeah, I'm alright. I just needed some time to think. I'm Megan." Ray reached across the seat for a packet of cigarettes and pulled one out with his lips. He seemed in no hurry. "Want one?"

"No ... um actually, yeah, I wouldn't mind. That'd be great thanks." I suddenly had a craving for a cigarette. I hadn't even thought about having a smoke since I gave up a year or so ago. But right now, I wanted one and I was going to have it!

"Hang on a sec." Ray pulled the car off the bridge and off the track a little. He opened the door and got out offering me the packet. I took a cigarette and Ray lit it for me. He lit one for himself and leaned his tall slender torso against the car. He had a rugged look about him, like he had seen some rough times. He smiled at me, his eyes glimmering with a touch of amusement as he watched me draw the smoke in deeply.

It felt good. I'd forgotten how good it felt.

"You look like you needed that."

"Yeah, I think I did. Stupid really, as I've given up. But I just feel like one today."

"Huh. I haven't tried to give up the smokes. I'm trying to get off the booze though." Ray looked relaxed as he enjoyed his cigarette and eyed me thoughtfully. "You're one of the students, aren't you? Going to that Bible College up on the hill?" he asked squinting at me through the blue smoke.

I nodded but didn't feel like talking. I just wanted to enjoy this cigarette. It was helping to numb the confusing pain ... for the moment.

"How long have you been here?" I asked.

Ray frowned as he thought for a moment. "Coupla months, I guess. I got a big scare. Made me realize I needed some help, you know. Yeah, I really needed help. I went to the crap house and got the shock of my life. Scared the be-Jesus out of me. It was full of blood."

"Really? Yaark! That sounds awful."

"It wasn't good, I can tell ya that. It wasn't good at all. It was after me big birthday bash." He chuckled to himself. "I turned thirty ya know."

"But how did you end up here?"

Ray looked at me shaking his head as though he still couldn't believe it. "Ran into some guy in the street that day and he invited me to church. I'd never set foot in a church in me life before. Still can't believe I did it. But I was scared. I thought maybe God was trying to tell me something, you know." He chuckled and grinned. He held his lip awkwardly trying to hide his missing tooth. It turned his grin into more like a smirk. But his brown eyes looking directly at me, seemed genuine … warm even.

"Wonder what Mum would say if she knew. Lordy, what would she say?" He shifted his weight to his other foot and dragged on his cigarette again, chuckling to himself.

"Anyway, ended up having a chat with Kevin after a mate set it up for me and he said I could hang out here for a bit, while I clean m'self up. So here I am. I've got a caravan over by the dam." He nodded his head in the direction of the campground.

"Oh. There seems to be a few people living down there." I paused and looked at my watch. The time had flown. "Well, I'm actually due back in class right about now." I stubbed out my butt with my gym boot. "I should get back, but gee thanks for the smoke! I enjoyed it more than I should've."

"No problem. Any time. Nice chatting with ya." Ray had finished his smoke too and moved to get back in the car. "Ya wanna lift?"

"Nah, I need the walk. See you 'round."

"See ya." He winked at me through the window as he drove off. I smiled and waved. He had been a welcome diversion from my inner turmoil.

My mind turned to Cat and Stella as I strolled back to the classroom. A pang of regret made me catch my breath.

What an idiot I had been! Of course they'd been telling me the truth all along. Why hadn't I believed them? How do I fix this?

I determined to go and visit them next time I was in Brisbane. I hadn't spoken to them for a long time. They deserved an apology. Perhaps talking to them again would relieve some of the physical pain that stabbed at my insides relentlessly now as I walked.

I sat with the phone at my ear, listening to the ringing tone, hoping that Jane would answer. As I waited, I pondered how much had changed since meeting that awkward girl all those months ago. It had never occurred to me that Jane would become such a close, trustworthy friend. It had been a joy to discover the hidden Jane. In fact, getting to know her had changed my perspective. I'd realized it was worthwhile getting to know the quiet one who stands in the corner, the one hiding in the shadows. I'd learned that if you made the effort, you never knew what jewel you might uncover. Getting to know Jane had been like that.

The ringing stopped and I heard the receiver being lifted. "Hello?"

"Jane, I'm so glad you're home. I need to talk to you."

"Hi Megan. Nice to hear from you. Are you alright?"

"Yes, no … I don't know. I'm confused. Have you heard?"

Jane was silent momentarily. "About what?"

"Kevin and Andrea. Have you heard about them?"

"Yes I have Megan. It's awful. How do you know?"

"They told us at Bible College today. Arthur Carson came up and told us. He said it would be announced in church. I'm sick to my stomach. I don't know how to react."

"Mmm Megan, a lot of people are feeling like that."

"How did you find out?"

"Well, it's strange Megan, but Andrea called me. I went round to her place. It's awful what's happening to her."

"What … what's happening to her? Arthur said she'd gone to Adelaide."

"She's going to Adelaide. Listen, I can't say much. It's all supposed to be secret. But Andrea's asked me to go with her."

"With her? Really? To Adelaide?"

"Yes."

"Are you going?"

"Yes."

"Wow."

"I can't tell you what a state she's in. She's sworn me to secrecy, but I can tell you that she's pretty low. She needs a good friend at the moment."

"Oh Jane."

I'd never told Jane about Cat and Stella. In fact I'd never spoken to anyone about that whole situation since I'd walked out of Andrea's office that day. Robert and I had kept that secret between us. We'd never even spoken to each other about it again. That was about to change as he was next on my list to call.

"Look Megan, you've been a great friend to me but I'm going to have to go away for a while. I'm going away with Andrea. I'm not sure exactly how long, four to six weeks, something like that. Promise me you'll write."

"You're going with her? I don't know what to say, Jane. Of course I'll write to you."

"Somehow I think it's what I'm meant to do. I *have* to do it."

"Wow. I guess I'll just have to say goodbye then, for a while. When do you go?"

"First thing in the morning. I'll be in touch when I can …

when I know where we'll be living."

"Okay Jane. I'll be thinking of you. Bye."

I hung up the phone feeling close to tears, another loss. Listening to Jane had made me feel a bit sorry for Andrea. It added to my confusion.

Slotting some more coins in the phone, I dialed Robert's number, hoping he, too, would be at home.

Chapter Twelve

It had been a whole week since the news had broken. I'd been oscillating between wanting to abandon everything and trying to find a focus on God again. The investment I'd made in my Bible College fees had been an influence. I still felt numb and in shock, but Phillip Hannigan was growing on me. He certainly seemed committed to taking over Bible College. He had been here every day and I had to admit he had been a great encouragement. He was helping me to get my eyes off Kevin and Andrea and onto God. He had made me realize that I had put both of them on some sort of pedestal. It was clearly not a good thing to do. It was like worshipping someone. I needed to be worshipping God. Worshipping another person was obviously flawed.

It was Friday again, but we knew not to expect Kevin. Somehow, knowing he wouldn't be here today made the wounds feel fresh again. I was sure we were all thinking the same thing.

How could Phil compete with Kevin's lectures on moving in the Holy Spirit?

The mood was somber as we started our usual morning prayer vigil. Sandy led, her voice droning in a monotone. It was difficult to focus. Peter must have been having trouble too, or at least he wasn't praying with his eyes shut. He rather rudely interrupted, calling out, "Hey, It's Kevin! Wonder what he's doing here?"

We all rushed to the window to look, prayers forgotten. Sure enough, Kevin and Phil were getting out of the car and making their way towards the lecture room. I could feel my pulse quicken a little and there was a murmur around the room as the students took their seats.

Kevin looked a little sheepish as he entered the room. I'd never seen him like this before. I couldn't help but think how hard this must be for him. He needed some guts to be walking through that door. But then, he'd probably had lots of moments like this over the last week or so. Phil followed him through the door and let him take the floor. Everyone was quiet in their seats, waiting, watching.

As usual there were empty desks at the front. Kevin leaned on one clutching his compendium to his chest with his arms folded.

"Good morning students," he paused as he collected his thoughts. "This is hard … one of the hardest things I've had to do lately." He took a deep breath, sighed and laid his folder down on the desk. Looking up, his eyes scanned the room. He made direct eye contact with each of us, pausing for that split second. It made you feel he wanted to say something personal to you. His eyes were dense with emotion.

"I have felt great pain over the last few weeks. It's hard to tell you how much pain. It's such a great loss to me to have to give up teaching this class. You know, coming up here has been the highlight of my week. I so much want to continue to share with you what God has shown me. Unfortunately that can't be for the moment. But I want to encourage you all not to lose momentum, not to lose heart. You need to take this opportunity here at Bible College and make the most of it. You've taken time out of your lives to be here and study God's Word. You may never get a chance like this again in your life. So I want to encourage you to remain true to your commitment in being here. This is your opportunity to learn, learn, learn … to learn about yourself and to learn about God. This is your opportunity to ask all the hard questions about life and God. This's a time and place to prepare you for the ministry that God has for you."

He stood up and seemed rejuvenated, like he had eased a weight on his chest. No one said anything. We waited. Kevin moved around and stood next to Phil and put his arm around his shoulders. Phil grinned, a little embarrassed.

"I'm so grateful to God that he has given us Phil! Students, this is good news for you. I can't tell you how much I admire this man. His knowledge and devotion to the Word is exceptional. He is known around the world for his insights into end time events in particular. I couldn't be putting you into better hands if I'd tried to orchestrate things myself!"

He smiled a little as if to himself. "Fortunately God was in control all along and as a result, Phil is now with us full-time. I'm overjoyed." He shook Phil a little in his excitement and appreciation. "His whole family has moved to Australia and they're all excited to be in the church. They're here to stay." Phil nodded and grinned. Kevin let go of Phil and looked directly at us again.

"I'll let you get on with your class now. I'm leaving knowing you are in good … no, *great*, hands. I encourage you to give it your best, your all. I've got some other things to tend to around here. I want to talk to a few other people. I mightn't be in the class room for a bit, but I'm still going to be around." He moved towards the door. He looked a little awkward, like he wasn't sure exactly how to exit. He hadn't given anyone a chance to speak. I guess he didn't want anyone to ask uncomfortable questions. He was almost out the door when he pulled up at the last minute and looked around the room once again. His eyes rested on me. "Oh Megan. I'd really like to have a word with you after class. Perhaps you could meet me outside in the mess hall?" He nodded his head as though I had agreed and kept walking out the door.

I was stunned, frozen in my seat. There had been no opportunity for reply. He wanted to talk to *me* after the class. He was gone.

Phil seized the moment and diverted everyone's attention. "Okay. Time to start work. Moving in the Spirit. Let's get down to business." He was handing out soft covered booklets titled *Moving in the Spirit*.

I was only half listening. It was hard to concentrate. Kevin wanted to talk personally to me.

Why?

Maybe he was going to apologize for that time so long ago in his office. I felt as though a cold stone had suddenly been dropped in my stomach. It was hard to focus.

◊ ◊ ◊

I didn't rush out of the room at the end of class. Strangely, no one said anything to me about Kevin's invitation. Even Sandy seemed in a rush to be somewhere and just smiled at me on her way out. I packed up my papers and books slowly. I was feeling nervous but also intrigued. One part of me wanted to rush to the mess hall to see if he was waiting, but another part of me felt cautious, wary.

I picked up my papers, Bible and books and made my way out. Once at my room, I threw everything onto the bed before making my way down to the hall.

The double doors into the mess were banging a little in the

breeze as I walked through. It was a busy place at meal time but there was always someone around any time during the day. It was a center point for this little community. Pots were clanging in the kitchen as the cook got ready for lunch. I could hear him calling out orders to his helpers.

My eyes did a quick scan of the room, my stomach still twisting. Kevin wasn't there.

Had I heard him correctly? Had I understood his invitation?

I replayed his words in my mind and convinced myself that he had said he wanted to meet me here. I walked over to the urn and made myself a coffee. The stacks of fresh bread in the corner looked inviting. I decided to wait for lunch; it was only about an hour away.

I was still stirring in the sugar when I heard the door on the other side of the mess bang open. I looked around in time to see Kevin walk in looking a little disheveled. His hair was sticking out in odd places probably due to the breeze outside and his obvious haste to get to the mess hall.

"Sorry Megan. I got a bit held up down by the caravans chatting with folk. How are you?" His words seemed to gush out a little too quickly as he strode across the hall towards me, breathless. "Good, you've got a coffee. Come over here and let's have a bit of a chat."

He stopped at one of the mess tables away from the kitchen where a little sunlight was shining on the table. He pulled out a chair for me. He scanned the room to see who else was around. He lowered his voice a little as he spoke. "I have to be very careful now. I want to talk to you in private, but that would be inappropriate so I have to make sure we chat in a public place. I don't want people to think I'm trying to hide something."

I looked at him, puzzled, trying to absorb what he had said as I sat down. I didn't care who could see us. It didn't seem important to me. What I wanted to know was why had Kevin singled me out? What did he want to talk to me about? I couldn't remember having a conversation privately with Kevin ever before – just Kevin and me. Though I felt I knew him from listening to him on the platform at church – telling stories about himself and his past and listening to his sermons. I wondered now whether I really knew him at all. He had always seemed larger than life on the platform. But here he was sitting opposite; talking just to me.

The news of his illicit affair with Andrea had been a shock, particularly to me. Over the past week I'd been trying to sift through my reactions and emotions. I was trying to understand my response.

How do I feel?

I didn't know. It seemed maintaining my confidence in my faith in God was the only constant in the midst of all this turmoil. Taking a sip, I looked at Kevin over the top of my mug, waiting to hear what he would say next. I felt a little guarded but also privileged. He hadn't wanted to talk to any of the other students alone that day. He wanted to talk to *me*.

"How have you been?" he asked.

"Okay I guess," I lied, remaining guarded.

"Megan, I wanted to talk to you about your future after Bible College. I've been thinking a lot about it and I wanted to share some of my ideas with you."

"Oh?"

"Yes, I've been watching you and you have great potential. I know God has big plans for you and I know how dedicated you have been to the youth group, NSC and to your studies here. You're doing very well. Andrea spoke highly of you too."

He didn't wait for any reaction. He just kept talking.

"You know that the church has bought the property next door to here – the one called Calvary?"

"Yes, I've heard about it. I know you've been looking for

donations to help buy a herd of goats," I said.

"Yes, that's right. I want to set up a dairy to milk goats. It's the perfect place to take people who need help; people who are really sick and need to get away from their environment for a while - for people who need help to get back on their feet. I've been thinking especially about drug addicts. I want to build a drug rehabilitation farm. The kids that go there can work on the farm and get spiritual help, counselling as well. Milking the goats will be a kind of therapy. Plus, of course, there is the potential to make money selling the milk. It can help to run the place."

Kevin was becoming more and more animated as he spoke. He sat forward on his chair. His furrowed brow reflected his intensity. His eyes were gleaming, alive and they were set on me.

"I can see how it will all work in my mind's eye. God's given me a vision. I can see the whole thing. Andrea thought it was great idea too. She was excited about it." He sat back in his chair again and momentarily relaxed a little, a shadow passed across his face and he sighed. Then he looked at me, leaning forward again.

"I want you to run it."

I must have been visibly shocked. "Me? Are you serious?" The thought of taking on such an enterprise seemed so far out of my reach and capability; I could only react in shock.

"I've never been more serious in my life. You have so much potential. I know you can do this. You'll need some help and support, of course. But you have a gift over your life. I know God has big plans for you."

I put my mug down on the table and looked back at him. He looked like he meant what he was saying. He talked with his whole body; with such energy ... infectious energy. He went on to paint a graphic picture of how he saw life working on the farm. I felt as though his words were soaking into me gradually, creeping under my skin, penetrating my head and heart.

I pondered. If he really believed I could do this, maybe I could. The idea was intoxicating. I could feel a sense of excitement strangely mixed with fear rising within me. It seemed like a crazy idea, but maybe, just maybe, with God's supernatural help, I could do something this big. Maybe this was my purpose in life.

We talked on for a while, or rather Kevin talked – I mostly listened. I lost track of time. I was finding it impossible not be carried away by his enthusiasm and vision. He really wanted to help broken people and he believed *I* was the best choice to help him realize this dream.

Suddenly the noise around us in the mess hall intruded into our conversation. It was lunch time. Kevin seemed to notice at the same time. I looked up. People were milling around getting plates and cutlery, waiting for the buffet to open. Everyone was keeping a respectful distance from us but I could see their side-long glances. Kevin stood up and I knew the conversation had come to an end.

"Hey Megan, I think we'll have to wrap this up for the time being. I've got lots more to talk to you about, so how about we meet again next week? Maybe we can find a better spot – somewhere public but where we can talk a bit more freely."

I felt stunned and a little in awe. "Okay then, I guess. I'll see you next week then? I'll have to think about things in the meantime. I might even see if I can get down to Calvary and have a look around."

"Great idea. You do that. Till next week then." His warm smile was infectious and he reached out his arm to shake my hand. I stood up, smiling back. As I shook his hand, it was as though we had reached an agreement and were shaking on it. "Thanks for your time, Megan. See you next week." With that, he turned and left the hall, smiling and nodding to people as he moved past them on his way out.

Whatever Kevin might have done, he still carried a presence wherever he went. Students and other members of the community at Araluen gave Kevin plenty of space as he passed, returning his smile.

It had been a puzzling day. I needed time to digest all that Kevin had said. But I couldn't help feeling tremendously complimented that he had singled me out in such a way; that he held me in such high regard. He obviously saw more in me than I saw in myself. There was much to reflect and think about.

Talking with Kevin hadn't resulted in the apology I'd been anticipating. There had been no discussion about the past at all. No, it had been something entirely different, purely focused on the future. Unexpectedly, I'd been caught up yet again in Kevin's charisma and enthusiasm.

Chapter Thirteen

I took my coffee cup outside to the wash-up area to rinse it out. I was still lost in my thoughts when Sandy appeared at my side.

"That looked interesting," she said.

"Hmm. It was," I replied. I finished rinsing my cup but didn't bother drying it. We walked back into the mess hall to get lunch. It was the usual luncheon meat and salad. The mess hall wasn't a very good place to talk privately, so I didn't say much as we ate. We agreed to meet in our room later. I needed to talk with someone about the things Kevin had said.

Sandy was out cleaning up her dishes when I opted for another slice of bread with peanut butter. While at the bread counter, I noticed Ray sitting on his own eating his lunch. After applying a rather hefty helping of peanut paste onto my lovely fresh bread, I walked over to Ray's table.

"Mind if I join you?" I asked.

"No mate, not at all. Sit down." He grinned at me. I could see his tongue trying to conceal his missing tooth, rather unsuccessfully.

"How's it goin'?" he asked. "I heard you have a new preacher up there in the college."

"Yeah, we do. It's a big change, but I like him. We all miss Kevin though."

"Yeah, heard about all that messy business. Gotta expect it though. A man's a man."

"You reckon?" I was shocked at his comment. "It was hypocritical though."

"Yeah, probably you're right. But I still like him. He's been good to me, letting me stay here and all."

"How are you going with your drinking problem?"

"Good mate, good. Good while I'm here anyway – there's nothing to drink." He laughed as he answered. "Some of the guys down at the camp go into town sometimes for a few, but I don't go with them. Don't know what I'd do. So I've been hanging out here mostly."

"Good on you! But you were coming back from somewhere the other day."

"Yeah, I've been helping out Andy a bit. Nothin' else to do. He looks after all the grounds around here. It's a pretty big place. I picked up some stuff in town for him. Kept away from the pub though. Don't trust m'self yet."

"Andy? Yeah, I've seen him around. He always looks like he's in a rush. He doesn't even say hello."

"Ha, ha. He's probably too scared to talk to you. You bein' one of the students up on the hill."

"Really?" I replied, a little shocked. "Scared of us? Why?"

"'C'mon, you're joking aren't you?" His face was stony but amused. He took another mouthful of lunch. He seemed to be studying my face as he chomped, gauging me. "You students keep to yourself … too good for the rest of the folk living here."

His words pulled me up a bit. I hadn't thought about it before. But I had to be honest. Ray was the first person I had talked to other than the students and staff at the college since I'd been here. Araluen was home to a lot of other people, but they kept to themselves and so did we. But I hadn't realized that until now.

"I guess we do keep to ourselves. That isn't very nice though, is it?"

"Whatever. Jus' the way it is." He shrugged and kept eating his lunch. "Nice that you came over for a chat though."

"Ha, I appreciated that smoke you gave me the other day. I felt bad afterward though. I've given up you know. Dumb thing to do, really."

"You looked like you needed it."

"Yeah, it was all the bad news about Kevin. It got to me."

"Anytime. If you wanna chat, feel free."

"Gee thanks. Anyway, I'll let you finish your lunch." I stood up to go and realized I hadn't touched my bread and peanut butter.

"Ya might as well finish that." He said pointing to my bread with his knife, grinning. The playfulness in his eyes caught me off guard and for some strange reason made me feel a little vulnerable.

I sat down again. He was very different from anyone I'd known before and I liked talking to him. His rugged face looked marked somehow, scarred, yet not without charm. I had a sense his life experiences had been very different from my own which made getting to know him tantalizing, intriguing. Though his build was slim, I could see the ripple of his muscles move as he ate his lunch.

"If you want another smoke, you're welcome to pop down to me caravan … anytime." He said.

"No, no. Don't tempt me!" I replied, laughing. "I don't want to start it up again." His eyes were laughing too, but I knew his invitation to be genuine. I peered at him quizzically. "You know, it's kind of hard to imagine you in church. That must have been some experience you had ... that you told me about the other day. Have you been going to church?"

"Yeah, a few of us go into Gympie on Sunday mornings." He looked up from his lunch and looked at me carefully. "It's a lot to take in all this stuff. I'm tryin' to get my head around it."

"Really? I'm happy to talk about it if you like."

He put his cutlery down though he hadn't finished his lunch and leaned back in his chair. "That might help actually. I don't get some of the things that go on there at times."

"Really, like what?" I asked.

He leaned forward, pushing his plate aside, lunch forgotten, his face intent. "Well, I can't understand why those people fall down at the front. What's that about? It's freaky. What's goin' on?"

He was looking into my face, waiting, his dark brown eyes probing.

"Oh, okay. That is different isn't it? I found it scary at first too, but then it happened to me."

"Really?" His eyes widened, waiting for more.

"Yeah, I didn't want to fall down, seemed a bit nutty to me. But when Kevin prayed for me and he put his hands on my head, I felt this nice feeling flow over me. It was easy to fall down."

"He didn't push you?"

"No way! I just sort of felt relaxed and wanted to lie down and keep the feeling. It made me feel close to God. Things were going on in my head and I felt like God was talking to me. It was like I could see things clearly for that moment."

"Wow. Still sounds pretty weird, though. I'm not sure about it."

"Well I wouldn't worry about it too much. It's something that happens sometimes. It doesn't mean anything if it doesn't happen to you."

"That's a relief. I don't want that happening to me."

I smiled. "I felt like I was surrendering to God when it happened. I've been trying to change my life for the better."

Ray looked at me, puzzled. "Wadda *you* got to change?"

I laughed. "You're joking, aren't you? So much has changed already, but so much more to do! But I'm getting there I guess. I love studying the Bible at college. It's interesting. I love it."

"Well, you're alright by me." He seemed distracted for a moment by something across the room. "Look, Megan, I gotta go now. Bin great talking to you though. Have to do it again. You make a lotta sense. I gotta go." He picked up his plate and stood up. I stood up too.

"Sure. See you round," I said and we both went our own way. I could see a woman waiting for him across the room.

Sandy was waiting for me when I got back to our room.

"Hi! Sorry about that. I got chatting with that Ray guy at the mess hall. We never talk to a lot of the people around here much, do we? Hadn't thought about it before."

Perched on her bed, Sandy looked at me. "Whatever. I guess not. Don't think I really want to talk to that lot, though. Talk is most of them are hiding out here from the police. Kevin's a bit of a soft touch, they say." Sandy didn't seem interested in talking about Ray. "What I want to know is what Kevin had to say to you."

Jumping on my bed, I got comfortable, lying back and propping up my head with my arm. I told her all about Kevin's plans for Calvary down the road and how he wanted me to be involved.

"That's fantastic, Megan. Now you know what you'll be doing at the end of college. I wish I knew what I was going to do." Sandy pouted as she spoke. "I have to admit ... I am a little jealous."

"Jealous! Don't be ridiculous. I'm terrified." But secretly I was chuffed at her response. Running a drug rehabilitation farm did sound rather a prestigious undertaking. "God will tell you what he has in mind for you, I know. You have so many gifts."

"I guess so."

We chatted about Phil and the way things were going. The mood in the Bible College generally seemed to have settled since the shocking news of the week before. I think we were now all resigned to the fact that we were here, so we might as well get on with it. There wasn't anything else we could do.

Though it came into my mind as I talked to Sandy, I didn't mention that I'd known about Kevin and Andrea's relationship. I'd kept that secret for so long, it seemed easiest to keep it that way. I didn't know what else to do, so I decided it best to maintain the status quo.

Chapter Fourteen

I approached the campsite cautiously. The people here seemed to keep to themselves and I felt uncertain about approaching them.

The layout seemed haphazard with a combination of tents and caravans set up. Washing hung on a makeshift clothes line. A pregnant woman with long dark hair was lugging a bucket of water as I drew near, switching it from hand to hand. Her hair was lank and unkempt. Her bare feet appeared with each step as her long Indian cotton skirt swished around her legs as she struggled with the bucket. She eyed me suspiciously. I recognized her as the lady who had called Ray away at lunch the other day. I couldn't help wondering if they might be together.

"G'day," I offered when I was within hearing range. "I'm looking for Ray. Do you know where he is?"

"He's down by the rubbish dump helping Andy, last I saw him." She tilted her head in the direction of the dump as she spoke, peering at me quizzically. Though she didn't say it, I felt her eyes saying, *And what the hell do you want with him?*

Her general countenance made me feel uncomfortable, so I decided not to strike up a conversation, but turned in the direction of the dump. I'd never been there before; in fact, I didn't even know one existed. I set off in the direction she had indicated with the tilt of her head.

"Thanks!" I threw over my shoulder as I left.

I didn't have to look far as I could hear the banging and crashing over a rise, not far from the camp site. Andy was operating a small tractor, trying to bury some of the rubbish with the blade while Ray was trying to get a fire going to burn some cardboard boxes. Ray was surprised to see me approaching.

"Hi mate. Wadda ya doing here? You desperate for a smoke or something?"

His question made me chuckle. "Hi Ray. No, no, that's not what's on my mind at all. But now that you've offered ..." I was shocked at myself. I had not thought about having a smoke at all since that day a couple of weeks ago, but now that I was here talking to Ray, the idea suddenly seemed quite attractive. Impulsively, I took a cigarette from his proffered packet. I was aware that the tractor had stopped working behind me and I could feel Andy's eyes on us.

Ray lit the smoke for me and then lit himself one. He kept a watchful eye on the smoldering pile of rubbish. I could feel the heat emanating from it.

I dragged on the cigarette before speaking further. It was Virginia. I hated Virginia. I much preferred Menthol. I wondered what I was doing, but I didn't stop. I waved at Andy who was still staring.

"Listen Ray, I don't mean to hassle you, but I need to ask a favor."

"Yeah? What's that?"

"I want to go down to Calvary, the new property next door. Do you ever go down there? How do I go about getting a lift down there some time? I just want to have a look around."

"Oh sure. I go down from time to time to pick things up or take things down. Lotta work going on down there at the moment; lotta buildings going up."

"Would I be able to go with you one trip? It'd have to be in the afternoon 'cause we're in lectures all morning."

"Sure. Next time I'm goin' down I'll give you a yell at lunch time. How's that?"

"That'd be great. I'd really appreciate it. There's a chance I might be working down there at the end of college and I don't know much about it."

Andy had the tractor moving again, but I sensed his eyes still on me.

"Sounds interesting." Ray took another drag on his cigarette. "What ya gonna do there?"

"Not sure yet. Have to talk to Kevin about it more. He wants to make it a refuge for people in trouble, for people who need to get away."

"That explains things a bit. They're building blocks of some sort. I guess they're for someone to live in."

I could feel my face burning from the heat of the fire and the hot sun. The cigarette was making me feel dizzy and the Virginia flavor felt rough in my mouth.

"Well thanks, Ray. Let me know when it's a good time to get down there, then." I stubbed out my cigarette and looked up again. "Thanks again for the smoke," I turned and walked off. I gave a bit of a wave to Andy as I left. I could feel them both watching me as I walked away.

◊ ◊ ◊

I loved feeling wind in my hair on the back of the utility as we lumbered down the track towards Calvary. The track was washed out in places, so Ray had to ease the truck along steadily while I clung to the rollbar on the back. We couldn't get up much speed, but that didn't detract from my enjoyment. Being up on the tray of the ute gave me a wonderful sensation of freedom - something about being outdoors, in the cool breeze, unprotected.

We approached a fence and Ray pulled up and jumped out to open the gate. I couldn't help noticing his muscular arms as he closed the car door. He looked up and grinned.

"I can get that." I said as I scrambled off the truck, wishing I hadn't worn a dress. I had put on so much weight since being at Bible College; I didn't have many things that still fitted. But my wrap-around white Indian dress was a favorite. It helped to hide my growing curves. At least, I hoped it did.

Ray got back in the cab and I opened the farm gate. I felt embarrassed fiddling with the latch but managed to master it.

"Hop in the cab," he said.

"Nah, I like it on the back." I managed to climb back on reasonably daintily by sliding my bottom onto the tray first then swinging my legs up while holding my dress. There was no way I was going to miss out on a ride like this.

We pulled into Calvary and Ray had been right; there was a lot of activity going on. Construction was well advanced on what looked like some sort of accommodation similar to what I was living in at Bible College. Central to all the activity was a lovely old Queenslander. It was a traditional weather-board farm house with the usual verandah most of the way around. It looked a little worse for wear, but still added character to the scene in spite of paint peeling back here and there.

Ray had some things in the truck he had to drop off, so he pulled up next to one of the sheds at the front of the house. A middle-aged man, who must have heard the vehicle approach, came out of the doorway and called, "G'day!"

Ray helped me off the back and started untying the rope which secured the boxes on the back. He called something to me, but a motor running in the shed smothered his voice.

"G'Day, 'ow ya goin? I'm Nigel." The middle-aged man had pulled off his hat and extended his hand towards me. What little hair he had was sticking up at odd angles, wet with sweat. His shirt was having trouble staying secure in his pants, probably due to his generous girth. Nigel and his wife Mary were running the existing diary operation at Calvary.

"Hi! I'm Megan. I'm up at Bible College and wanted to come down and have a look around," I said as I shook his hand. His smile was warm and friendly and I felt pleased to meet him.

Nigel nodded his head like he was taking in what I had said, chewing it over in his mind. "Sure. We're just finishing up in the dairy at the moment. Have a look around." He turned to Ray. "Got that stuff okay?"

"I dunno. Andy gave me some boxes to bring down to you."

"Great. Thanks for that. Put 'em in here and I'll get to them when we're finished." He looked around at me again and called, "See ya!" as he tipped his hat. I could hear his feet squelching in his gumboots as he trudged back into the dairy. I wanted to go in and have a look. I'd never seen one before.

"Can we go in there?" I asked Ray.

"Nah. Not much to see at the moment. They've finished milking. I can bring you down another time if you like. They're at it every day ya know," he said, grinning to himself. "They're building a new dairy over there … for goats. Kevin seems to have some crazy idea about a goat dairy. Goat milk's gettin' pretty popular he reckons. I dunno m'self. Never tried it."

"Yeah. I've heard about that." The thought of trying to milk goats sounded fascinating to me. I didn't know anything about farm life, but I'd always wondered about it, wondered what it might be like.

"Anyways, I've gotta get these boxes off for Nigel."

"Okay. I'm going to have a look around."

I left Ray to his work and wandered over to what I guessed would be the accommodation block. It was still in progress; the rooms more like empty shells with a few pipes sticking out here and there. I found it hard to imagine what it might look like eventually. It was quiet with no builders around. I guessed they were working on the goat dairy.

Rubbish was strewn around inside and out and I could see where the builders must have had their meal breaks. Lunch wrappers flapped in the breeze, trapped under broken bricks and chunks of cement.

I wandered through the openings where doors were yet to be installed, trying to picture the type of people that might end up here. I tried to imagine myself here looking after them, talking to them, counseling them.

How the hell would I know what to say to them? How would I even know how to help them?

Kevin seemed to think I could help them. I remembered his words and could visualize the intensity on his face as he had said, *'You have so much potential. I know you can do this. You will need some help and support of course. But you have a gift over your life. I know God has big plans for you.'*

I sighed deeply and repeated it in my head, *'God has big plans for you …'*

It all seemed overwhelming — the thought of *me* running a drug rehabilitation farm. I wouldn't know where to begin. But I wanted to please God. I wanted to fulfill my potential and do the very best that I could do. Perhaps this was my destiny, the path that I had to take.

I realized I had come to the last room in the block. I stood at the window opening which looked back towards the house and the sheds. I could hear the builders at work, hammering and someone using an electric saw. A gentle breeze touched my face. I thought about my own life and the stupid choices I had made in the past. I had seen some of the dark side of life. Perhaps that would help me to understand others still struggling to make their own better choices.

I sighed again, wondering if I had what it would take to fulfill Kevin's dream.

Is this really God's will for my life?

Chapter Fifteen

I kept lifting up the lid of the kitchen urn and peeking in as I waited for the water to come back to the boil. I wanted to make myself a nice, hot cup of coffee. I couldn't help grinning to myself a little as I waited.

There was no denying that I enjoyed being singled out by Kevin. This was the second week in a row that he had arranged to meet with me after class. He had popped into the classroom only briefly to encourage the students this morning but still taken the opportunity to set up a meeting with me again.

He seemed a little more relaxed this week. I couldn't help feeling he might be enjoying having a bit more freedom. He had been 'stood down' from his role as senior pastor but I wondered what that really meant. He wasn't preaching from the platform anymore and he wasn't teaching at Bible College but he did seem to be very involved in the developments at Calvary next door.

I kept an eye on the double doors, expecting him to appear at any moment. I wasn't disappointed. The doors swung open and Kevin, at his usual bustling pace, burst in, eyes scanning the mess hall, looking for me.

"Megan, Megan. Good to find you. How are you?" His face was aglow and he was smiling warmly as he took my hand in his with a firm grip. Before I could answer, he said, "Let's find a better place to have a chat. What about your room? Where is it? If we sat outside it, would we be in public view? I don't want any chins wagging. I have to be very careful, but I want to be able to talk freely. How would that do?"

Taken aback and feeling a little confused, I said, "My room overlooks the mess. That's it up there. Pretty much anyone can see us there." I pointed through the window to my room on the hill overlooking the mess hall, knowing Sandy had gone into town for the afternoon.

"Perfect," he said, following my gaze. "I'll grab a coffee."

I chatted to Kevin about my visit to Calvary as we walked up the steep drive.

"Good. It's coming on, isn't it? I've even found someone to run the new dairy. Yes, it's all coming together rather nicely. It's in God's plan. Things always come together nicely when they're in God's plan, don't you think?" He grinned at me.

"I guess." I said, still feeling uncertain. I kept my eyes down and kept walking.

When we got to my room, Kevin arranged the seats outside carefully to make sure we could be easily seen. He pulled them well away from the door.

"Can't be too careful," he said. It made me feel a little uncomfortable and I looked down at the mess hall wondering what eyes might be on us. I felt confident that someone would be watching us. I wondered what they might be thinking. I wasn't sure what I was thinking about this.

We settled into our seats ready to talk. I wanted to raise my concerns about taking on a commitment like Calvary when I felt so inexperienced. I decided to start with, "I think I'm going to need some sort of special training —"

"Training? The Holy Spirit's the best trainer there is. You'll be fine, Megan, I know you'll be fine." He took a brief look around and then set his eyes on me with a sense of urgency.

"Megan, I really need someone to talk to. I can't talk to anyone. I know you and Andrea were good friends. I know you'll understand. I know you're someone I can trust ... really trust." He was staring at me, intensely. He sat forward in his seat a little. One of his eyes winked gently, occasionally as he talked.

I didn't say anything. I just sat staring at him, unprepared for this sudden shift in tone.

"I loved Andrea from the depth of my being. I still do love her. Having her taken from me has been the most painful thing I have ever experienced. I feel like ... like I'm being torn in pieces."

I had nothing to say, so I sat and listened, wide-eyed. It was as though a flood gate was opening. Kevin had things burning inside him that he obviously needed to talk to someone about. Here I was, sitting right in front of him. He had chosen me to tell his deepest, innermost thoughts. I felt frozen in time. It was as though my own feelings turned to stone. I was there to listen, and listen only. I swallowed my sense of shock and tried to take in what he was saying.

"No one can imagine what it's like for me. No one can imagine what it's like to spearhead a move of God like this. It is such a pressure, such a burden, such a struggle. All the things we've done ... all the things NSC has achieved ... there has been a price. I've had to pay that price.

"If I could only describe to you what that pressure is like ... give you a glimpse of the weight I carry. It is immense. The devil wants to stop me ... stop me any way he can. The devil brings such pressure against me; emotional pressure like you can't imagine. Andrea could see it. She really wanted to help me. She tried to help me. She *did* help me. She made it bearable. Somehow, with her by my side, I had renewed energy, renewed vigor. I could cope. She helped to ease the pain."

He sat back in the chair. There were no tears in his eyes, but his pain and agony were palpable. I was looking into Kevin's innermost personal turmoil. I had no idea what to do, what to say or how to react. So I just sat and listened, wide-eyed and stunned.

"My life with my wife is a shell, an empty shell. Can you imagine what it's like to be trapped in a marriage with the wrong woman? It's torment. It's hell on earth.

"I was such a shy, shy man. I lived in the bush. I talked to cows and horses all day. I didn't know anything about girls or how to talk to them. I met Sue at Bible College. She seemed nice. I don't remember how it happened … how it happened that we got married. But it did. We don't even talk. We live in the same house together, but it's not really living together. We're strangers in the same house."

He leaned forward again and tucked his feet under his chair. His eyes were boring into mine. The lines and creases on his cheeks seemed to have deepened. His toughened skin seemed stretched and strained.

"God talks to me. He has given me so many ideas, so many plans, so many dreams. Sometimes I can't sleep at night. God talks to me and shows me things, visions. I haven't even started yet with all the things he's put in my head and heart to do. God has asked so much of me … everything.

"I thought he would understand about Andrea. I thought that he knew I needed her … that I couldn't do it without her. God meant for us to have a mate. That's why he created Eve. A man needs a mate. I needed Andrea."

He sighed deeply, looking at the ground.

"We were so good together. They have been the happiest

times of my life."

He looked up at me again, the pain evident in his eyes.

"But I understand now that I deceived myself. You have to believe me, Megan; I thought it was okay. I really thought God understood and would make allowances for me for all the things he has asked me to do."

"But now I see that it wasn't okay." He leaned back, cradling his chin in his hand. He shook his head slowly from side to side. His eyes looked away, glazed and staring. He was lost in his thoughts, lost in his private agony. "Poor Andrea, she's hurting. I know she's hurting so much."

The silence hung heavily between us. Still I sat as stone, my coffee mug cradled on my lap untouched. It was cold now.

"Have you spoken to her?" He was looking directly at me again, waiting for an answer. I wasn't sure I could move. Everything felt frozen, frozen in time.

Somehow I managed to stir myself and looked down at my coffee mug. I took a sip to gather my thoughts and get my body moving again, even a little.

"Me, uh, no. I haven't spoken to Andrea, no." I felt confused and unsure of myself.

Why hadn't I spoken to Andrea?

It had never crossed my mind to speak to her. In fact, the mention of her name made saliva form in my mouth in distaste. I remembered spitting on the ground at the mention of her name the day we heard the news of the affair. I hadn't wanted to think about Andrea. I didn't want to think about her now. I knew on some level that I needed to forgive her but I hadn't reached that place yet. I needed more time.

But somehow now, I had been taken to another place, a new place, a place I didn't understand. I was being forced to see Andrea's situation from a different perspective. I looked at Kevin, but said nothing further.

What do I feel?

"You must, Megan. She'll be so lonely down there. She's with a bunch of strangers. She's hurting. I know she's hurting. She needs her friends. That girl, Jane, who went with her. What a blessing she was, willing to do that. Both Andrea and I are indebted to her. But she can't stay with her forever."

I'm sure my mouth must have been gaping, but Kevin didn't seem to notice. I was trying to take in what he had said. Andrea needed *me*? My mind couldn't seem to absorb the words. They bounced off.

Kevin stood up suddenly. Someone standing outside the mess hall was calling him. He waved back and yelled, "In a minute." He looked back at me. "Megan, I have to go now. I can't tell you how important this has been to me, what a difference it makes for me, to be able to talk. We'll talk again soon." He tapped my knee with his hand casually as he moved to leave. I went to stand up, but he was gone.

I leaned back in the chair and sipped my cold coffee, dazed. I needed a cigarette.

Opening the door to my room, I rifled through the bedside table and found the packet of Alpines stashed there a few days ago. I didn't want to smoke, not really smoke. I just wanted to have the occasional one; at least that is what I kept telling myself.

I stuffed them in my study folder and cradling the folder in my arms, I set off down the track. Smoking wasn't appreciated by the other students and I didn't want them to know I was indulging. I wanted to find a quiet place to think, alone.

Kevin's words were spinning around in my head as I walked. I still couldn't believe he had taken me into his confidence the way he had. I was trying to find my feelings; trying to understand myself.

One thing I knew, however, was that I couldn't talk to anyone about this. I couldn't betray Kevin's confidence given to me so freely, so confidently. His trust in me was compelling.

Away from the Bible College buildings, I found an old tree stump out of sight and lit up a cigarette. I drew in the smoke deeply.

What just happened? Why did Kevin choose to bare his soul to me?

I felt sure he had not revealed these thoughts to anyone else. I now held the strictest confidence of a very powerful and influential man.

As I sat on that log and enjoyed my smoke, another emotion bubbled to the surface, finding its way through the cold stony feeling that had been choking my chest since Kevin had opened his personal floodgates. Another emotion had emerged that sealed with surety my need to keep Kevin's confidence absolutely secret ... I felt honored to have been singled out by Kevin. I couldn't deny that I was flattered that Kevin had chosen to share *his* secrets with *me*.

It was now my responsibility, my duty, to protect Kevin. He needed me. As the blue smoke from my cigarette curled around my face, I realized that whatever I felt about Andrea had to be put aside. For some reason I couldn't explain, what *I* felt was not important now that I had shared Kevin's intimate pain and suffering.

Chapter Sixteen

"I need to pee," Sandy said, looking at Alan.

"Okay, okay. Do you want to pee by the road or can you wait until we need petrol?" He replied, looking a bit annoyed.

"When do we need fuel?"

Alan looked at the gauge, "We've got about half a tank."

Sandy pulled a face. "Better stop before that." She looked up ahead for some trees or bushes she could hide behind. We had been driving through flat country, more like a desert than anything else. There didn't seem to be many discreet spots for peeing around here.

"I'm getting hungry anyway. Let's stop at the next town. Who's got the map?" Peter said over the back seat.

"It's here," I said, pulling it open. "Next town should be, um ... Wilcannia. Have you noticed any milestones lately?"

"Nup," was all Alan could manage. I'd been dozing in the back, so hadn't been paying attention for the last hour or so.

"Maybe we need to swap drivers again," I said, worried Alan might be zoning out with fatigue.

"Nah, I'm fine. Might be good to stretch the legs though. It's so hot. I really need a drink."

It was hot, even though we had all the windows open. I could feel my dress sticking to my back.

"What's the time?" asked Peter as a trickle of sweat escaped his forehead and rolled down his cheek. He wiped it away and flicked it in my direction.

"Hey! Yuk! Cut it out."

"Thought you might need some help waking up."

I found it hard to be mad at his cheesy grin and mischievous eyes. Sandy was looking over her shoulder at us, "It's nearly eleven."

We'd been driving all night and everyone was getting weary of sitting in the car. We all needed to stretch our legs.

"How far have we come and how far to go?" Alan asked.

I looked at the map again and had a rough guess. "Well, it looks like we are well over half way; probably around 700k's to Adelaide."

"That's still a long way, another whole day's drive," Alan was watching the road as he talked. "It'll be dark when we get there. Andrea'll be waiting for us, wondering where we are."

It had been Alan's idea to visit Andrea for the weekend, but the only way to get to Adelaide for a weekend was to drive nonstop for 24 hours – both ways. Now that we had finished Bible College we had the opportunity to take a short break before moving on to the next phase of our lives.

We had felt as though we were on a great adventure when we set off for Adelaide. Now we were just hot and thirsty.

Everyone fell silent again. I gazed out the window, planning to look for a milestone to see how far it was to Wilcannia. But my mind soon drifted. I thought about Andrea and wondered what it would be like to see her again. Most of my friends in the youth group had forgiven her 'indiscretion', as they called it. Others in the youth group hadn't been able to forgive so readily. Some had even moved on to other churches. Those that had decided to stick around missed Andrea and the fun we used to have in the youth group.

I felt swept along by their warmth and concern. Also Kevin's words had echoed in my head many times since our conversation months ago. *You must talk to her, Megan. She's so lonely down there. She's with a bunch of strangers. She's hurting.* I guess I did feel some empathy for her. It must have been hard being forced to leave the way she had. She didn't even have time to say goodbye to anyone. She had been whisked away in the middle of the night to a strange place. I couldn't imagine what that must have been like, being ripped away from family and friends. It must have been agony and I'm sure she felt guilty as well. I hoped her new pastor had been good to her.

I sighed deeply. A flash of movement caught my eye, "Hey, there's an emu! Look, over there. It's heading right for us!" A lone emu was striding at top speed on a trajectory straight for the car.

Alan eased off the accelerator. "Wow. It really is heading at us," he said as he slowed down and pulled off the road. The emu passed with amazing speed and dexterity, crossing the road not far in front of us.

"Stupid thing. If I hadn't stopped it would have crashed into us. I'm sure of it."

Sandy jumped out of the car. "I'm gonna pee and no one's going to look! Megan, you tell me if any cars are coming."

"Sure!" It was nice to get out of the car and stretch my legs. There was no car in sight. The road was so straight you could see for miles until it disappeared into the shimmering horizon. "Nothing coming either way," I called. Now that the engine had been turned off, the eerie silence of the bush enveloped us. A soft breeze brushed my face as I squinted in either direction, keeping watch, whilst trying to avoid looking at Sandy as she squatted not far away.

"C'mon Sandy. Let's get moving. I'm hungry all of a sudden." Alan was already getting back into the car.

"Hey! I've got a great idea," I said as it suddenly dawned on me. "We mightn't have any water, but we've got ice melting in the Esky!" I don't know why I hadn't thought of it earlier. I'd been cradling the Esky on the back seat for the last few hours.

"Oh man, what a great idea. Give us the keys, Al. I want to get my towel out of the boot."

Peter dipped his towel in the melting ice and wrapped it around his head.

"You look like you belong in the desert!" I teased. He lifted his head and strutted around, knowing we were all wishing we had a cold wet towel too. At least we could suck on some ice. It was a godsend.

"C'mon. Let's get going." Alan urged us all back into the car.

I woke to the sound of the phone ringing. I rolled over in my sleeping bag. The lounge room floor was hard but I was so exhausted after our long drive I didn't care. Andrea had picked up the phone and was kneeling on the floor talking in whispers. I guess she didn't want to disturb us. I tried to zone out the noise and drift back to sleep.

But whether it was the silence of the early morning which offered nothing to smother Andrea's hushed conversation or whether it was the sense of strain in her voice, I couldn't help tuning in and listening.

"Yeah, they're here. They arrived about ten last night, pretty wrecked ... No ... not really ... You shouldn't call like this. ... It ... It's got to stop ... I know ... Yes it *is* hard, *very* hard ... for me too. ... Don't say that!" Andrea was struggling to keep her voice as low as possible.

My foot was itching. I really wanted to scratch it but I held my breath instead. I didn't want Andrea to know I was listening. I tried to keep my breathing slow and easy, like I was asleep. I felt pretty sure by her tone and the few words I could make out that Andrea was talking to Kevin. I didn't know how I felt about this. I guess it wasn't a surprise after all the things Kevin had told me over the last couple of months about how he felt about her. It was no surprise to me that he was having difficulty giving her up. But I also felt sure that they weren't *supposed* to be talking to each other. I suspected such contact would be considered breaking the rules of Kevin's forced probation.

I could sense that Andrea wanted to get off the phone.

"Stop it please. I really need to go now … No, it's not that … He's been very good to me … STOP IT … Please. … I've got to go … now. I'm hanging up. … Bye." She put the receiver down quietly and tiptoed back to her bedroom.

It was such a relief to scratch my foot. I rolled over on my back and looked at the ceiling thinking about Andrea and Kevin.

I suppose they can't get into too much trouble now that they each live in different cities thousands of kilometers from each other. Maybe that's why the church board sent Andrea so far away.

I lay there remembering how painful it had been leaving Don when I had first made the decision to become a Christian. It hadn't been easy and the only way I had managed to stick with it was to believe that he was better off without me. Well that is how I had worked it out in my head. It had helped at the time. I didn't think about him so much these days.

Kevin was obviously still thinking about Andrea *and* he had her phone number. I wondered how he had managed to obtain that. Perhaps Andrea had given it to him or perhaps someone else knew they were still talking to each other.

To take my mind off them, I started rehearsing what I was going to say tonight. When we had told Andrea we were coming to visit her, she had asked if I would speak to her new youth group on the Saturday night. As I was going over what I had prepared in my mind, sleep drifted over me again.

◊ ◊ ◊

At last Andrea and I had a few minutes alone to talk. She had brought us to a hamburger shop for supper after the youth meeting and the others were up ordering.

"How did I go?" I asked Andrea, wanting to know what she thought.

She looked at me with her soft caring eyes and flashed a knowing smile, "You did really well, Megan. You spoke well. You'd obviously prepared well and it was amazing that the topic you chose to speak on was very much in line with what I'd been teaching them in the last few weeks."

"Really?" I was taken aback. Perhaps I had heard from God when I had chosen what to speak about. I had felt passionate about it. I wanted to understand God's judgment and understand truly how he wanted us to behave in judging others around us. I had worried she might find it a bit radical. It seemed confusing at times, trying to understand God's forgiveness and yet having a responsibility to judge people according to God's Word.

"The only thing you need to learn is to build a rapport. When you first got up, you jumped straight into reading the word and delivering your message." She frowned a little as she talked, but her eyes were genuine and encouraging. "Yes, you need to tell your audience something about yourself. Give them an opportunity to warm to you, to know who you are."

"Mmmmm," I responded thoughtfully. "I guess that would've been better, wouldn't it?"

"Yes, you watch when you hear a new speaker in future and see what they do. You have to make your audience feel relaxed with you in front of them."

I sighed deeply. "That might've been easier if I hadn't been feeling so nervous!"

"Of course, but you'll get the hang of it if you practice."

"Kevin has such big plans for me. It scares me."

Andrea's eyes darted towards me at the mention of Kevin's name. She held my gaze as she said, "I'm sure he knows what he's doing."

"Maybe, but I feel I'm so inexperienced to be taking on such responsibility." I could sense that Andrea didn't want to continue this conversation. I pushed the thoughts of Calvary aside and replayed her words of encouragement in my head. I was on a high. It was great feedback on my first attempt to teach from the Bible. It made me feel a little more confident about tackling the challenges of Calvary.

Alan, Peter and Sandy re-joined us and we chatted about Andrea's new youth group. It was obvious they all loved her, just as we had. Andrea's leadership qualities would ensure her success wherever she went. It didn't surprise any of us that she had been so well received.

The memory of the phone ringing that morning jumped into my mind. No one had mentioned that call. I didn't want to talk about it with the others. I had decided to tuck it away, deep down inside. I seemed to be accumulating secrets these days. I didn't know what to do with them all except that it seemed important to lock them away and keep them safe. I didn't fully understand why, but I had a sense that for some reason I had been chosen as a guardian of secrets about Kevin and Andrea. I had some sort of responsibility to keep these secrets. It seemed important not to fail them.

The feedback from Andrea and the others was very encouraging. I felt a little hope for the future and a smidgen of a boost in confidence. Maybe, just maybe, I could manage a drug rehabilitation farm at the age of 22.

◊ ◊ ◊

As we stood at the car saying goodbye, Andrea slipped an envelope into my hand.

"It's for Jane," Andrea said, her voice lowered. "Can you pass this on for me? I'd really appreciate it. I've missed her."

"Sure." I took the letter and shoved it into my shoulder bag.

"You know Megan, you did a great job helping Jane fit into the youth group."

"I don't know. I think Jane probably would have done alright on her own anyway."

Andrea took my arm. "Don't underestimate yourself, Megan. You did a good job."

"Okay. Thanks. I guess," I said shrugging, embarrassed.

Andrea turned away then and walked back into the house. I exchanged glances with the others, each of us knowing Andrea was feeling emotional and that she didn't want us to see her that way. She had not discussed her personal feelings at any point during our visit. The conversation had been congenial but light-hearted. But seeing Andrea take off like this made us all realize how hard life must be living down here so far away from all her friends and family. Yet she chose to keep her pain to herself.

On that somber note, we climbed in the car, sad, but also glad that we had made the effort to visit her.

As Alan pulled the car onto the street to begin the mammoth drive home, I gazed out the window. It occurred to me that I had never spoken to Andrea or Kevin about how they had lied to me all those years ago. They had never apologized to me, but then neither had I ever challenged them.

Weird.

I sighed deeply and leaned my head against the window trying to think about something else.

Chapter Seventeen

I preferred working in the mess hall. Sometimes I felt my bedroom claustrophobic. It was nice having a room to myself now that Bible College had finished and Sandy had moved back to Brisbane. Kevin had agreed I could keep my room rather than live down at Calvary. It was a relief to know I had somewhere to escape, a refuge.

But, for some reason, the sound of the cook working in the kitchen behind me helped. I could think better here than when alone in my room. I was tempted to go into the kitchen and chat with him. I knew he was leaving soon. But I resisted and tried to focus on the job at hand.

I chewed my pen as I tried to visualize life at Calvary and tried to imagine what a typical day might be like. I wanted to design a program that laid out what we would do each day. Now that the new year, 1979, had begun, it wouldn't be long before residents would arrive.

There wasn't much written on my note pad.

The days would start early milking the goats with each of the residents on a roster. I thought it would be important to keep everyone busy in a productive way. We also needed to develop a counselling program so that the residents had regular opportunities to work through their problems. It seemed we needed a mix of emotional, spiritual and practical support.

My attention was diverted momentarily as I pondered what we should actually call the residents. Residents seemed a little too formal. The thought of calling them inmates made me chuckle but of course that would be inappropriate, even though some of them may well have spent time in prison.

I could feel the knot tightening in my stomach again as I looked at my note pad. Not many ideas had been forthcoming. *How the hell can I design a program like this when I have no idea what I'm doing?* The regular internal dialogue was threatening to start up again.

Ray startled me as he pulled out a chair on the opposite side of the table.

"What ya doin'?" he asked. "You look pretty serious." The interruption was a welcome relief.

"Working on stuff for Calvary. Kevin wants to get it started in a few weeks." I put my pen down and leaned back with a big sigh.

"Oh yeah," Ray said, nodding his head. He had been working outside. I could see a stream of sweat rolling down his left temple. "I think the builders are nearly finished down there. Have you met the new guy running the goats? He's a blast."

I nodded as I replied, "Yeah, Geoff — Geoff Iverson. I do know him. Actually, I've known him for a while. He was friends with my brother Michael when he lived in New Zealand."

"Really? I could tell Geoff was a Kiwi. He seems alright. He's got lots of energy, that's for sure — always runnin' somewhere."

Ray's observation made me laugh. Ray was right. Geoff did have lots of energy and he was enthusiastic about running the goats even if he had never done anything quite like that before. In fact, Geoff was enthusiastic about everything he did.

"I really like Geoff's wife, Julie. She's diabetic, you know," I said. I'd never known anyone with diabetes before and found Julie an interesting person. She had an intensity, a passion for life and for Jesus that I hadn't seen in anyone before. Perhaps it was because she struggled so much with her health. She had nearly died a few times. "Funny but my brother Michael ... the one who knows them ... is coming to Araluen soon. Guess he and Geoff'll get on okay."

"Is that right? What's he gonna do?"

"He's coming to take over the kitchen. He's a professional cook — studied when he was in New Zealand."

Ray chuckled and leaned forward, lowering his voice, "Well, between you and me, that's probably a good thing. The old clown in there doesn't serve up the best at times ... ya know what I mean?"

"You reckon? He's not so bad." I looked down at my paper work, thinking I really should be working on my program for Calvary. I didn't want to bore Ray, but what he didn't know was that Kevin had appointed Geoff and Julie not just to build up additional enterprises at Calvary, such as running the goat dairy, but Geoff had also been appointed to help me. I'd finally managed to convince Kevin that my lack of experience was a problem. Geoff and Julie were to be my support, helping me in the overall leadership of the rehabilitation farm as well as managing the goat business. Having my brother Michael around would help too.

An awkward silence settled and I tried to think of something more interesting to talk about but nothing came. Thankfully Ray started the conversation up again.

"Not sure how Geoff and Nige'll get on, both trying to keep Kevin happy running the different dairies."

I shrugged. I hadn't thought much about such politics. "What, you mean the goat and cow dairies? Should be alright shouldn't it? They're separate buildings, different animals."

Ray shrugged back. "Just sayin'."

"Nige's got the farm house. Geoff'll be living down here at Araluen." It seemed a reasonable separation to me.

Ray shrugged again pulling a funny face. Before I could understand his insinuation, he changed the subject. "Kevin had a chat with me the other day."

"Really?" I said. "What about?"

"He wants me to go down to Calvary too — instead of living here. He said I would get more help down there with giving up the booze."

"What do you think about that?" I asked feeling panicked. *How the hell I would go about helping an alcoholic? What would I need to do?* My stomach churned.

"Well … it depends," he said.

"Depends on what?"

"Depends on whether you're the one that's goin' to look after me or not?"

I felt puzzled. "What do you mean?"

"Well Megan, you know I like talking to ya. You're the only person that really understands me 'round here. It ain't easy for me to trust people. I don't trust too many people at all ya know. I trust you. I'm not gonna go talking to any of those other clowns, no way!"

I could feel a blush creeping up my neck. "I don't know if that'd be possible, Ray. It's most likely that guys will be working with guys and same for the girls."

Ray's eyebrows pulled together in a frown. His eyes narrowed. "Yeah, but I have to be able to talk to somebody I can trust. There isn't much point otherwise, is there?"

What he said made some sense, but somewhere a little bell was ringing in my head, making me feel wary. But I liked it that he wanted to talk to me and seemed to like me. It made me feel empowered. It also helped my confidence in thinking about taking on this challenge; helped me believe I might actually be able to help people. Getting people to trust you was an important first step and I seemed to have achieved that with Ray without even trying.

"I don't know, Ray. I really don't know. I'll have to think about it."

"Anyway, somethin's gonna to have to happen. Kevin said I can't stay here. It's either Calvary or I'm outta here."

I was surprised to hear that. Kevin hadn't talked to me about his plans for Ray or his plans for any of the folk living in the camping area at Araluen. When I thought about it, there were probably others down there that might be candidates for Calvary.

"Are you ready to leave here? You haven't had a drink, have you?"

"No I haven't, but that's 'cos I'm livin' here. Don't know how I'd go if the pub was just around the corner. Ya know what I mean?"

"You might be stronger than you think."

"Maybe, but I'm not sure I'm ready to try."

"I don't know what to say, Ray."

"Ha! Megan lost for words. Never seen that before …" He wasn't hearing what he wanted to hear, but he still seemed amused. "Anyway, I have to do a run in the truck to take the milk down to the dairy factory, north of Brisbane. Was wondering if you'd like to come with me? Get you outta here for a bit. Whad'ya say? It'd be a good change of scenery."

The offer caught me by surprise.

Ray kept talking, "Geoff thought it would be a good idea to take someone with me. He wants to have options. The goat's milk has to get to the factory twice a week. We can't keep it around any longer than that. C'mon. You can learn to drive the truck." He was grinning now.

"Um, Ray, I dunno. Me, driving a truck? I've never done that before. How long does it take?"

"Coupla hours. You'll be back for tea."

The thought of spending a couple of hours with him was tempting. Even though we had got to know each other a little he still seemed mysterious and an opportunity to get to know him more was attractive. I closed my notebook and stood up. "Okay, I'll come. Give me a minute."

"Great." Ray stood up too. I'll meet you at the front gate in ten."

"Okay."

Ray was waiting in the truck with the door open when I came out. He had a tape deck sitting on the bench seat in the front and it was blasting. I climbed in the passenger's side and he asked, "Do ya like Fleetwood Mac?"

"I'm not sure." They sounded familiar, but I didn't really know them.

"Stevie Nicks … hottest chick in the world." He said, grinning with his cigarette in his mouth. "I'm in love with her," he said, laughing.

He turned the volume down a bit as he got the engine going. "We have to get cracking," he said. "Have to get the milk down there while the fridge is still cold. We can only just make it, so no time to lose."

I frowned. "Doesn't it keep cold while the truck is running?"

"Not this baby," he said. "Has to be plugged in to get cold. We've got about an hour and a half max and then it won't be cold enough to keep the milk fresh."

He showed me how the gears worked. You had to press the clutch pedal in and out and in again to get the gear stick to move smoothly; *double clutch* he'd called it. "Wanna have a go?" he said, looking at me, grinning, eyebrows raised.

"Not really. Is Geoff serious about me having to drive this truck?"

"Yep."

"But don't you need a truck license?"

"Only if the truck is over a certain weight. You can drive this baby on your regular license."

"Really? Oh, I don't think so … Not right now. I'll give it a go another time."

He pulled the truck out onto the road and out of Araluen as we started the trip. He turned up the music again and it filled the cabin. I took a deep breath and relaxed my head against the window, wistfully enjoying the mood stirred by the music. I wound down the window and let the wind blow over my face.

I reached for my shoulder bag and got out one of my menthol cigarettes. I didn't treat myself to them very often, but I wanted to enjoy this afternoon and this trip. I sat back and watched the scenery go by, listening to the music as we headed out on the Bruce Highway towards Brisbane. Ray had been right. It was great to get away and I wanted to listen to more of this Fleetwood Mac. I had become an instant fan.

The wind in my face, the mood, the music, the cigarette and the sense of getting away from Calvary for a while, were a perfect tonic.

◊ ◊ ◊

I must have dozed for a bit and was jolted awake suddenly as Ray hit the brakes. I looked out the window and realized we were getting closer to Brisbane. The traffic was much heavier.

"Where exactly is the dairy factory?" I asked.

"Not too far. It's in Caboolture, so we turn off pretty soon."

Fleetwood Mac was still blaring. Ray had the tape on automatic rewind and he was singing along from time to time. I watched him as he enjoyed the music. Then his face dropped suddenly and he stopped singing. He was squinting at something in the rear-view mirror, watching closely. I checked the side mirror out of my window and could see a police car coming up behind us. It would soon be right beside us. Ray was visibly shaken.

"What's wrong?" I asked.

"Nothin' nothin'. Don't like cops, that's all." He was trying not to look at the cop car. I could see beads of sweat break out on his forehead. He slowed the truck down and the police car headed off in front of us. Ray took the next left turn and pulled over and stopped the truck. He seemed traumatized.

"Ray, what's going on? What's the matter?" He turned off the tape recorder.

"I need a minute, that's all."

"Why're you so worried about that police car?"

He turned and looked at me a little accusingly. "Why do ya think?"

"Are you in trouble with the police?"

"Not here, not here, I'm not. But I've got some outstanding warrants back in Victoria. Could get me into strife if they stopped me, ya know. Just don't want that to happen. It'd ruin everything." He looked out the front of the truck again and I could see he was trying to calm himself.

I didn't know what to think. It had been a long time since I'd been hanging around anyone on the wrong side of the law. I looked at Ray and couldn't help wondering what other secrets he might hold. I couldn't deny that he had always seemed a little dark, but, crazily, that only seemed to make me more fascinated.

Ray laughed to himself and pulled out another cigarette. "We better get this milk to the factory." He started up the truck again.

"What sort of trouble are you in, Ray?" I asked.

He looked at me and shook his head. "Believe me, Megan. You don't want to know; you really don't want to know."

"I do want to know. What have you done?"

"Nothin' nothin'. Don't you worry your pretty little head about it. Hey, you know what?"

"What?"

"I told me Mum about you. I haven't talked to me Mum in a long time. I rang her the other day. See what a good influence you are on me?" He nudged my leg with his hand. I wasn't expecting the contact, but his hand felt warm. It lingered momentarily before he pulled it away. "I told Mum I'd met a really nice girl. I even told her you were a Christian." He laughed out loud, throwing back his head. "I don't think she believed I was serious, but I told Mum you were helping me get straightened out."

I looked straight ahead through the windscreen of the truck. I wondered who this man really was who was terrified of the police. *Was he a criminal?* It seemed quite possible. He came from a background I knew nothing about, but I felt pretty confident it wasn't favorable. Yet, curiously, I felt eager to learn more about him and his past. Despite some internal caution and instinct, I wanted to understand him and to do that, I needed to know more about him. Once I understood him, then I might even be able to help him.

Somehow, for some reason, I had managed to win this man's trust and it seemed I might be in a position to influence his life for the better.

As Ray got the truck back on the highway I gazed at him

thoughtfully. He was calm now and focused on his driving. He was confident maneuvering the vehicle despite the sticky gears and seemed to have shrugged off the fear of seeing a police car at such close quarters.

Staring at him now, it moved me deeply to think that I might be able to make a difference in his life, *save* him, even, from some horrible path he had been following; help him find new direction. I was tempted to reach over and touch his face, but I resisted.

Was this what God wanted me to do with my life? Why else would I be able to win the trust of someone like Ray if I wasn't meant to help him?

Right or wrong, I was hooked now. I wanted to know his hidden secrets and I wanted to help him.

I was getting pretty good at keeping secrets these days.

Chapter Eighteen

"Megan! Wake-up! Megan. Can you hear me?"

My eyes shot open and a rush of adrenalin pulled me out of my sleep in an instant. "Yeah!" I called as I pulled back the covers. Nellie, my favourite counselor, was standing at the door without her usual smile and relaxed countenance. Instead, her face, framed by her curly brown hair, was taut and drawn.

"What's wrong?" I asked.

"It's Simmo. He and Tanielle had a fight. He pulled a knife on her."

"What?" It was hard to take it in. *Pulled a knife?*

"Nigel's got it under control. He rang the mess hall. Tanielle wanted to talk to me."

"Is she alright?"

"Yeah, I guess. Just shaken. It's good she wanted to talk to me, though. Don't you think? I feel good about that. Means she's starting to trust me."

I stood in the doorway staring at Nellie. Had I heard right … a knife? What should I do now? I had no idea how I should respond, so I stood staring, dumbfounded. Finally I found my voice, "What's happening now?"

"Nigel said it's all under control. He managed to calm Simmo down. They got the knife off him and searched his room. He's in his room now with the light out. He was pretty upset."

I still didn't know what to say. Nor did I know what to do but was glad that Nigel and Mary were on hand to stablize the situation. The trainees had already adopted them as pseudo parents, something for which I felt deeply grateful at this moment. "Do we need to go down there?"

"Nah, Nige said that would just make it worse."

We stood staring at each other in the moonlight. Nellie ran her hand through her soft curls and rubbed the back of her head. "Megan, it scared me. What if he'd actually stabbed her? What would've happened then?"

"God. I don't know. God." The thought made my throat tighten. I stood there dumbly, trying to think of what to say but still nothing came. It was as though my brain was frozen. I couldn't think. We only had three trainees and already we were in a crisis.

Nellie demanded my attention again. "I needed to talk to you, that's all. I managed to get Tanielle calmed down. She's sleeping in the old farm house with Nige and Mary. *I* need to calm down! It's freaked me out." Nellie's soft eyes were searching mine, looking for some support. It was easy to respond.

"Sure. Let's get a coffee." I pulled a sweater over my head and slipped on my thongs, putting my arm loosely around her waist, glad to have a trusted friend working with me through this big mess. As we moved down to the mess hall, I couldn't help thinking about my smokes in the drawer next to my bed. I wanted one. Now. But the desire to turn and get them was replaced just as quickly by a staggering cloak of guilt. I nearly tripped. Nellie mustn't know of my weakness.

"You alright?" Nellie had stopped in her tracks and was peering at me in the dark.

"Yeah, I'm fine. Just tripped on a stone or something."

Don't think about it, you bloody hypocrite. Don't think about smoking ... especially not right now!

◊ ◊ ◊

As we opened the door to the mess hall, we found Mitch, my least favorite counselor, huddled over the kitchen urn. It had been switched off for the night and he was waiting for it to come back to the boil. The bad news must have spread fast. He looked up as we approached and I was struck by Mitch's thinning head of hair. He seemed too young to be going bald, only a few years older than me.

"Hi! What a night!" he said, pulling up his track pants as he peered into the urn yet again.

"Yeah! I agree, what a night! Have you talked to Simmo?"

"No, but I talked to Nige. I think I know what happened." Mitch looked at me, rubbing his neck as he talked. I'd never seen him this tense before.

"What? What do you think happened?"

"Simmo had a pretty bad day today. I took him to the doctor's in Gympie. He found out he's damaged his brain due to glue sniffing. He's done some permanent damage to his right arm. He doesn't have full movement anymore and it's never going to come back."

"Oh Lord!" I said, chewing my bottom lip. "That's awful. The poor thing. Of course he would have been upset!"

"Actually I think he took it pretty well, overall, considering. Yeah, it was a shock, but I think it made him realize more than ever that he has to stop, that he has to change his life. I think he really wants to change now. Still, I guess it's understandable he had a short fuse tonight."

I took a deep breath, thinking again how much worse this could have been if he had actually done some damage with that blade. It made me feel sick.

Happy the urn water was finally hot enough, Mitch made himself a coffee. His forehead was still pulled in a worried frown as he talked. "I've been worried about Simmo's temper. I've seen it brewing. I guess I knew it would erupt sometime. I've been working on some strategies and ideas, things I might be able to get him to do when he gets himself into a rage."

"Really? Like what?"

Mitch looked at me, his eyes narrowing. He didn't rush to respond.

Our hot drinks made, we moved over to one of the tables in the mess hall. No one seemed in a hurry to leave. I guess we were all trying to come to terms with a catastrophe avoided.

I wanted to hear more about Mitch's strategies. No doubt he had been taught them during his social work studies. If he'd share, Nellie and I could benefit. My trainee, Angela, was prone to losing her temper too. I asked again, "Tell us about your idea."

"You know, the usual stuff," Mitch shrugged off my question.

My mouth pulled into tight line and I realized I was clenching my teeth. Mitch knew very well I had no idea what "the usual stuff" meant and he was enjoying a sense of superiority. Unfortunately, it was a sense I couldn't deny him. His training made him better equipped to be developing strategies for traumatized trainees. Knowing this made me feel awkward, which Mitch no doubt enjoyed.

I had to force the thought of a cigarette out of my mind again as I sipped my coffee, trying not to stare Mitch down.

No one spoke as we sipped our drinks. I couldn't help wondering what else Simmo might do in a rage. It was disconcerting and for a moment my head spun, as though the ground moved beneath me. It was a constant struggle to maintain confidence in my ability to establish order, or some sense of progress, in running this drug rehabilitation farm.

Finally Mitch spoke again, "How are you doing with Angela? I think you're going to have to watch out for her, Megan." Mitch's challenging tone caught me off guard yet further.

"What do you mean?" I said, but immediately wished I hadn't. This wasn't the sort of conversation I wanted to have in front of Nellie. But the question was out now. I didn't wait for Mitch to respond further. "Actually, I feel like we're finally getting to know each other. She seems to be listening and really trying."

"How is it going with her little boy? What's his name again?" Nellie asked. She seemed almost back to her calm, cheery self. Her diversion was welcome relief.

"His name's Jake. He's such a cute little boy. Two is such a funny age. He makes me laugh, the things he gets up to. Angela loses her temper with him though. I can see she scares him." I eyed Mitch over the top of my coffee mug. The knowing smirk on his face made me want to push him back in his chair.

"I think you've got more problems than that," Mitch said leaning forward, his face intent. "Angela likes you a lot, Megan. I can tell. I think it's unhealthy. I mean, she likes you a *lot* ... in the wrong sort of way. You can see how jealous she gets over you and your time. What're you going to do about it?"

Mitch had a good point and unfortunately he was enjoying putting me on the spot. The truth was I didn't really know what I was going to do about it any more than I knew how to handle Mitch. Angela's growing affection for me was troubling. On the one hand, it was important that Angela trusted me, but I was unsure about the boundaries of that trust in this counselor/trainee relationship. If Mitch had advice for me, I didn't want to hear it, not right now anyway, not after such a traumatic evening.

Fortunately, the conversation was interrupted as Geoff rushed in the door. "I just heard what happened. Is everyone alright?"

I took a deep breath before replying. "We're all fine. The trainees are all fine. Nigel, God bless him, has everything under control. I'm so glad Nigel and Mary are living in that farm house down there. We really need them."

"I don't envy them, I must admit. I'm happy working the goat dairy. But a knife! This changes a few things." Geoff's eyes were wide. "We're going to have to search all their gear, implement some stricter controls to make sure this *never* happens again. We can't take the risk."

We all nodded solemnly in agreement. I think we were sick of talking about it. We seemed to be going around in circles. Finally, I suggested, "Let's talk about it tomorrow at our leader's meeting. We'll need to talk to the trainees. I'm sure the three of them will want to have their say. A search is a good idea. Let's talk again once we've all had a good night's sleep. Thank God the drama is over and no real harm was done."

Mitch was sitting back in his chair now, arms folded tight across his chest. No doubt he felt frustrated that I had managed to evade his earlier challenge.

"There're goats to milk tomorrow. I think we need to get to bed." I stood up and took my cup over to the sink. I needed some space to think. The events of the night were unsettling — knives being pulled, uncontrolled anger, challenging staff members – typical of so many things at Calvary.

How do I deal with all these problems? The only thing on my mind as I climbed the path back to my room was the packet of

Alpine in my drawer. I'd have to sneak out the back somewhere private to help calm my nerves. But the worst thing was I didn't know where to go to find the answers I needed. Perhaps a private talk with Geoff might help.

Chapter Nineteen

Despite having to rise early to milk the goats, I enjoyed these crisp fresh mornings. The lawn below me was dripping with dew as I waited for Geoff for our weekly get together. I had grown to love this verandah on the farm house at Calvary. It had a great view of all the improvements. You could see both the cow and goat dairy, the trainees' accommodation and most of the sheds and buildings which spread out from the house like the spokes of a wheel.

I could hear Nigel's voice as he yelled to his off-sider in the cow dairy, their voices muffled by the sound of the pump as they cleaned up after milking.

Though the house was a bit run down, Mary and Nigel had made it cozy enough. I could hear Mary cleaning up the breakfast dishes in between calling to her girls to get ready for school. It helped the trainees to have a regular family around. Mary was a great cook and seemed to like spending time with the trainees. I had noticed them responding to her motherly role. It seemed to provide some balance in the overall operation, having them around all the time, living there.

I could see Tanielle and Simmo chatting as they shared a cigarette outside their quarters. It was good to see that they had reconciled since the drama a few nights ago.

A cool breeze swept in and I pulled my sweater close across my chest. I was tempted to go back to the kitchen and cook some more toast, but I resisted and kept my eye on the goat dairy, waiting for Geoff to emerge. I could do without that extra bit of toast. Being more active with the goats was helping with my figure and I could feel in my clothes that I had slimmed down a bit.

I looked forward to my regular chats with Geoff. He was always encouraging and supportive. It was the only time I really felt I could be myself, that I didn't have to pretend that I knew what to do.

Geoff rushed out of the shed in his usual haste. He called over his shoulder giving instructions to someone still in the dairy as he jumped on the bike and headed towards the house. Even though life at Calvary had settled into a routine, I still felt like we were sitting on top of a volcano that might erupt at any moment. I never felt fully in control of what was going on.

Geoff leaned the bike on the garden fence and came in striding, taking the stairs two at a time. He still had his gumboots on.

"Mornin'," he said as he pulled off his hat. It was an authentic Akubra with a broad brim and made him look the part of the genuine farmer. His hair was flat and wet with sweat despite the cool fresh morning. He pulled a chair over and grabbed one for me. "Are you fine to chat here this morning?"

"Sure."

"I've got a problem with one of the milking lines in the shed. I'm going to have to get it fixed today ASAP. Don't want to have to pull my boots off."

"Fine with me."

He looked at me, pushing thoughts of the dairy out of his mind. "How are you going?"

"I'm okay I think, I guess. Things seem to be going along alright at the moment. No major dramas recently. Thank goodness!"

He nodded his head in approval. "That's good, really good."

"How are things going for you?"

He pulled his head back and looked me in the eye, surprised to have the attention turned on him. "Busy busy. Lot's to do."

"How's Julie?" I knew she struggled with serious health issues.

"Up and down. But it's always been like that," he grinned at me.

"Geoff, I'm sorry to hear that."

"Yeah, she's a battler, but looking after the boys is pretty much all she can do these days. That takes all her energy and then some. What's happening with the new arrivals?"

"Seems they may not be coming now. It hasn't been confirmed yet, though. Kevin said he'd be up here this week. I hope to get more information then."

Geoff nodded as he listened. "Probably just as well. We need to get a few more things sorted out around here yet, get things a bit more settled."

"Yeah, I guess. It's good that Nellie and I have one trainee each, but I don't imagine we can keep it like that. Mitch seems to be managing with Simmo so far. He said he's ready to take on another one."

"Well that's good. Hey Megan, I really need you to learn how to drive that truck and help with getting the milk down to Caboolture. It's critical to our business and we need options for people to get it to market. It wouldn't be a permanent solution but do you think you could give it a go until I can work something else out?"

"Me driving the truck?"

"Yeah, it's not hard."

"Really? Okay, I guess I can give it a go. When's it due to go again?"

"Today, this afternoon."

"Alright, I'll chat with Ray about it and get Nellie to look after Angela."

"Good! Let me know how you go managing the drive."

Geoff's eyes were drawn to the goat dairy again. I could see he was anxious to get back to work. He looked at me, "Anything else then?"

I shrugged. "Not really. I'm not sure whether I'm handling Angela the best though. You know she says she *likes* me. I'm still ignoring it and working with her as though she never said it. Don't know what else to do."

Geoff must have picked up the strain in my voice. He leaned towards me and looked into my face. Then he reached out his hand and touched my cheek tenderly. His movement took me by surprise, but I didn't pull back. His hand lingered, stroking my cheek. I stared into his face, moved. Someone had noticed and cared how I was feeling.

"Megan, you do try hard don't you?" He pulled his hand back suddenly and stood up abruptly. "We need to talk about you and Angela more. But now probably isn't the best time. Let's meet here tomorrow, same time."

"Alright, that's probably a good idea," I said, standing up as well. "In the meantime, I'll give driving the truck a go."

"Thanks Megan. If I don't get this line fixed, it will cripple our production. I need to get back to it. But remember, I'm here if you need me … anytime."

"Okay, I know. See you later."

Geoff was off and down the stairs. I frowned as I watched

him go, puzzled at his unexpected act of tenderness. I touched my face where he had touched me.

Should I have reacted differently?

I watched him jump on the bike and tear off back to the shed, wondering what was going on inside his head. I didn't want to think further about it, so I pushed it out of my mind and decided not to read anything into it.

He's just trying to support me the best way he can.

I was pleased to hear Fleetwood Mac playing again as I climbed into the truck beside Ray. Listening to them would make the trip even more enjoyable. I wanted to buy my own tape deck after the last trip. Music was such great therapy and helped to create a vibe and mood. I'd been trying to save but the $50.00 a week I earned was a meager salary despite the fact that the church provided food and board. It made buying a new tape deck out of reach. I couldn't save like I had before I came to Bible College. I had been earning well over $200.00 a week then and had saved all I needed for the twelve months at college. Doing God's work required more sacrifices than I had anticipated.

"Ah, nup … you're driving this time." Ray pulled open the driver's side door and climbed out.

I always like a new challenge and was prepared to try driving the truck, but that didn't mean I didn't feel nervous about it. I climbed in behind the steering wheel and Ray got in the passenger's side.

"Get the feel of the gears before we start," he said. "You have to push the clutch in, then pull your foot off it and then push it in again … sort of quick like."

I gave it a go slowly at first and then got the feel of it. It didn't feel that much different from driving a car.

"You don't need to do that all the time, only if you're having a bit of trouble. C'mon, let's get started. Rev her up."

I turned the key and the motor started with a bit of help from the accelerator.

Well, that wasn't as hard as I thought it would be. Perhaps I had been worrying about nothing.

"Now pull her out onto the road and let's get going." Ray was enjoying watching me; amused at my cautiousness. Driving the truck was like steering an elephant. It was cumbersome and slow to respond to commands. I took things at a steady pace.

We pulled onto the Bruce Highway and climbed to about 50 miles per hour. I didn't have to worry about managing the clutch while cruising so I thought it a good time to get a conversation going.

"How've you been going?" I asked Ray, trying to see his face with a few sidelong glances.

"Not bad, I guess. Haven't spoken to Kevin for a while. I heard he's coming up this week."

"Yeah, he is. Still no drink?"

He looked across the cab at me. "Nup. No drink."

"Do you still think about it?"

"Sometimes, but then I think about that day I saw the blood and I don't wanna drink anymore."

"That must've been awful."

"You reckon? It was a shock, that's for sure. Not good, not good at all."

This was an opportunity to find out more about Ray, about his past, but I didn't know how to steer the conversation in that direction. We drove in silence for a while.

"Have you spoken to your mum lately?" I asked, wondering if I could find out more about his family in Victoria.

"No, no, I haven't called her again." He laughed at the

memory. "Would've taken the old girl a bit to get over that last call, I'd reckon."

"I'm sure she'd like to hear from you again."

Ray looked across the cab at me. "Can't go calling me Mum all the time. She wouldn't be expectin' to hear from me again. It's not safe. I took a risk calling her."

"Really? Why? Why can't you call your Mum?"

"Megan, it's no joke. Things are tough for my family. I have to stay away. It's not safe."

I couldn't look at him because I needed to keep my eyes on the road while maneuvering the unfamiliar vehicle.

"Ray, that sounds terrible. I can't imagine what this's about."

"Painters and Dockers, that's what it's about."

"Painters and Dockers? The union?"

"Uh huh."

"What, is that some sort of mafia or something?" I didn't know much about it, but it stirred a distant memory of things I'd heard on the news.

"You could say that." Ray was shaking his head, reluctant to say more.

"But why can't you call her? Why do you have to stay away?"

Ray was looking at me and I gave him furtive glances as we cruised down the highway. Fortunately there wasn't too much traffic.

"My brother —" Ray paused. I looked at him and could see his face twisted as though in pain. He face was drained and his skin color ashen. He turned his head away, looking out the window before continuing. "My brother … what they did to him."

"What, what'd they do to him? Ray, what …?"

He looked at me again and I was shocked to see his eyes. They were dark and intense, packed with emotion. He was recalling a painful memory. "It'll shock you, Megan. You won't believe what they did to him. It'll shock you." He stared out the window again.

"What'd they do to him, Ray? What'd they do?"

Ray sighed and kept looking out the window before he continued. "They … they chopped him up into little pieces and …" He choked on his words. Though he wanted to say more the words wouldn't come out. He shook his head in disbelief; his emotions threatening to overwhelm him. His hands were shaking as he opened and closed his fists. He didn't look at me, but tried to regain his composure. I could see the whites of my knuckles as I gripped the steering wheel; trying to keep my eyes on the road while stealing glances at him, waiting to hear more. I had heard the words, but they were difficult to comprehend, to believe.

Finally he turned to me ready to continue. He was calm now and strangely in control. His face was blank and his voice even. "They cut him into pieces with a chain saw, put his bits into plastic bags and shoved him in a freezer." His hands were clenched into two tight fists. "I can't go home."

We both looked out the windscreen, driving in silence for a moment. Then unexpectedly he smashed his fists into the dashboard. "Fucking mongrels. They're fucking mongrels." He smashed the dashboard again and again.

I was shocked at his outburst. It frightened me, but I gripped the steering wheel trying not to imagine what had happened to his brother. It was shocking.

Ray didn't want to talk anymore. He sat looking out the window. My mind was trying to process what he had said. I had wanted to know more about him. Well, now I did. I had thought Ray came from a very different background from me but I had never imagined anything like this. What he had just told me was the sort of thing you read about in the newspaper; heard about on the TV. It wasn't something that had happened to someone you knew, not to somebody *I* knew.

Chopped into pieces … my God. It was unimaginable.

"I can't go back, Megan. I'm running for my life. I mustn't go back no matter what … ever."

"So being at Araluen has been helping you in more ways than one," I said as the realization dawned on me.

"You could say that," Ray was nodding his head as he answered. "They're fucking mongrels, Megan. They'll do anything. You can't imagine the things they can do, *will* do, if they get a chance."

I felt stunned. Ray had told me ages ago that he trusted me but now he had basically put his life in my hands. We drove on in silence for a while. The air was heavy and I knew I needed to stop asking questions, that enough had been said. Understanding what he had shared was like looking across a chasm and trying to make sense of what I could see on the other side, a world so different from what I had ever known. Mafia and chainsaws were a far cry from my middle class upbringing in Chelmer, Brisbane.

But the craziest thing about it all was that I wanted to traverse that chasm and find out more about this foreign life, Ray's life.

I had always wanted to experience life to the fullest, to see and breathe life in the extreme. I guess that was why I had been drawn to the drug scene and Kings Cross. Ray had given me a tiny peek into a different life and, as horrible and frightening as it sounded, it was also exciting. He had been talking about murder, murder in the first degree, yet I still wanted to know more.

Ray's vulnerability had the strange effect of drawing me closer to him even more powerfully than ever. Crazy as I knew it was, I had an overpowering desire to take him in my arms and hold him and comfort him and tell him it would be alright.

Ray turned his head to look at me. "Megan. I can't believe I've met you. I never thought I'd meet a girl like you in me life … ever. A good girl like you. A good girl like you with me … that's magic. Best chance in my life to get it right … to put things right. That's why I had to tell me Mum about you. Why I took the risk to call her. I had to tell her I had a chance to put things right."

It was hard to concentrate on the driving. Suddenly I felt I was being swept along by forces outside my control.

"Ray …" but I didn't know what to say. A bond had been forged. It scared me and yet thrilled me, at the same time.

Ray reached across and laid his hand on my thigh. "Megan, I've never known anyone like you before. I don't want to lose you."

His hand felt warm. I liked him touching me and I didn't want him to take his hand away. We finished the trip in silence. The cab was warm and comfortable. It was easy to be in his company.

It was just on dark when we arrived back at Araluen and climbed out of the truck. Our goodbyes were awkward. I knew I would see him again around Araluen, but all I could think about as I walked away was: *When am I going to spend some time with Ray again like this?*

Chapter Twenty

I took a big swig of my coffee eyeing Kevin through the steam. His confidence and air reflected his full reinstatement to running New Start Centre. His brief "punishment" for his indiscretion with Andrea seemed way behind him now. He had several major endeavors underway, Calvary being one of them. I searched his face for signs of weariness. One deep crease on his left cheek provided meager evidence of stress but his eyes were alive with excitement as he shared his plans.

"I've got more goats on the way. I've managed to secure some more funding. I'm thinking of going into Angoras this time. I hear the wool sells at a premium and there's a high demand. We'll get some more milking nannies too. I've been working to build interest in the goat milk. It has world-recognized health benefits — did you know that?"

He didn't wait for my answer. "Amazing ... awful stuff, I think. The problem is, we need to educate the market here about the benefits. It's pretty expensive, though ... top of the range ... great earning potential."

He looked away, his eyes a little glazed as business ideas

churned around in his mind. Then he looked at me as though remembering I was there. "Remind me to talk to Geoff about the Angora idea. He'd have to manage it. We'd have to set up a shearing shed. I imagine it's like shearing sheep. Don't know, though. Geoff'll have to find out all about it."

Although I was impressed with the pace at which his mind worked, I wanted to turn the conversation to issues more relevant to me. "What's happening about the new trainees? Are they coming?"

Kevin leaned forward, seemingly forcing himself to focus on me, reigning in his thoughts.

"Yes, yes. Well no, actually. I've thought a lot about it and I think we need to move cautiously before taking on any more folk. I want this operation to work long term so I don't want to over stress things prematurely … at least until we get things a bit more developed and settled. These goat enterprises should provide great therapy, don't you think?"

Again, he didn't wait for my response.

"We can give the trainees some life skills; give them some ambition. Not only will they receive inner healing while they're here and have their broken lives put back together, but they'll get some skills and training that should make them employable as well. Working with animals is good for them, isn't it?"

"Well … yes, I guess. But it's hard to get them out of bed. I'm not sure they see it the same way we do, working them like that. I think they feel a bit like free labor."

Kevin looked at me, astonished. "Really? How I'd love to get in that goat dairy myself and have a go. I'd have me a time I would, if I could." He sighed deeply. "We're giving them such a gift, but I guess they need time and therapy to really appreciate it."

"That's for sure. But Kevin, the problem is that I don't really know what that therapy is … how to go about it."

"Megan, don't you worry about that. God'll show you the way. All you need is the Holy Spirit and a willingness to listen to him and the courage to give it a go. God will bless you and equip you with what you need for the job. God is right behind this endeavor, I know it. He's the one who inspired the whole idea from the start."

He leaned further forward and took one of my hands. "Megan, you don't know your own talents. I see in you a quality, a strength, that I don't see in many people. You don't know your own potential. God has big plans for you. This is just the beginning."

I put my coffee cup down on the floor beside my chair and blinked at him, trying to take it in, trying to believe it. He let go of my hand and sat back.

"So no new trainees?" I asked again.

"Well … we have all the folk down in the caravan area. I want to break up that little community. There've been some reports … some issues. Some things have come to my attention." He sighed. "Unfortunately sometimes people take advantage of your best intentions. You give them an opportunity; cut 'em some slack … you give 'em an inch and they take a mile."

I frowned, wondering what he was talking about. Some of the Bible College students had believed the campers were hiding from the police, but I hadn't heard anything but vague rumors. However, knowing what I now knew about Ray, there was likely truth in them.

"So some of them may be transitioning to Calvary?" I asked.

Kevin looked at me. "I thought about that, but I think under the circumstances, they need to move on. They are welcome to be part of the church community, but their time for living here has come to an end. There are too many close together and I don't think it's been productive or helpful for any of them in the long run. I don't want any of them here any longer."

I desperately wanted to say, *"What about Ray?"* But some internal instinct cautioned me to hold my tongue.

As usual, our conversation came to an abrupt end, before I felt we had covered everything I needed to discuss. Kevin's time was in great demand and there were many people he needed to see when he visited Araluen and Calvary. He was being called away by someone standing outside the mess hall. He needed to move on to his next appointment.

"Sorry Megan, that's it for today. Hopefully I'll be back soon." He stood up and took one of my hands in both of his and shook it gently. "You're doing good, you're doing real good. I have every confidence in you. Keep up the good work." He turned on his heel and was gone; his tornado-like energy diverted elsewhere.

I picked up my cup of coffee. It was cold now, but I sipped at it anyway going over some of his words. Kevin had managed to pump me up again. As usual after spending time with him, I felt like I was a balloon inflated so full of hot air that if someone poked a pin in me, I'd burst. It wasn't a nice feeling. It usually took me a few hours to get my feet back on the ground. I tried to reconcile what Kevin said with how I saw myself. They didn't connect very well but as usual his energy buoyed me along.

I resigned myself to keep applying myself to this difficult task even though I found it hard to measure how I was going and whether I was achieving anything positive. I barely managed to get through each day.

I tried to focus on my dishes as I cleaned up after dinner, but I couldn't help scanning the room for Ray. I hadn't seen him since the trip in the truck at the beginning of the week. I knew Kevin had told the camping community to move on and some of the tents had been taken down.

Where was Ray? Has he left without saying goodbye?

I almost jumped out of my skin when I felt a warm hand grip my elbow. Ray was standing close to me, waiting for me to look around.

"Got a minute?" he said.

"Sure. Just a sec." I put down my tea towel and stacked the still-wet dishes hastily together and took them into the mess hall, dumping them on the crockery table. I hoped no one noticed us walk away together as I followed Ray out the door towards the dam.

We didn't speak as we walked but his arm touched mine several times. I could feel the heat emanating from his body despite the cool evening. Each brush sent a little shiver over me. I kept pace with him, hoping for further fleeting contact.

The air seemed even cooler as we approached the dam. Ray was still in his work clothes, a long-sleeved shirt rolled partly up his arm.

I pulled my cardigan closer around me. The light of the mess hall dimmed in the background as we walked. Only the reflection of the waning moon on the water provided ambient light, just enough to find somewhere to sit. I could barely see his face, but I was glad of the darkness, as it gave us some privacy. We sat side by side looking at the dam.

I stilled the questions in my mind, waiting for him to speak. Then footsteps nearby interrupted our silent reverie. I felt my heart jump a beat and spun around in my seat. I didn't want Geoff to see me here talking to Ray but it was impossible to make out anyone in the darkness. Whoever it was had moved on.

I turned back to watch the moonlight playing on the surface of the water. "I'm leavin'," Ray announced.

I turned to look at him, not really surprised, yet his words still made my heart speed up. I could feel the pulse in my temples accelerate. "Really, do you have to?"

"Yep, saw Kevin the other day. He said I have to go to Calvary or leave."

I sat watching him, but didn't say anything. I didn't know what to say.

Ray returned my gaze. "Megan, Calvary isn't the place for me. I just can't see m'self down there with those other clowns. It's not for me. Time for me to get outta here."

"Where will you go?"

"I'll fix m'self up in one of those boarding houses in the Valley. It's cheap rent. Hope to find me a job doin' somethin'. Andy said he'd put in a good word for me."

"What about the booze?"

"I'll be alright, I reckon. I think I'll be alright. Can't keep hidin' out here anyway. It ain't real. I have to get back to things."

We sat looking at the dam for a bit. You could hear the odd splash as a fish broke the surface of the water.

"Megan, I want to know if you'll come and visit me some time. You bin good to me. You make a lotta sense and I like talking to ya. Will you come and visit me?"

I felt a heavy weight pressing on my shoulders and chest. The difficulty of our circumstances hung in the air. I was enjoying sitting close to Ray and being alone with him. I wanted to sit even closer. But that alarm bell was ringing inside my head again. I was breaking one of the golden rules in counselling ... never get emotionally involved. Even though, technically, I had never been appointed as Ray's counselor, he was here as someone in need of support and guidance. I was here in a leadership capacity, trying to orchestrate and manage the work of God, helping needy people. It was dangerous territory. But being close to him was alluring. It wasn't just that I found his ruggedness attractive; it was also the sense of danger, the forbidden.

"Megan, it can't end like this. I have to know that I'll see you again. You are my hope for the future. Knowing you has changed my life. I'm a different person 'cos of you. You're the only one that really understands me. Just tell me I'll see you again." Ray's voice was taut, waiting for my response.

"Ray, I want to, but …"

"I'm not asking anything else, just that you'll come and visit me. You must get time off. You can't work all the time. What do ya say?" He reached his hand across and placed it softly, but firmly, on my thigh. "What do ya say?"

The alarm bell was still ringing, but the feeling of his hand on my thigh muffled it.

"I guess there wouldn't be any harm in coming to visit you." I stared at the water as I spoke. Ray stroked my thigh briefly before he withdrew his hand. His touch sent shivers over me. I didn't want him to take his hand away, but my reaction also frightened me.

"Good girl. I knew I could count on you. I knew you wouldn't let me down. Megan, you sure are one helluva girl."

"How will I know where you are?"

"I'll write or ring as soon as I get a place. It'll be in the next day or so."

"When do you go?"

"Tomorrow. Andy's offered to give me a lift to Brisbane. He's appreciated me helping him out. Pretty good of him really seeings how he's got as much as he can handle, keeping up with the grounds 'round here."

"Tomorrow?" It seemed so sudden. My shoulders slumped a little further under the growing weight. On one hand, Ray leaving was a good thing; it silenced the warning in my head. But on the other hand, I felt a sense of loss. The opportunity to see and understand his world was slipping away.

I would miss this closeness and the sense that he needed

me. I wondered how he would handle the temptations around him, away from the security of Araluen.

We heard footsteps behind us again. This time it was several people coming down the path to the dam. Our privacy was about to be disturbed and it made me agitated. I needed to cut this interaction short.

"Okay, I'll wait to hear from you then. I really have to get going, Ray." I didn't want to be seen alone with him like this; it wouldn't look right. I swung my legs around the log and stood up. Ray stayed where he was, looking at the dam.

"Ray ..." He looked at me and I rested my hand on his shoulder briefly saying, "Bye."

Ray put his hand on mine and held it there. "Well, I'll be looking forward to seeing you again soon Megan. Not sure why you're in such a rush. But if you have to go ... I'll call as soon as I can. It's not 'good-bye' it's 'see ya'."

Though his hand was warm, I pulled mine away gently, reluctantly. "Okay then, see ya."

He turned back to the dam. He didn't seem to care who was coming down the path, but I did care. I turned away and headed off before anyone could see me. I didn't want to take any further chances. I walked all the way around the dam before heading back to my room. My cheeks were flushed with the cool air and maybe ... yes, maybe, Ray's touch had something to do with it.

I sat in the moonlight outside my room for a long time. Thoughts were bouncing around inside my head like a ball in a pinball machine.

Should I visit Ray? Probably not a good idea. But he will need some support when he leaves here. There is no harm in seeing him ... only to encourage him. Why do I feel I have to convince myself? Why do I feel like I'm in a battle?

Though I had never discussed it with him, I felt confident Geoff wouldn't approve of me going to visit Ray. *I'm not talking to Geoff about this. I'll work it out on my own.*

The pull, the wanting to see Ray again, weighed heavily on my shoulders. Some other sense in me was also at play which was much more guarded and cautious. Then I thought again of Ray's touch on my leg and the memory sent a shock wave through my chest. What a dilemma!

When I finally went to bed, sleep was slow in coming. At some point I managed to reassure myself that nothing wrong was ever going to happen; I wouldn't let anything happen. I had too much responsibility looking after Calvary and the trainees depended on me, as did the other counsellors. I was determined to do the right thing.

I'll probably never hear from him again anyway.

I slept fitfully.

Chapter Twenty-One

I must have been dozing. The knock on my door jolted me awake. I put my Bible aside and opened the door. Michael was standing in the rain trying to shelter under his umbrella. "Call for you again Megs … in the hall."

I looked at my watch. It was nearly 9:00 pm.

Not again.

I wondered if it was Angela having problems with Jake or perhaps some other drama unfolding at Calvary. This was the second night in a row I'd been called urgently to the phone.

I sighed and, grabbing a coat, shared Michael's umbrella as we walked down to the mess hall.

"You must've been working late again," I said as we walked.

"Yeah. I was sorting out paperwork and trying to get my orders ready for tomorrow. You're lucky I was there to pick it up."

"Or unlucky maybe …" I said, wondering.

He shrugged. "Well, let me know if you need anything," he said as he returned to his work in the kitchen.

I walked over to pick up the phone which was dangling down the wall.

"Hello, Megan here." I said. No one spoke back, so I raised my voice a little, "Megan here. Anyone there?" The sound of the rain on the tin roof of the mess hall wasn't helping. I tried once more, "Hello, anyone there?"

"Meggie, Meggie, is that you darlin'?"

An electric shock went through me. It was Ray. "Yes?"

"Oh darlin' it's so good to hear your voice. Sorry it's taken me a coupla days to get to ya. Things've bin a bit harder than I thought. How are ya?"

"I'm okay, I guess." My body started trembling at the sound of his voice. I wasn't sure why. *Why is he having this effect on me?*

Ray had contacted me. Whatever concerns I had about this man, I was excited to hear from him.

"Listen love, I haven't got much time. Gonna run out of coins on this machine. Bin waitin' for ya to come to the phone. Have ya got a pen and paper?"

"No I don't," I said looking around to see if there was anything nearby. There was nothing.

"I've gotta give you my address. You'll have to memorize it. It ain't hard. Are you ready?"

"Okay."

"I've got m'self a room in a place on Brunswick Street in the valley. The place is called the Guest House. I'm in room number 11. The street number is 921. Got that?"

"Room 11 at the Guest House in Brunswick Street. What was the street number again?"

"921. You gotta remember it, Meggie. I'm waiting for you to come and visit. You be down next week?"

"Um, I'm not sure, Ray. Maybe."

"This machine's gonna cut out any minute. I know the milk has to come down on Thursday. I'll be expectin' ya then.

Come down after you drop the milk off. I'll be --" The phone was beeping in my ear.

I stood stunned, still holding the receiver.

Ray called me.

I slowly put down the receiver, then raced into the kitchen looking for a pen and paper.

"More trouble down the road?" Michael asked as I rummaged around his work area for a pen and paper.

"No, not tonight, thank goodness. It was a friend, but they got cut off. Didn't get much chance to talk." I scribbled the address down as I spoke.

"Hey Mike, really appreciate you picking up that call and getting me in the rain."

"No worries. You're lucky I was still here."

"Yeah, I know. Thanks again. Hey, maybe you're working too hard. Anyway, I'll see you tomorrow." I hugged his shoulders.

"You want the 'brolley? It's still raining."

"Nah, I'll run up the hill. Can't be that bad."

I jogged up the path back to my room, trying to keep the piece of paper dry, thankful the rain had eased. I tucked the address safely in the front of my Bible and sat on the bed, amazed, but thrilled, that Ray had actually called me.

The thought of going to visit him sent another shock wave of exhilaration through me.

It can't hurt to go and visit him and make sure he is okay. It can't hurt.

Anyway I wouldn't get an opportunity to do anything until next week, so I tried to put the phone call, the address and the opportunity out of my mind and went back to reading my Bible.

◊ ◊ ◊

The sun was well up as I strolled down the track. It was nice to walk to Calvary sometimes instead of driving one of the utes. It gave me a chance to think and clear my head. There was always so much going on, it made my head spin at times – the traumas and dramas with trainees; getting the counselling team to work together and, of course, the primary production enterprises Kevin kept initiating. His vision to have Calvary support itself financially added another whole dimension of complexity.

I pulled up the sleeves of my sweater, the chill of the morning forgotten as I soaked in the sun. A movement to my left startled me briefly, but it was just a wallaby, disturbed. He bounded off into the bush.

Sometimes it seemed the people involved in running Calvary were tripping over each other. It was clear that Kevin had placed me in charge, but sometimes I felt others were competing to be in control. I wondered whether it was because I was so young. Did they have no confidence in my ability? Mitch frequently made comments that made me feel he doubted my leadership.

Maybe he could do a better job; he certainly seems to have plenty of good ideas.

I could hear the farm bike in the distance and felt surprised at how far the sound travelled. I wondered if it was Geoff moving the goats around.

Geoff seemed pretty confident running the primary production side of things. He researched many ideas for Kevin and shared his passion for making the enterprise work. Kevin trusted him and Geoff seemed to love the farm life and was always racing around at a mad pace. I don't think I had ever seen him walking. There was no doubt that he filled his days to the maximum.

Geoff also took his role in supporting me seriously and I certainly appreciated having someone like him close by. I looked forward to our weekly meetings and felt I could be myself; that I didn't have to pretend I knew what I was doing. I wondered what we would talk about at our meeting today. I looked at my watch, making sure my pace was right to be there by 10. I had plenty of time.

As I stopped at the gate to open it, I could hear the bike much closer now and realized someone was coming towards me on the track. I waited with the gate open. It was Nigel. He must have finished the morning milking. His large frame rather consumed the bike seat and he didn't look very confident as he putted along. With each bump, his bulk seemed to heave and leap such that I thought he might fall off. It made me giggle, so I turned my head so he couldn't see my face.

"G'day," he said as he pulled up at the gate, straddling the bike with his legs outstretched. "Not used to these things, ya know. We always used horses back home."

"Hi. Everything okay?"

"Yep, yep. Ran out of bread so the missus sent me up to get some for lunch."

"I could've brought it down for you."

Nigel pulled off his hat and scratched his head. "Yeah, didn't think about that. Forgot it was Tuesday today. No worries though. I'll be back in a jiffy."

"Okay, see ya soon."

I closed the gate behind him and followed his progress for a moment as he avoided a stick and just missed a stump hole. The bike swerved and leaned so far to one side that I thought he must fall off. He didn't, however. He managed to straighten up and continue along the track towards Araluen.

I liked Nigel and Mary and they seemed to be enjoying running the farm house. Their household was the center of activity at Calvary and they pretty much knew everyone's comings and goings each day.

They had taken this commitment seriously and I knew they wanted to serve God by trying to help these needy kids. They wanted their family life to be a role model for the trainees and had put a lot on the line, bringing their children into this environment.

I could no longer hear the bike. I sighed and my mind turned to Ray's phone call. My heart rate jumped immediately and a shot of excitement bolted through my chest. His words echoed in my head, *"I'm waiting for you to come and visit. See you next week."*

He likes me and wants to see me.

I could hear my heart thumping in my ears as I thought about him. I wanted to see him again and, in some strange way, felt I *had* to see him again.

There can't be any harm in just going to visit him.

The thought of pulling up the truck outside the 'Guest House' sent a shiver down my spine.

The farm house was in sight now, so I broke into a jog. I didn't want to be late for my meeting with Geoff.

I could hear Geoff's voice in the kitchen as I climbed the verandah stairs. It wasn't very often that he was waiting for me. I followed his voice, looking forward to a cup of coffee after my walk.

"G'day Megs." Geoff sidled up to me and put his arm around my shoulders briefly as he greeted me. Mary was working at the sink cleaning up after breakfast. The morning tea was still on the table.

"Grab a cuppa and we'll sit out the back this morning. Should be a bit warmer there."

"Okay, sure." The water in the electric jug was still hot, so I poured a coffee and grabbed a piece of chocolate brownie from the table before following Geoff down the hallway. The old farm house was split down the middle by a hallway which opened onto the verandah at each end of the house. It was impossible not to notice how chaotic the bedrooms were as we passed them. The carpet had virtually disappeared under a blanket of clothes and other items, some of which were oozing into the hallway. You had to watch where you put your feet. Housekeeping obviously wasn't one of Mary's priorities.

Geoff sat down on the top step. The stairs at the back of the house led down to the laundry and I could see the sheets flapping on the clothes line in the back yard. I sat down next to him. It was a bit cozy but at least we had some privacy.

"How are you going?" Geoff asked.

"Okay I guess."

"What's up?" He said.

"Well, I'd like to talk about Angela. You know I've told you before she said she likes me. You know … in that sort of way. Not the *right* way."

"Yeah, sorry Megs. You've mentioned that before and we've never talked it out have we? How's it going?"

"Well, I think it's okay, but I'm not sure. I've never had to deal with something like this before. We seem to get on well. I feel I have her respect. I think she's listening to me. She's had a pretty rough time, you know … in her life. She's trying to bring up that little boy the best she can." I looked at Geoff's face. "I don't see I can do anything else except keep doing what I'm doing. I treat her the same way I would treat any trainee. Do you think that's okay, or is there something else I should be doing?" I wanted to hear what he thought.

"Well Megan, I'm not sure. I don't see you together that much. I'm not around all the time, especially when you're with the trainees. I suppose … as long as you don't encourage her."

"I don't encourage her, but I do care for her … care about

her straightening out her life. She might take that the wrong way."

"Then you can't be responsible if she takes it the wrong way. I think we have to see how it goes for the time being. Keep an eye on it and if things aren't going well, we can always put her with another counselor, Nellie maybe."

"That would have to be a last resort. I've spent so much time building my relationship with her. That trust comes at a price."

"You're probably right. I don't think you can do much more than you've been doing." He put his hand on my shoulder, lending his support and encouragement. "I'm sure Angela will be able to work through these things as she learns more about God's way and works through the major issues in her life. There're probably other things more important at this stage. But I do think we should be mindful of it though. It's good to keep these things out in the open. Keep your heart and your attitude in the right place and I think you can trust God to do the rest. I'm sure it will come right."

I looked out over the back garden. "I hope you're right."

We both sat in silence for a few moments. Then I sighed deeply.

Geoff looked at me again. "Is there something else on your mind?"

It shocked me that he could read me so easily. I chewed my bottom lip, my mind racing. I felt safe with Geoff, but I also felt unsure about telling him what was on my mind.

"Megan if there's something troubling you … you know that's what I'm here for. You can tell me. What is it?"

I sighed deeply again. "It's nothing really …"

"C'mon Megan. There's obviously something on your mind. I can see by that furrow on your brow." He rubbed his thumb gently across my forehead. It lightened my mood a little.

"Well ... there is one other thing ..." I paused looking at him again, searching his face wondering whether I should take this next step in trusting him.

"Yes?" He said waiting expectantly for me to continue. "What is it?"

"I heard from Ray Klein, remember him? He rang me the other day."

Geoff's reaction surprised me. His body stiffened. I had taken him by surprise. "Ray? That character? He rang you? What did he want?"

"He wants me to go visit him sometime."

"Really?" Geoff stood up abruptly. He went down a couple of steps so that he could look at me directly. "Megan, that'd be crazy." He was searching my eyes. "Tell me I don't need to tell you that'd be crazy."

"Crazy? We used to have some good talks. I think he needs some encouragement now that he's left here."

"Maybe he does. In fact, I'm sure he does, but you shouldn't be the one to encourage him. That would be very unwise." He put his hand under my chin, lifting my face towards him, looking directly into my eyes. "Megan, you aren't thinking seriously about this are you ... visiting him, I mean?"

I stared back at him, but didn't answer. My silent response seemed to anger him and he dropped his hand. "Listen Megan, I've got a lot of time for you. I think you try really hard here and are having a go at a very difficult job. It would be difficult for anyone. I know it's tough, but you visiting someone like that Ray character is absolutely stupid. I give you much more credit than that." His whole body and demeanor had changed. His anger and curt response startled me. I felt he was overreacting, but said nothing. I leaned forward and cradled my chin on my hands.

"Megan, tell me you aren't going to do anything crazy like trying to find that guy."

I shrugged. "Okay, okay. It probably isn't such a good idea. I just thought he could do with some encouragement, that's all, now that he's away from all the support he had here."

"Well, even if he does, that's *his* problem now, not yours. He's the one that left here after all." I could see Geoff's shoulders relax a little, but I wished now I hadn't told him.

Geoff looked at his watch. "Listen, Megan, I've got to go. I've organized to talk to Nigel about some of Kevin's latest ideas. He'll be waiting for me in the cow dairy." He sat down beside me again. "Listen, you're doing great. Put that Ray guy out of your head and focus on what's going on here. This's where you're needed. This's where God wants you, right here. Okay?"

"Okay."

"You tell me if he bothers you again, won't you?"

"Okay," I said and sighed again. "You better get going. I'll see ya later."

Geoff got up to go, then paused, staring at me without saying anything, before racing off at his usual pace. I watched him go, regretting that our meeting had ended on such an unpleasant note.

I didn't feel that Ray had been bothering me. It had been a mistake talking to Geoff about it. *Why did I even bring it up?*

He obviously didn't understand. I stayed on the back step for a while, still cradling my chin and gazing over the back yard. I couldn't understand why Geoff seemed so mad. It didn't make much sense.

Chapter Twenty-Two

Geoff was waiting at the truck when I arrived.

"Good to go Megan. Sorry you have to keep doing this. I hope to have something sorted out pretty soon ... been working to get some more staff. Should have it sorted next week."

"I don't mind Geoff. Actually, I like taking the truck now that I know how to drive it."

"Ha, that's good Megan. But it's not the best having you go off. You need to be around. Never know what's about to happen around here." He winked at me as he shut the driver's door.

I shrugged. His words hung in the air and made me feel uncomfortable ... as though I might be trapped at Calvary forever. I waved goodbye as I made my way to the exit. It wasn't quite the same without Fleetwood Mac blaring from Ray's portable tape deck, but it was exciting to be getting away for the afternoon. My stomach jumped with excitement as I pulled onto the highway. I wound down the window and let my hair fly in the air even though it was a bit cool. It enhanced my sense of momentary freedom.

◊ ◊ ◊

It was a relief to have dropped off the milk and fulfilled my responsibility for the day. I looked at my watch. I had made good time. Sitting in the car parked outside the milk factory, I pondered my next move. Taking the truck into Brisbane city presented a new challenge. It would be quite different from driving up and down the highway.

Trucks move around the city all the time. It can't be that hard.

I mapped out a route in my mind. It should be a matter of following the Bruce Highway right into the city center.

Finding Brunswick Street should be pretty straightforward from there.

I pulled the piece of paper out of my pocket and looked at the address again before flattening it on the dashboard of the truck.

921. I just need to remember 921.

I kept reciting the number in my head as I backed out. Pulling up at the turn off to the Bruce Highway, I hesitated momentarily. Geoff's angry face popped into my mind and I could hear his words, *"You tell me if he bothers you again, won't you?"* I crunched the gears and jerked the truck forward, following the sign to Brisbane. Geoff had been wrong; Ray wasn't bothering me at all. Geoff didn't understand. It was a free country and I needed an afternoon off. There was no harm in going to visit Ray … just to see how he was going.

◊ ◊ ◊

Fortunately the Guest House was in a quiet section of Brunswick Street and it was easy to find a parking spot for the truck. I felt nervous as I slipped out of the cabin.

Would Ray even be home?

As I stood on the footpath, I tried to smooth some of the creases out of my dress. It was nice to stretch my legs after the long drive. I ran my fingers through my hair to straighten it as best I could without a brush.

I looked at the entrance to the Guest House. It was dark and dingy. All the windows were closed except for one with tattered curtains flicking in the breeze. I climbed the brick staircase tentatively, hoping to see Ray appear at the door so that I wouldn't have to go inside.

I stepped inside the door looking for a reception area, but there was none. Someone was listening to the races on a transistor radio. The front door opened onto a long hallway with rooms on either side. I took a few steps straining to see the numbers on the doors so that I could find Ray's room.

"Meggie. I don't believe it. You came." My heart stopped for a split second as I spun around. Ray was standing in the doorway behind me, on his way into the Guest House. He was grinning from ear to ear.

"Meggie me girl, you came! Aren't you a sight for sore eyes? Come here. Come here." Ray reached his arm towards me. "C'mon girl. Let's get out of here. Let's go for a walk. It's too dark in here. I want to get a good look at you."

He grabbed my elbow firmly and shepherded me back out the front door, moving confidently and smoothly. It was nice to feel him beside me, but I also felt a little anxious. This was unfamiliar territory. I let him steer me back to the footpath.

"C'mon girl. Come with me. I couldn't believe me eyes when I saw the truck sitting there. 'Me girl's come to see me.' was all I could think. 'Me girl's come to see me'." Ray's excitement at seeing me was helping to settle my nerves. He was ecstatic and there was a noticeable spring in his step as we set off down the footpath towards New Farm. He held his arm loosely around my waist as we walked.

"Where are we going?"

"Well Meggie, I think this calls for a celebration. Don't you?" he said smiling down at me. "Let's go get a drink and celebrate. There's a great local just a few doors down."

I stopped in my tracks. "Ray! You're not drinking again, are you?"

"Settle down Meggie, settle down. It's fine. It's fine. I'm not *drinking* drinking ... not like I used to. Just have a couple of beers now and again. That's all." He winked at me, amused at my reaction.

I remained stationary, searching his face, trying to understand what he was saying.

"C'mon girl. Don't get me wrong. I'm not going back to what I was before. I'm a changed man. Coupla beers ... it's harmless."

I continued to stand my ground, peering into his face.

"Meggie, Meggie, you know me. I had a big scare, a really big scare. Given up that heavy drinkin' and won't be going back to it neither. Hey girl, I was listening. I took it all in up here." He tapped his head as he spoke. "Don't you worry about that; took it all in. C'mon. Let's go. Gee it's good to see you."

He rubbed his hand playfully across the top of my head, then put his arm around my waist again and gently nudged me forward. I took a few reluctant steps and then slipped into his walking rhythm.

Ray chatted as we walked. He told me how he came to find the room at the Guest House. It seemed he had made a few new friends since leaving Araluen.

I found his enthusiasm at seeing me intoxicating, so much so that despite my confusion at hearing that he was drinking again, I could feel myself relaxing as we walked. I couldn't remember knowing anyone ever express so much excitement in seeing me. It was a new experience, but one that I was very much enjoying. It felt good to be so appreciated.

"Things are going well for me, Meggie; new life. Soon I'll be earning some serious dough. Got a great opportunity in the pipeline, I have. Can't wait to tell you about it." He stopped and pulled me slightly closer to him as we stood side by side. "And you've come to visit me. Best day ever." He squeezed me briefly and then we set off again.

It seemed as though some barrier that had been between as at Araluen had been removed. Meeting Ray like this on the street in the middle of Brisbane was very different from our stolen conversations at Araluen. There, I had always felt that we were being watched, that we were under scrutiny.

Here, in the middle of Fortitude Valley near the center of Brisbane, there were no eyes on us; no one around who cared who we were or what we were doing. I liked this feeling of anonymity and independence. Life at Calvary could be stifling at times. My anxiety forgotten now, I relaxed, determined to enjoy Ray's company. His warmth and enjoyment at seeing me was infectious.

Ray led me into his "local" and we pulled up a chair in the lounge. It looked as though it had been recently renovated and was tidy enough.

"What do you want, love?" he asked.

"Um … I don't know. I don't know what I want." I hadn't had an alcoholic drink for several years. Actually, I hadn't even been inside a pub for a very long time. "What're you having?"

"A beer, of course." Ray tipped his head and widened his eyes as though I was asking the most ridiculous question. "I'm no pansy. I'm having a beer, of course."

"Oh, okay. I might have a gin and tonic then. Haven't had one for a long time." I racked my brains trying to think of some reason why I *shouldn't* have a drink. I tried to think what rule or regulation stipulated that I wasn't allowed to consume alcohol.

What the hell. I'll only have one; one drink can't do any harm.

I waited at the table while Ray got our drinks at the bar. The room was empty except for two middle-aged ladies sitting in one corner smoking. I watched them as I waited for Ray. Every now and then they would lean towards each other and giggle uncontrollably at some private joke.

Ray came back with our drinks and sat opposite me, still grinning in delight at seeing me. He lifted his glass towards me, "Cheers Meggie. It sure is good to see you."

I felt a stab of guilt as I picked up my glass and took a sip.

Great drug rehabilitation supervisor I make ... sitting in a pub having a drink ... with an alcoholic.

It tasted good, refreshing. I put down my glass and eyed Ray across the table from me. I had never seen him looking so happy, so free. He seemed positive about his life and I could only deduce that his time at Araluen must have benefited him.

"Do you miss being up there, at Araluen?"

He threw back his head in a laugh. "Miss it? No way. No, Meggie, I don't miss it at all. Glad to be getting on with my life. I do miss Andy, though. He was a good bloke." He pulled out a cigarette as he talked. "How's it going up there?"

"Okay I guess. There haven't been any major dramas lately. We have a new trainee arriving on Monday, should be interesting. Don't know all his details yet."

"You'll handle it girl. You got what it takes."

I twisted my mouth, unconvinced. "I don't know. Sometimes I think everything is going okay and sometimes I wonder what the hell I'm trying to do there."

"Well Meggie, you sure made a difference to me. I'm a different man now, all 'cos of you. I can see a future for m'self now. Things were pretty bleak before."

I shook my head. It was hard to believe I had made *that* much difference to his life. "Have you been to church?"

Ray took a sip of his beer and grinned at me. "Nah … I thought about it but that NSC's too big for me, too many clowns running around. I don't need it now. I'm on the straight and narrow. No going back for me. I'm a changed man." He patted his chest and leaned back to drag on his cigarette.

"That's good Ray. That's good to hear. I wanted to make sure you were doing okay … since leaving."

"As long as I got you Meggie, I'm a new man." He leaned forward. "I gotta tell ya, Meggie. I've got an opportunity. It's pretty exciting." He lowered his voice as he spoke so I had to lean forward to hear him.

"What is it?"

"Mercenary training camp. Heard about it from a friend of a friend. It's like, you know, Special Forces training. You train for specialist type jobs."

"Mercenary?" I said, my eyes widening, wondering if he meant what I thought he meant.

"Yep, can make a lot of money. Ya gotta know the right people, though."

I could hear what he was saying, but it was hard to take it in, to believe it. I sipped on my drink as I listened and watched him, trying to understand. I was looking into that other world again, across the chasm.

Sometimes Ray was talking so quietly and quickly, it was hard to pick up his words and follow what he was saying. I had to ask him to repeat things a few times. It was all very confusing, but what seemed clear was that Ray had been given a very lucrative offer and that he felt it was a timely opportunity. He would have to go away for a while and he couldn't disclose the exact location.

Though I didn't want this time with Ray to come to an end, I looked at my watch when we had finished our drinks. "Ray,

I need to get the truck back. It's going to be dark by the time I get home."

"Sure Meggie, sure. Hasn't been long enough though. It's early days yet with this training camp stuff. Just talk for now. Nothing is going to happen tomorrow like." He reached across the table and grabbed my hand. "Can never spend enough time with me girl, though. Ya gotta come and see m'room, see me new home before you go. C'mon."

We left the pub and walked side by side; Ray's arm around my waist. He held me a little tighter this time, with a confidence, a surety; as though I belonged to him. I felt needed, appreciated, that I belonged. I leaned into him a little as we walked. He looked down at me, "Gee it's good to see ya, Meggie" and held me even tighter.

It was as though he was drawing me to him, into his life, into his private world. I had no defense, drawn by his sense of need. It was as though I was bobbing on an ocean swell and my feet couldn't touch the bottom; a swell that was compelling me towards him. Knowing that Ray needed me and wanted to be with me created feelings I had never experienced before. My insides were on fire. It felt magical.

It was only a short walk from the pub back to Ray's room, but I lost track of time. For this moment, nothing else mattered except to enjoy being with Ray, being close to him. We reached the Guest House and climbed the stairs. He guided me down the hall, holding me as close to him as possible the whole time. He stopped briefly outside his door as he unlocked and opened it, holding me all the while.

The door was barely shut behind us and he had me fully in his embrace in one fluid movement. There was no moment to stop and look around his modest room. Frighteningly, I responded to his embrace, overcome with the desire to be as close to him as possible. It felt like we had always been together, we belonged. His arms were around me holding me close. I could feel his firm tight muscles under his shirt, his warmth encompass me.

Being this close to him alone, ignited a response in me I wasn't expecting. The affectionate hug had moved almost immediately into something different, something quite different.

I no longer felt in the midst of an ocean swell but rather that I was riding atop a tidal wave.

"Oh Meggie, what a woman, what a woman. I can't believe I've found you. I've found m'self a good girl. I'm not going to blow it this time. I'll treat ya right, You'll see. I'll treat ya right."

Ray moved me gently towards his bed as he continued to embrace me. I knew exactly what was happening, but I didn't want to stop it. I could feel myself responding to him in every way. His touch seemed to have opened floodgates and I couldn't contain the emotions and feelings that were now welling up and tumbling out, out of control.

I was out of control. I knew it, but I had no defense, no way to stop this tidal wave.

I didn't want to stop it.

I lay down on Ray's bed.

Chapter Twenty-Three

My knuckles went white as I gripped the steering wheel. I let go and banged the wheel, furious.

What have you done? What the hell have you done? You stupid girl!

Ray had been asleep when I'd left the room. I'd tried to tidy myself as quietly as possible so as not to disturb him as I crept out. It was dark. Driving the truck at night would be a new experience. I fumbled to get the key into the ignition, my hands trembling.

I have to get home. I have to get home now.

I kept stealing glances at the entrance to the Guest House, wondering if Ray would appear in the doorway as I tried to get the truck started. He didn't. The truck didn't start straight away and needed the accelerator pumped several times.

How do I turn on the lights?

I fiddled with every knob and stick I could find and finally managed to switch them on and was able to pull the vehicle away from the curb. I looked at my watch, 7:35. It felt much later.

Trying not to think too much, I concentrated on navigating the truck through the city and back to the Bruce Highway. There was a cold stone sitting in my belly; an icy feeling that was spreading slowly up my chest as I drove. It hurt. A right only lane forced me to turn unexpectedly and I had to loop around the block and double back. I swallowed hard, trying to contain the icy feeling as I searched for the correct lane to get out of the city. The traffic was a little heavier now than it had been earlier and I had to trek carefully as visibility was limited due to the size of the truck.

It was a relief to reach the main arterial road out of Brisbane, which eventually became the Bruce Highway. The multiple lanes made it easier to navigate and I felt I was at last on familiar ground, on track to get home safely.

But that relief was momentary as the icy feeling took further hold. The pain in my chest could no longer be ignored. I had to face it, face the truth. I had to face what I had just done, what had just happened.

I had slept with a man ... something that was absolutely *not* supposed to happen again until I was married!

You idiot!

Where was the warmth of Ray's embrace, the unrestrained passion that had so totally overwhelmed me only a short time ago? Caught in the moment, it had felt so right at the time, the desire to be with Ray ... to be in his arms. I had belonged there.

But sitting in the truck driving home now, that passion was but a memory, a memory fast being replaced by a dark icy shadow.

What have I done?

Looking back at the scene in Ray's room, the realization of my foolishness was crushingly cruel. The icy shadow was rising up my chest and had now reached my throat. I felt it constrict, tighten. There was nowhere to hide. The enormity of what I had done came crashing down upon me, forcing the air out of my lungs as though someone had sat on my chest. I groaned.

"Oh my God, oh my God." The words hung in the air. Then tears came tumbling down, unannounced.

"I'm a hypocrite. I'm such a hypocrite."

I gripped the wheel tightly and forced myself to concentrate on driving. The tears welling up made it hard to see at times. I had to blink and wipe them away to keep focus on the oncoming traffic and lights around me. My mind turned to Calvary, the trainees and my counselling team. A sob gripped my chest and I groaned again.

I've let them all down. I wanted to help them and now I've let them all down. What sort of a disappointment am I?

My sense of failure threatened to consume me. Here I was trying to help these young trainees rebuild their lives and overcome difficulties. I was trying to give them hope.

What hope can I give them if I can't even keep control of my own life?

A fresh stream of tears bubbled up and poured down my cheeks. My nose was running. I had no handkerchief or tissues in the truck, so had to wipe my face with my sleeve and hands as best as possible. I lost sense of time as the truck lumbered on towards Araluen, my concentration challenged.

I care about those trainees. I don't want to hurt them.

Stickability and determination were characteristics I had been reaching for in my life since getting involved at NSC. I had determined to make sacrifices in order to serve God to the very best of my ability.

What do I do now? Do I go back and pretend that I've done nothing? That everything is okay?

But even as those words went through my head, I knew that I could never do that. I could never be such a hypocrite. I didn't want to be that sort of a leader – one that pretended to be someone they weren't. Such a thought was abhorrent and it made me shudder. That's what Kevin and Andrea had done, pretended for so long. I vowed not to be like them, not to repeat their mistakes.

Then what do I do?

No idea came as I posed the question to myself, only a fresh flood of tears and the cold steely pain crushing my chest as I drove on in the dark.

◊ ◊ ◊

Araluen was eerily quiet as I pulled the truck into the entrance. Even the kitchen was dark as I parked outside the service entrance. I slipped out of the truck, leaving the keys in the ignition, as usual.

The night air was chilly. I shivered. There was no one here to accuse me, yell at me, or abuse me. No one was troubled by my late return. Only my own guilt and the pain in my chest threatened me, stood as my silent accuser. My face was dry now, the tears had stopped some time ago. Only the icy darkness remained.

I sighed deeply, letting the cold night air bite into me momentarily before moving. I made my way up the hill to my room struggling to lift my feet with each step, as though I carried a great weight.

Without changing, I flung myself onto the bed, wrapping myself in my bed cover in an effort to stop the shivering. I lay there, staring at the ceiling not thinking for a while, trying to keep my mind blank. My mind wandered as I searched for some explanation, some understanding as to how I had managed to get myself to this life shattering, devastating point.

I had given up my job, my career, studied the Bible and dedicated myself to full-time work for the church – to serve

God. I had worked so hard to try to make Calvary work and to live up to Kevin's expectations of me in spite of all my misgivings and feelings of uncertainty.

I pulled the cover closer around me, but the shivering continued.

I had worked hard to get the trainees to trust me so that I could speak into their lives and influence them for the better. I'd tried to change myself, so that I could help others.

But have I changed myself? Can I really help them?

It seemed that in one evening I had lost control and virtually thrown away all that I had achieved. I rolled from side to side, frustrated. The cover came loose.

I can't sleep like this. I have to decide what to do.

I could find no peace within, no way to reconcile the events of the evening. There was no place for a relationship with Ray Klein in my Christian life, my Christian walk. And there was certainly no place for a relationship with Ray Klein in my life as leader of the drug rehabilitation operation.

There was no excuse for my behavior. I had fallen into sin and the guilt was sitting on my chest, crushing me. There seemed no escape. I needed to make a decision. I had to determine some course of action to try to alleviate the pain. It was killing me.

What choices do I have?

I thought about what I had learned about repentance. I understood that repentance was both a decision and a determination to change. It wasn't enough to get down on my knees before God and say that I was sorry. That would be too easy. I had to determine to change.

And yet, even now, as I pondered all this, I knew that the pull to be with Ray was still strong. I couldn't deny that I wanted to see him again, not today, not right now, but I did want to see him again. I unraveled myself from my bed cover and slipped partially off the bed so that my knees reached the floor.

"Please God, tell me what to do now. Help me. Tell me how to deal with this situation. I want to do the right thing. I want to fix what I have done, but everything seems so mixed up right now. Tell me what to do."

The tears started again and tumbled down my face as I waited in the dark for some divine inspiration. All I could hear was the pounding of my heart.

"God, please forgive me and tell me what to do now."

My knees were hurting on the concrete floor but still I waited for some divine epiphany, some way to make sense of the evening's events.

How do I resolve this conflict?

Finally, my knees almost numb, I crawled back into bed and lay flat on my back and closed my eyes. My ears were ringing as if I had been listening to loud music. I still needed to make a decision, to determine an action. I had to *do* something.

Then inspiration came at last. The Bible said, "Confess your sins one to another and pray for healing."

I know what I can do, I can talk to Geoff. I can talk to Geoff.

A wave of exhaustion overcame me. At last, I had a plan, an action, some direction. At least it was something definite. Though the pain in my chest did not subside, I felt the tension ease marginally.

Chapter Twenty-Four

It was a sorry sight looking back at me in the mirror. My eyes were puffy and my hair a mess. It was hard work trying to draw out the tangles with my brush. The cold feeling was still sitting on my chest, so I tried thinking about the routine for the day at Calvary.

The morning goat milking would be over by 7:30 and Geoff would go to the house for breakfast with the trainees. Geoff's day from that point was always different, depending on what needed fixing or investigating. The trainees would be busy with their duties until their counselling session at 10:30 on the verandah at the house. Angela would be expecting to see me then.

I felt a stab in my chest at the thought of Angela waiting to talk to me about her daily problems. How could I counsel her when I was such a hypocrite? The thought made me want to vomit.

I had to talk to Geoff before then. It seemed the best time to catch Geoff would be after breakfast, before he started his day's activities. I looked at my watch. It was just after 7:00 am.

Maybe a coffee will settle my tummy down a bit.

◊ ◊ ◊

I could hear laughter as I climbed the stairs. To hear this joviality emanating from the dining area at the farmhouse was jarring. We had finally managed to establish a sense of community. It made the pain in my chest intensify and climbing the stairs more difficult.

I paused on the top step and patted my puffy eyes, hoping that no one would notice them. I didn't want to go inside. Hopefully Geoff would come out and I could speak to him without seeing the others.

I stood frozen in that position for several minutes, undecided what to do next. Footsteps coming down the hallway set my heart thumping. Nigel emerged, pulling on his hat.

"G'day Megan. Wasn't expecting to see you here yet. You alright?"

"Morning Nige. Yeah, I'm fine. Just wanted to catch Geoff."

"Yeah, he's finishing up I should think. That's if my Chrissy lets him go this morning. He's been winding her up a bit today." He chuckled as he pulled on his gumboots. "Go on in." He looked at me quizzically momentarily, then set off down the stairs.

"Sure, see ya later," I said, not moving to go inside. The thought of seeing anyone else made me shiver. The sound of further footsteps in the hallway caused my heart to speed up again. I swiveled around. It was a relief to see Geoff. The tension in my shoulders gave a little.

Geoff looked surprised to see me as he reached for his gumboots. "Hi Megan. What's up?"

"I need to talk to you … urgently."

Geoff's eye's narrowed a little and he frowned. "Right

now?"

"If possible. It's really important."

He scratched his head. "Hmmm. Julie's expecting me. We're off to town to do some shopping."

"Geoff, something's happened and I need to talk to you … *now*. It shouldn't take long. We just need to … to find somewhere private." I looked around and added, "Really private."

Geoff's frown deepened. "Okay, then. How about you drive back in the truck with me? That private enough?"

"That'd be good. Means I'd have to leave the ute here, but I'm sure that won't be a problem." I pointed to the utility I'd left parked near the garden gate.

"I'm sure we can fix that. C'mon. My truck's down near the goat dairy."

I followed Geoff down the stairs feeling nervous. *How am I going to tell him what a stupid thing I've done?*

It was hard keeping up with Geoff, as his walk was more like a jog, but I managed to keep pace. The speed helped ease the pain in my chest a little. I waited in the truck as he rushed into the dairy briefly. It was a useful respite, but my thoughts kept swimming around in my head as I tried to think about what I might say.

How am I going to get this out?

Geoff jumped in the cab and revved up the truck, crunching the gears as he reversed onto the track.

"Okay Megan. What's up?" Geoff watched me as much as he could while navigating the truck, his concern reflected in his quizzical frown.

"Geoff, you're not going to like what I'm about to tell you. It's really bad. *I've* been really bad. I don't know what to do, but I have to tell someone. I have to tell someone I trust." My eyes stayed fixed on him as I talked.

My face must have looked severe as Geoff pulled up the

truck in the middle of the track. Thankfully we were out of sight of the main house. He turned off the ignition and gave me his full attention. "Okay. I'm all ears. What's up?"

I took a deep breath. Not being able to hold his gaze further, I looked out the windscreen.

"I've done the worst thing imaginable. I'm sick to my stomach. I can't undo it. I don't know how to put it right."

It was Geoff's turn to sigh this time. "C'mon Megan. It can't be that bad. What's up?"

"Well … you know I told you I heard from Ray."

"Y…es." I could feel Geoff's body stiffen. He shifted in his seat, but he said nothing further and waited, staring at me.

"Well, I took the opportunity to go and see him … yesterday … after I dropped off the milk. I know you didn't think that'd be a good idea and I realize now, you were probably right. I took a risk. Things got carried away … really carried away." I turned my head towards him again. I wanted to look him in the eye as I summoned all my courage. "Geoff …" I hesitated a moment longer.

"Yes?"

"Geoff … I slept with him." I could feel the tears banking up behind my eyes as shame threatened to overwhelm me, but I held them back and continued to hold Geoff's gaze waiting for his reaction.

He held my stare momentarily, then turned his head away. All the air escaped from his lungs as though someone had squeezed him hard. His shoulders sagged. Neither of us spoke.

The pain in my chest had eased ever so slightly. It was a relief to have shared my guilt. But the relief was short-lived as the enormity of my actions threatened to consume me again and I wondered what would happen next.

It was unusual to see Geoff speechless. He continued to stare out the window, silent. I didn't know what else to say so

I sat and watched him, waiting. Eventually he started up the engine again.

"Megan, I need some time to think about this ... what it means. I have to admit, I'm shocked ..." He turned to look at me. "and ... um ... well ... disappointed." His words cut like a knife. He got the truck moving again, but he didn't move out of second gear. We crept along the track. "Megan, do you have any idea about this man? Do you know who he is and what he's really like?"

"Well, I don't know. I think I know, but I ... um ... um ... I'm not sure, I guess."

"I don't know much about him, but I suspect he's dangerous. You're a fool to pursue any further contact with him. For your own sake, Megan, you have to leave it alone." He took his foot off the accelerator and stopped the vehicle again as he turned to me and put his hand on my leg. "Promise me, Megan. Promise me you won't have anything further to do with him."

I could feel a tear squeezing out, refusing to be contained any longer. Geoff didn't know Ray and he certainly didn't understand how we felt about each other. I said, "But God can help him. God can help anyone. Ray is trying to get his life sorted out."

"Of course God wants to help him, but that doesn't mean *you* need to be the one to make that happen. Think about what this means to Calvary and your position here. This is very serious."

"I know."

"I'm going to have to think about this and," he turned to me as he continued, "I'll have to talk to the others in leadership around here as well."

Involuntarily, tears tumbled silently down my cheeks unrestrained. The realization that Geoff wasn't going to keep this conversation confidential was shattering. "You have to tell other people?"

"This has to be dealt with in an open and proper manner."

I sat immobilized, saying nothing.

"Damn it! Damn it! This is all Kevin's fault." Geoff's face reddened and he thumped his fist on the dash. His outburst took me by surprise, startled me. "It's Kevin's fault. That's why this's happened. It comes from the top. It always comes from the top."

I didn't understand what he meant. I gathered he was referring to Kevin and Andrea in some way. It was puzzling.

I sat quietly, lost in my own misery - guilt and humiliation tumbling around together. Telling Geoff and confessing what I had done had not brought the relief I had anticipated. I felt naked and exposed. Others would find out.

"What should I do in the meantime?" I asked, feeling desperate, vulnerable.

"What?" Geoff seemed lost in his own thoughts momentarily, my question pulled him back.

"What do I do now? Do I go to my counselling session with Angela?"

"Um, oh, I see what you mean. I don't think you should do that Megan. Why don't you get Nellie to take Angela today, until I've had a chance to think this through? Maybe you should take a bit of time off for now."

"Okay." I wiped my cheeks with the back of my hand.

"Listen, I'll catch Nellie before Julie and I leave and ask her to fill in for you for a couple of days."

"Okay." I nodded my head, glad that I didn't have to talk to Nellie myself. I wanted to crawl into a hole somewhere and die.

We drove the rest of the way in silence. I decided to ring Jane when I got back. I needed to talk to a friend.

Chapter Twenty-Five

I could hear footsteps up the path before I heard the knock on my door. I opened it straight away, anxious for an end to this painful wait. The last two days had been agony. Geoff was standing back a little as the door opened. His face was drawn and his jaw clenched.

"Megan, we need to talk, but I don't want to talk here. Can you come with me? I've got the key to one of the lecture rooms. It's more suitable."

"Sure," I said, grabbing my jacket to follow him.

I watched him as he strode in front of me, missing his usual warm and friendly demeanor. Although I had considered over and over whether telling him had been the right thing to do, I always came to the same conclusion. There had been no other choice, no other option. I had been obedient to what the Scripture said.

I sighed deeply, wondering what would happen next.

Geoff looked uncomfortable as he sat opposite me. In contrast, I felt strangely relaxed. It didn't seem possible that things could get any worse.

Despite the coolness, the room smelled stale. I looked at the window considering whether to open it or not.

"Megan, this is hard for me."

My attention drawn back, I looked at Geoff a little puzzled, saying nothing.

I thought it was hard for me.

"I've had to think long and hard about what you told me the other day. It's been a tough few days ... for all of us."

My reflex was to feel angry but I held my tongue. This wasn't about him. Geoff kept talking.

"It's hard for me to tell you this, but I have to. It's the only way I can see to resolve this situation and get everything out in the open and back on track. Things've been heading very, very much in the wrong direction. It's been as much my fault as anyone's. I think I understand why you did what you did."

He stood up and paced the room as he talked. I wasn't sure where this was going. I sat back in my chair, folded my arms across my chest and listened, waiting.

"But in the end, on Judgment Day, we all have to stand before God. Ultimately we are all responsible for our own actions and we all stand before God, alone. You have to face up to *your* actions and so do I and so does Kevin."

I just nodded my head in agreement. What he said was true. I had to find my own peace with God and accept His forgiveness for what I had done. I needed to get my life back on track and back in control. That was why I had gone to Geoff in the first place.

"But it gets more complicated when you're in a leadership position. You have a responsibility for your own life, but you also have a responsibility to those you're trying to lead. What you do also influences others ... dramatically. That's why it's critical that we deal with your situation by the book. We have to do it right."

My heart sank. I didn't know why, but his words sounded

ominous.

"I don't think NSC did things right last year. They didn't get it right and that's why I think we're in this predicament here now, today."

He sat back down, perching on the edge of his chair. He leaned towards me, his eyes fiery. "Megan, they swept what happened between Kevin and Andrea under the carpet instead of bringing it out in the open properly. The church members were only ever told *part* of the story. Because of that, it's now become a festering sore affecting so many members of the congregation." He stood up, pacing again.

"I believe it's affected you. I think you have fallen into this situation, this temptation, because you haven't been under the right covering ... the right leadership. And Megan, it's affected me too."

He sat down again. He was so wired, hopping up and down, that I had to place my hand over my mouth to contain a giggle. He reminded me of a jack-in-the-box. If it wasn't such a serious situation, I would have laughed out loud. Regardless, he had my attention. I was wondering what was coming next.

"I was appointed in a leadership capacity here too. Kevin wanted me to shepherd, guide and help you set up this drug rehabilitation operation. I've failed in that role Megan. *I've* failed too."

"Geoff, it's not your fault I did a really stupid thing. What're you talking about?"

"But Megan, the problem is ... I've been in the wrong too. You don't know this, but ..." Geoff was having difficulty getting his words out. "The trouble is ... I've had feelings for you. I've been caught up in this festering sore too. *I'm* part of the problem. I've been thinking about you in a way that I shouldn't have been."

I wasn't sure I had heard correctly. I sat frozen, not

breathing, shocked; staring at Geoff. He sat opposite me, quiet now, giving me time to digest his words. Pain was evident in his countenance. He was deeply disturbed and he was finding it difficult to talk openly.

"So you see Megan, I'm guilty too. I know nothing happened between us, but that doesn't change the fact that it was in my head. That was the problem, it was in my head. I've told Julie all about it now. She was mad as hell. But we've worked through it … we're working through it."

He punched his thigh with his fist.

"So stupid really. I just got my head in a bad place. I was so worried about my boys. Julie's been so sick, so ill, you see. She could die at any time. She's been to the brink of death so often. Without a kidney transplant … well, there isn't much hope. We don't like to talk about it much, but I was losing hope and worried about my boys. I let my mind get carried away."

He punched his thigh again, his face stricken with guilt. I shook my head, watching him, not believing what I was hearing. We were both silent for a time.

The memory of him touching my cheek a few weeks ago, flashed into my mind. It had felt strange at the time, but I'd shrugged it off, thought nothing about it again. I hadn't been looking for that sort of attention from Geoff, never even considered it. Sure, I liked him and appreciated his support, help and guidance. He was a lot of fun, and quick witted. He had been a good friend … but I'd never thought of him in *that* way.

What the hell?

Geoff sighed deeply. "But I've got it all out in the open now. Getting things out in the open breaks their power. Things hidden in the dark fester. Julie and I are straight again now and I've got my head back in the right place … the place where God wants me to be. Megan, what you did was wrong.

We have to bring it out into the open too. For the sake of all these folk at Calvary we have to make things right."

Geoff was talking faster now. Still shocked, I kept listening, trying to stop my mouth from gaping.

"I've talked to Mary and Nigel and we've all agreed that the best course now is for you to confess what you've done. The Scripture says in James that we should confess our sins to each other and pray for healing."

"Haven't I already done that? I've prayed to God *and* I confessed to you."

"No Megan, I mean publicly confess what you've done. Because you're in a position of authority and leadership, your actions can't be swept under the carpet and hidden from view. It *must* be made public. You need to get up in front of everyone at Calvary, confess and acknowledge what you did. You have to do it in front of them all and admit to them that it was the wrong thing to do. Then everything will be out in the open. Then we can all move on. The power of this sickness will be broken … once and for all."

My jaw dropped open. "Are you serious?"

"I've never been more serious in my life! Too much has been going on behind shadows. To follow God we have to live right; we have to live in the light. It's a tough path sometimes, but if we want to live our lives for God, it *is* tough. The straight and narrow is the harder path to take, but we will be better people in the end. It will be an opportunity to cleanse your soul and show some genuine repentance for what you've done. It is a way for you to set an example for the trainees. There are so many reasons …"

It was hard to keep listening to what he was saying. My mind was distracted by an image of me standing in front of everyone: my counselling team, the trainees. I tried to picture myself telling them that I had slept with Ray Klein but it was too painful. The tears were threatening again. I placed my hand around my throat, trying to contain my emotions.

An elephant was sitting on my chest, suffocating me. I was drowning. I got up from my chair, turning away from Geoff, and stood at the window looking out. My sense of failure and guilt shrouded my every move. Geoff's confession, shared moments ago, seemed only to add to my confusion.

The pain in my chest was unbearable. I'd thought confessing to Geoff would provide the relief I needed to move on. Now I had been told it wasn't enough. I had to do more. It would be humiliating.

But ... perhaps it would take this pain away ... help me to begin the recovery and healing process. Perhaps I have to go this far to find repentance.

I had let the team down in every way and my guilt and humiliation were crushing the life out of me. Perhaps going through with this saga might relieve that sense of guilt. Perhaps such a confession might cleanse me somehow, wipe the slate clean. It might just work. I might be able to feel better again, if I can survive it. At the end of the day, I was ready to do anything to put things right.

I turned back to Geoff, resolved.

"Well, if that's what I *have* to do, I guess I *have* to do it then." The tears could be held back no longer. My destiny was set and my only hope was that going through this ordeal, would help me find peace again ... peace with God.

Geoff ignored my tears. His shoulders relaxed noticeably. "Good. You've made the right decision."

"The thought of going through with it makes me feel sick." The decision made, my mind became alarmingly clear all of a sudden. I realized something, something vital.

I need to get out of this place, out of this place forever and ... as soon as possible.

"Okay Geoff. I'm going through with this, but I want it off my back as soon as possible. It has to be today, tonight ...

now. I'm not waiting around with this hanging over me any longer. *And* I'm leaving straight after. I'll do my penance and then I'm out of here. I'm leaving Araluen." I made no attempt to wipe the tears streaming down my face.

I didn't want to continue this conversation any longer. There was nothing more to discuss.

"I'm going to my room to pack. You come and get me …" I looked at my watch, "as soon as possible. I'll be waiting."

I checked around the mess hall again. It was deserted. I picked up the handset to the telephone gingerly and I pulled out the piece of paper in my pocket with Kevin's direct, private number. I dialed, keeping one eye on the double door.

The ring tone seemed to drone on and on in my ear. I was about to give up when it answered and I heard a voice on the other end.

"Hello?" It was Kevin. "Who's this?"

I could feel my throat close as I tried to speak. *No time for tears.* "Kevin, it's me, Megan."

"Megan … just give me a minute."

I could hear some muffled sounds in the background and Kevin's muted voice. It was a relief when he came back on the line. The mess hall was still deserted, but I didn't know how long I would have this privacy.

"Megan, are you there?"

"Yes. Have you heard?"

Kevin sighed deeply, "Yes, I've heard. Unfortunately news like that travels fast. Are you alright?"

"No, I feel terrible. I messed up. I don't know how to fix it. I just want to get out of here."

"Humph. I can tell you, I know how you feel. But, Megan, you mustn't get involved with that man. You must listen to me. He's not a good person. He's not the right sort of person for you. A man like that will hurt you. He's not to be trusted."

I could feel my throat tightening. My time with Ray seemed like a distant memory and yet it had only been a few days ago. The sense of guilt had overtaken everything. It still weighed like a heavy sack on my chest. I couldn't wait for this night to be over.

"Are you still there Megan?"

"Yes, I'm here. They want me to confess … in public." I could hear Kevin catch his breath, followed by a quiet groan.

"That wasn't my idea you know. I'm not sure if that's the best thing in this circumstance. Geoff seemed adamant. You'd have to agree to such an action."

"I know. It's up to me. I've told them I'll do it. But once I have, I'm leaving. I can't do this anymore."

Kevin was silent. I could hear him breathing into the phone. Finally he said, "Megan, I don't know what to say. Where will you go? What will you do?"

"I'm not sure. I'll have to get a job. I need some time to think about things. Anyway, I've got to go now. I just wanted to tell you myself that I was leaving."

"I wish you didn't feel you had to do that."

I heard the mess hall door swing open. I needed to get off the phone as quickly as possible. "I've got to go. I can't talk any more, sorry. Bye."

"But I do understand --"

Click. I put down the phone before Kevin could say any more. I stood with my hand still on the receiver, frozen momentarily.

"Megan, are you okay?"

I looked up; it was Michael. He was moving some dishes to the serving area. "No, I'm not okay. I guess you've heard the news."

A frown crinkled across Michael's forehead. He dumped

the stack of plates on a table nearby and moved towards me. "I did hear about it. Geoff came to discuss it with me ... to get my opinion on what he should do."

"They want me to confess ... publicly."

"I know. Megan —"

"I've told them I'll do it. But I'm leaving afterward. I can't stay here any longer. I can't get up in front of all the kids and my workers and confess my sin ... be humiliated ... and then stay on as their leader. It wouldn't be possible. I have to get out of here."

"Geoff agonized over the decision. But he couldn't think of any other way to handle it. I had to agree with him ... under the circumstances. It's a tough call." He came around to stand beside me and put his arm around me, but I moved away.

"You think it's the right thing to do?"

Michael sighed deeply. "I do. I think you have to do it."

My shoulders sagged. I moved to sit on a nearby chair. I felt trapped, cornered.

"Michael, this thing with Geoff ..."

"Yes?"

"I don't know how it happened. I seem to attract this sort of attention, but I don't mean to. I don't look for it. I don't even want it. But when it happens, I don't think I handle it very well. Sometimes I get caught up in things, swept along."

Michael sat down beside me, his eyes downcast, listening.

"Even when I want to stop things, I don't. It's weird. What's wrong with me?"

He looked up at me, his eyes reflecting his concern.

"I don't know, Megan. Do you want me to pray with you?"

"No, not really. Not right now." I stood up. "I'm tired. I'm going to my room to finish packing. Say goodbye to Lorraine and the kids for me. I don't want to talk to anyone.

"Megan, if you want to talk, you know I'm always here."

"Yeah. I know. I just want to be alone."

Chapter Twenty-Six

I couldn't stop the tears as I walked out of the house at Calvary and down the stairs. Confessing in front of everyone had not absolved me, had not relieved the pain in my chest. In fact, it felt worse. I could hear someone on the verandah behind me, but I didn't look back.

"Megan, Megan, wait a minute." It was Angela. I stopped walking but didn't turn around. She rushed down the stairs and came up behind me. "You can't go like this. You can't just go like this. It's awful."

Still facing away, I said nothing.

"I don't care what you did. It doesn't matter to me. I think it's worse they made you do that … get up in front of everyone."

I turned to face her. "I'm sorry, Angela. I wish you all the best. You're a good girl. I'm sure you'll sort everything out. I'll miss Jake too. He's a great kid. I'm sorry I let you down."

"You didn't let me down! You have been a really good friend to me." Angela was visibly upset. Seeing her like this tugged at my heart. I moved towards her, put out my arms and drew her into a hug. She was crying too.

"Just keep going the way you've been going and you'll make it." I patted her back and pulled away, the silent tears still streaming down my face. This was too painful. I had to get away.

I could tell Angela wanted to say more, but she was too upset.

"I'll write to you. Nellie will look after you. You'll make it, Angela. I know you'll make it. I've got to go now. See ya … bye." I waved as I pulled myself away and turned to leave.

Geoff had brought me down to Calvary in his truck but I wanted to go back alone. I turned and waved goodbye to Angela one more time as I set off towards Araluen.

Despite the cold evening air, I warmed quickly as I broke into a jog. My HR Holden was packed, ready and waiting. I didn't want any more painful goodbyes. It was time to go. It was time to get out of here and put it all behind me.

I lost sense of time as I drove towards Brisbane. It was raining, which seemed congruent with my mood and sense of despair. My mind replayed snatches of the evening as I drove. Each memory brought a fresh set of tears.

The group had already assembled by the time Geoff and I had arrived. I remembered the scene as though I was outside myself, watching from above. I stood in the middle of the room as Nellie, Mitch, Tanielle, Simmo, Nigel, Mary and Geoff sat where they could: on the old lounge chairs, perched on the arms, or sprawled on the carpet on the floor. I had been surprised to see Geoff's Julie there too.

Geoff got the group's attention. "Everyone, Megan has something important to say. I'd appreciate if you could give her your attention, please. Listen up."

He had stepped back to give me the floor. It was awkward having everyone sitting around the room as it made it harder to know where to look. Though I hadn't wanted to make eye contact with anyone, my training for ministry and public speaking had already developed that reflex when speaking to a group. I could see myself scanning the room, briefly pausing to look at each person while I struggled to catch my thoughts, to think clearly, to find the words.

I groaned and tried to push the memory away.

The rain was heavier now and was making it difficult to see through the windscreen despite the wipers working at top speed. I slowed down and concentrated on driving, trying to push the memory of one of the worst nights of my life away. I didn't want to think about it anymore.

But the picture of me standing in the middle of that room crept center stage again and again. Even now, so soon after the event, I couldn't recall exactly what I had said. I wanted to let the memory sink into an abyss of forgetfulness. But something made me replay it in my mind, over and over. Perhaps I was trying to make sense of it all.

Why had I agreed to do it?

A scripture popped into my head, *"If we confess our sins he is faithful and just to forgive us our sins and to cleanse us from all unrighteousness."*

God said he would cleanse my sins. Well I've confessed them now. Why don't I feel clean? Rather, I still feel only terrible shame and embarrassment. I don't feel clean at all.

But then I remembered another scripture, *"And their sins and iniquities will I remember no more."*

God has cleansed me. He has forgiven me. I just have to forgive myself.

The rain had eased a little now, so I picked up speed again. The sooner I got home to Mum's the better.

The scene in the middle of the room at Calvary appeared in

my mind again. One thing I recalled now, very clearly, was the look on the faces of the trainees. Simmo, in particular, had been shocked but I could tell by his eyes that he was feeling for me having to go through the ordeal. I could tell he wanted to say something, but held back. Here I was, the counselor, the leader, admitting fault. I could tell by their expressions that the trainees were identifying with me. In this bizarre turn of events, I had become one of them, a peer. Their unmistakable support and compassion was moving.

I peered through the windscreen trying to figure out exactly where I was on the highway. I looked at my watch. It would be very late by the time I got home. Mum would be wondering where I was, though she would probably be in bed by now.

I didn't care that I was driving in the middle of the night in the rain. Every mile I covered was taking me further and further away from Calvary and Araluen. I wanted to stop the tears, stop the pain and start the healing process.

The sooner I get home, the better.

Once home, I pulled into the driveway, parked the car in the back yard and climbed the back stairs as quietly as possible, lugging one of my suitcases. The back door fell open just as I reached it. It startled me. Mum stood inside.

"I heard the car," she said. "I've been waiting for you. Are you alright? I was getting worried. It's so late."

I dropped my bag inside the door and let her put her arms around me for a welcome hug. The tears had stopped flowing. I had none left.

I sighed. "I messed up, Mum. It's been a rough few days. I need some time to think about things … everything."

"I'm sure you do darling. Come in now, anyway. You need

some sleep. I've made up your old bed. You can unpack in the morning. We can talk more then."

"Okay. I'm wrecked."

Mum followed me down the hall to my room and said good night. I flung myself on the bed, relieved to be somewhere safe and glad that Mum hadn't pressed me for details about what had happened and why I was here.

As I lay down on my bed, it suddenly occurred to me that as awful and humiliating as the whole ordeal had been, at least I didn't have the responsibility for Calvary any longer. For the first time in the last few days I felt something positive, instead of pain. I felt an overwhelming sense of relief. I had confessed. God had forgiven me. Now I could heal and the responsibility for Calvary and every person there was no longer mine. Somebody else had that pressure now, not me.

◊ ◊ ◊

Mum had left a few things on the table for me for breakfast, so I poured myself some cereal while she washed up a few dishes.

"Did you manage to get some sleep?" she asked.

"I did actually."

"That's good. Do you want some coffee?"

"Yes Mum, thanks."

She brought a mug of coffee over and sat down at the table, looking a little concerned.

"What're you going to do now?"

I sighed and put down my spoon and took a sip of the coffee. "I'll have to get a job again, I guess. I'll look for secretarial work. At least I should get paid some decent money again."

"Do you have any money saved?"

"Not much … just a few hundred dollars. Kevin didn't pay

me enough to save, just enough to survive." I looked around the room for the morning paper. "I'll have to go through the paper." Turning my eyes to Mum, I said, "Might have to stay here for a bit though. Is that okay?"

Mum gave me one of those looks as if to say "as if you had to ask" and said, "Of course. You know, Megan, I've been talking to John Fieldman about maybe converting this place into a community home. You know they've been setting them up around Brisbane for the youth group. It's such a big house and I'm here by myself these days, seems such a waste. It might be nice to take in a couple of young girls. What do you think?"

"Mum that's a great idea. Why not? I guess you would get some board as well. That's a really good idea."

"You being here might help too."

I looked directly at Mum, "Um, I don't know. Actually Mum, I don't think I'm much use at the moment. If you want to do this, you shouldn't rely on me. I need some time to think about things. I'm still working stuff out in my head."

"Well, I guess I could do it on my own."

"Of course you could Mum. You'd be great at it. Just get one or two girls in and see how it goes. It could be fun." I reached for the paper and turned to the jobs section and scanned the columns. Mum got up to continue with her morning chores and I looked around for a biro.

Pen in hand, I took the paper into the lounge room and spread it out on the floor for some serious study. As my eyes scanned the columns looking for suitable job titles, my mind wandered to Ray. I wondered what he might be doing and whether he had left for his training camp. He didn't know that I had left Calvary.

Should I see him again?

Seeing him could be risky, as I would be putting myself in temptation's way. Even so, it was difficult to shift the picture of his haunting face. Disturbingly, the pull to see him again was tugging. I felt so battered and bruised from the events of the last few days, perhaps spending time with Ray could help to heal my wounds - his passion and adoration for me, a healing tonic.

Chapter Twenty-Seven

It was as easy to find a park in Brunswick Street as it had been last time. I felt a bit nervous as I wondered where Ray might be.

Am I doing the right thing?

I felt pretty sure that most people would believe that I was not doing the right thing and yet here I was, seeking out this man again. Whether it was the intrigue of his mysterious life, the sense of danger and excitement, or his persistent admiration, something was pulling me to him and I was finding it difficult to resist.

The hallway was musty and eerily quiet as I knocked gently on Ray's door in the Guest House. Not knowing if he was even still living here, I put my ear to the door, listening intently. I could hear nothing, but I knocked again, a little louder this time. Perhaps he was asleep.

Footsteps behind startled me. I looked up to see a weathered man, dressed in ill-fitting pants with a stained tweed jacket, making his way down the hall trying to avoid eye contact. I drew closer to the door to let him pass.

Ray obviously wasn't here. There was only one other option and that was to see if he was at the local pub. It was the only other place I could think to look. If he wasn't there, I would give up and go home.

◊ ◊ ◊

As I put one foot tentatively in the doorway to the public bar, the smell of stale beer hit me. There were no women in the room, only a few men sitting on stools around the bar puffing on cigarettes and chatting. This was uncomfortable territory and I was about to withdraw when I realized the man sitting at the very end of the bar with his back to me, was Ray.

I paused at the door, half turning to leave, frozen, unsure what to do next. But my movement had attracted attention and everyone looked around at the same time. Ray had seen me.

"Meggie, Meggie me girl." He was up immediately and over to the door, beaming. He took me by the elbow with his usual confident manner. "C'mon round the back. It's not so nice in here. Let's go around to the lounge." He didn't say anything to the other men in the bar, or even cast a glance back at them as he steered me into the Lady's Lounge next door.

He had me seated in no time, all the while telling me how excited he was to see me, that he had tried calling me at Araluen and that he missed me. It was just the welcome I craved and it helped to settle my nerves. I could feel myself relaxing a little, soaking up his attention.

"What're ya drinkin' girl? Name your order." He said, winking, still unable to keep a straight face. "Gin and Tonic right?"

"Okay, that'd be great," I said, smiling back.

"Back in a jiffy."

Ray returned with my drink and his beer, which he must have retrieved from the other bar. "So good to see you, Meggie. Where have you been? Bin trying to call ya since the other night."

I shrugged, not knowing where to start or what to tell him.

"Can't see the milk truck up the road and it isn't Thursday. What's doin'?"

"I left Calvary. I left it for good. I'm never going back there."

Ray looked a little surprised but there was a glint in his eye that made me feel he might be pleased. "Oh, Meggie, that's a big change of events. You back here in Brisbane then?"

"Yep," I said nodding.

Ray let out a long breath and sat back in his chair. "Well, that does call for a celebration then, doesn't it! Means we can see a lot more of each other. This is good news Meggie, I have to tell you. This is good news."

"Not really Ray. It's not good news. It's not good news at all. I … we … did a terrible thing, Ray. Sleeping with you was wrong. It's not what a good Christian girl is supposed to do."

Ray threw his head back, laughing and took a few moments to compose himself before looking at me more seriously. "Meggie, that was the most natural thing in the world. Don't you worry your pretty little head about that! You and me, we was meant to be together. It's only natural. You don't have to feel bad about that … not at all." He put his hand on my leg to reassure me, playfully. It felt nice, but I also felt cautious. There was no way I was going to end up in bed with him … again.

No way. I didn't want to end up with a chest gripped by that terrible crippling guilt … again.

"Ray, it was wrong. I did a terrible thing staying with you that night. That's why I had to leave Calvary. I couldn't stay there and be such a hypocrite."

"Well, you know Meggie, I don't understand a lot of that church stuff. To me, what we did, between you and me ... the most natural thing in the world. But I'm not going to argue with you. It's not worth it. You can believe what you want to believe. Feel bad if you want to feel bad. I don't and I'm not going to."

He seemed so sure of himself, relaxed yet amused, though he tried to mask it, rather lamely, sensing my gloomy mood.

"What's happening about your training camp?" I asked wanting to change the subject.

"Good, good," he said. "Takes a bit for these things to come together properly sometimes. But it's lookin' good."

"When do you go?"

"Not sure, not sure Meggie. Could be any day, a week maybe. I'm waiting for a call." He looked around the room a little nervously. "Can't say much Meggie. Have to be very careful." He winked and smiled at me and touched my leg again. "Gees it's good to see you."

Again, I liked his touch. I moved in my seat, feeling uneasy, trying to think of what else to talk about.

"I'll get you another drink Meggie. Same again?"

"No Ray. It's my shout. What beer are you drinking?" I stood up pulling out my wallet

Ray spread his arms out and sat back, surprised but entertained. "Hey Miss Independence, Four X of course. What else?"

As I stood at the bar, getting our drinks, I decided I needed to get going as soon as possible. Ray's adulation in seeing me had not been disappointing, but the conversation didn't seem to be flowing like normal. I decided it was time to go as I made my way back to our table.

"Meggie, I called me Mum again the other day."

"Really?"

"She was shocked to hear from me again and told me not to call anymore. But I had to tell her about you. I had to tell her I had a really good girl for the first time in me life."

"Ray ..."

"It's true Meggie ... we can do anything if we stick together." He pulled his chair next to me and put his arm around my shoulders. Perhaps it was the gin, perhaps it was his apparent sincerity, or a combination of both, but it was as though a blanket had been thrown around me, drawing me to him. His confidence in our future was compelling. It also frightened me. I knew I was putting myself in temptation's way. I didn't want to take any more chances. It was time to say goodbye to Ray, get back in my car and go home. I sucked on my straw and sculled the rest of the gin and tonic.

"Ray, I need to get home. It's been good catching up, but I need to go now."

"Go. Go where? Where's home?"

"I'm staying with Mum at the moment till I work something out. I have to get a job."

Ray nodded his head. "That's good Meggie. That's good."

I stood up to show him that I meant it. Ray picked up his beer, which he had barely touched, and gulped it down in a few seconds. "I'll walk with you Meggie. I don't want you to go, but if you have to ..."

Ray tucked me under his arm as we walked away from the pub. He held my elbow with his other hand. We had to walk in the same rhythm to move in such a close embrace. It was nice to feel him close to me. It felt safe and I was glad that he was walking me to the car. We didn't talk much but enjoyed the close proximity. Nice as it was, it didn't change my resolve. I wasn't going to make the same mistake again. I was going home. Now.

I slowed down as we approached the car. Ray managed to turn me towards him in a full embrace as we stood beside the driver's door.

"Oh Meggie ..." Ray groaned as he held me to him. I could feel a familiar sensation rising. I pulled away and looked at him.

"Ray, I've got to go. It's good to see you. I'll see you again soon." I turned to break away from his embrace and he surprised me by pulling me to him again. I was locked in his arms. My face was now close to his and the smell of alcohol on his breath made me realize that he had consumed more than one or two beers. Ray was probably drunk.

"C'mon Meggie, just a bit longer. I can't say goodbye yet." Before I could say anything further, he had turned me, tucked me under one arm and held my elbow with his other hand in a vice-like grip. We were walking again, away from my car. His movement took me by surprise. I tried to pull away to look at his face, but his arms were like steel pressing me against him, steering me down the road.

"Ray, I want to go. I want to go home. What're you doing?" My heart was racing. I could feel it thumping in my ears. I was frightened now.

"It's alright Meggie. I want to spend a little more time with you, that's all. Can't blame a man for that, can you?"

I tried to slow down the pace and resist his movement by digging my feet into the pavement. He tightened his grip a little more and kept guiding me towards the Guest House.

"Ray, I want to go home."

"I know Meggie, but really you *are* home. Home is with me. I know what you came to see me for. Couldn't let you down now, could I?"

"No Ray, no. I didn't come for that at all! I just came to see you, to see how you're going. You've got it all wrong! I want to go home. Let … me … go." My voice louder now, yelling, I tried to wriggle out of his grip with all my strength. We were walking down the hallway and nearly at his door. He continued to hold me in that vice-like grip. I couldn't twist my arm free. I was pleading with him to let me go.

Somehow Ray managed to open the door while still restraining me. Once inside, he slammed the door shut with his foot. With one simple movement he tossed me onto the bed and, before I could take a breath, he was on top of me, trying to kiss me. I flicked my head from side to side avoiding his mouth, yelling, "Stop it! Stop it! Ray, let me go!"

He was unstoppable. Those muscles that I had so often admired were now pinning me down. It was hard to breathe with his weight on my chest. His knee forced my legs apart. One hand was pulling at my dress while the other hand pinned my shoulder and arm. I tried to push him off me with my free arm. I was so angry! I pushed and thrashed with all my might, trying to get him off me, but it was futile. I couldn't move him or stop him.

I'm trapped.

Ray's arm pinning me down was now on my throat. I couldn't scream anymore. No sound came out. The realization came that nothing I could say or do now was going to stop him. In fact, if I resisted further, he was going to hurt me, really hurt me, maybe even choke me.

Suddenly I relaxed. I stopped fighting. It was inevitable. I accepted my fate. This man was going to impose himself on me no matter what I said or did. If I fought any further I was only going to get hurt. I couldn't see Ray's face in the dark, but I didn't need to see it to know that this man was determined to have his way. Nothing I could say or do was going to change what was about to happen.

You bastard. I screamed in my head but I said nothing. I lay limp, quiet.

You fucking bastard.

I don't know why or how, but in that instant, my rage became contained and internalized. It manifested in a different way. I felt so angry that this man believed he could do whatever he wanted to me as though he owned me. He felt he had a *right* to do this to me.

You don't own me. You aren't going to take me! You fucking bastard.

Inflamed with indignation, it was as though a switch flicked inside me. My anger turned instead into an unrestrained passion - a crazy frenetic passion. I had turned on my own sexual response. My body was inflamed.

I'm going to take you, you bastard. You're not taking me!

I was battling again, but rather than fighting him off, I was challenging his sexual approach with my own sexual response. I was asserting myself in a completely different way.

I will not let you dominate me. I will not let you dominate me. You fucking bastard. You don't own me. You will never own me. I'll take what I want!

Time blurred as we pushed against each other, the instant frozen in my memory forever, until finally spent, I felt him relax and give way on top of me. His weight still pressed on me so that I could hardly breathe. I lay still, perfectly still, my heart pounding in my ears.

I lost track of time, waiting, wanting to be free but terrified to move. My body was on alert, on guard, but I was too scared to move. Gradually my heart slowed enough to be able to hear Ray's breathing.

He's asleep. Is he asleep?

I took shallow breaths, terrified that I might disturb him if my chest moved too much. I didn't want to wake him. I was terrified he might restrain me again and hold me captive.

I have to get out of this room.

A pang of fear exploded across my chest as he snorted in his sleep and rolled off me. I held my breath, waiting, wondering what would happen next. I didn't move.

He is asleep.

One of my legs was still pinned beneath him. Bit by bit I inched my leg out, waiting between each movement to hear his even breathing, to be sure that he was still asleep. Any movement he made or any change in his breathing made my heart skip a beat.

Finally my leg was free. Every muscle, every tendon, every nerve in my body was on alert as I worked to slip one leg then the other off the bed, trying to move as smoothly as possible so as not to disturb this sleeping monster. I was afraid to breathe. My lungs were bursting for fresh air, but it was imperative that I did not wake him. There was no telling what he might do. There was no trust, no confidence, and no hope of any reasonable understanding. Ray Klein was a monster and I had been a fool.

Once off the bed and free to stand I tiptoed, ever so slowly, towards the door. Every squeak and creek made my heart jump and race again. I held my breath and waited until I could hear his even breathing before trying to move again.

It was impossible to open the door silently. I stood poised, ready to run should he move, as I turned the handle and opened the door. He rolled over and my heart jumped into my mouth. I couldn't breathe and my throat was so tight, I felt I was choking. I stood frozen. His breathing remained even. I moved again, through the door and out into the hallway.

It took all my restraint not to break into a run until I crossed the threshold of the front door. Then I nearly fell down the stairs as I tried to run to the car. I slipped and caught myself on the rail. My heart pumping again, I pulled myself up, resisting the urge to look back.

I was trembling now, all over, uncontrollably. I fumbled

with the keys trying to get them into the car door. I dropped them.

"Fuck!"

I looked up at the entrance to the Guest House, terrified I might see Ray at the door coming to get me. There was no one. I picked up the keys and managed to get the door open. I felt a little safer once inside with the door locked. I took a breath and tried to still my racing heart while starting the car.

You fucking bastard.

The engine started with a roar and jerked forward. I had to ease my foot off the accelerator, telling myself to calm down.

Get out of here now!

I stole one last look at the Guest House door as I pulled away from the curb heading for home … and safety. Thankfully, Ray did not appear.

Chapter Twenty-Eight

The beeping of my alarm dragged me reluctantly out of a deep, blissful sleep. I could no longer shut out the noise. I reached over and turned it off and lay looking at the ceiling.

The memory of the night before, of Ray on top of me, forcing himself upon me, against my will, flashed into my mind. I groaned and rolled over, pulling the pillow over my face, trying to push the image away.

You stupid, stupid idiot! What did you think was going to happen?

Thinking back, it was obvious that my naiveté and foolishness had led me down a senseless path … yet again. That realization made me feel exasperated, sick to the stomach.

How could I be so stupid? How could I have expected anything else from a criminal for God's sake!

Kevin's words pounded in my head as through a loud speaker, "A man like that will hurt you. He's not to be trusted."

Why didn't I believe him? What was I thinking!

In the light of day, I had to confront my foolish recklessness and it was shattering. When would I ever learn?

What was the pull that I had felt so strongly to be with him? The memory eluded me now. *Was I under some kind of spell?*

Whatever it was, it was broken. Now it was crystal clear that Ray Klein was an evil man and had nothing to offer me at all. I had been carried away with my own importance and the belief that I could help him in some way. *Megan, the noble rescuer — absolute foolishness!*

I could see now that Ray had been out to get whatever he could for himself.

I doubt that he cares one iota for me. He probably doesn't even know how to care for a woman, any woman.

I realized that a man like that would have no problems lying and now doubted anything he had ever told me.

He is not to be trusted.

A soft knock on the door distracted me.

"Darling, do you want some brekkie? It's still on the table." Mum said through the door.

"Sure Mum. I'll be out in a minute."

I didn't feel like breakfast but I didn't want Mum to know anything was wrong either, so I dragged myself out of bed and pulled on my dressing gown.

In the kitchen, I put some bread in the toaster.

"What are you doing today?" Mum asked, looking up from her paperwork at the kitchen table. "Have you lined up any job interviews?"

I sighed. "Not yet, though I found a couple I can apply for. I'll have to get out the typewriter."

"It's in the spare room."

"Okay, thanks."

We both jumped as the phone rang. Mum went to answer it while I peered into the toaster.

"Hello … oh … yes … she's here," Mum was frowning into the phone. "Who's speaking please?" Mum jerked her head away from the earpiece, looking shocked.

She held it out to me looking concerned. "It's for you."

My heart jumped into my throat. The look on Mum's face made me immediately suspicious. I took the phone tentatively and put it to my ear. "Hello?"

"Meggie, Meggie, listen to me … don't hang up! Give me a minute to explain." It was Ray. I felt frozen to the spot.

"How did you get this number?"

"From the phone book of course. Bin ringing every White in the book to find ya. I'm desperate. I had to find you."

I wanted to hang up the phone. I couldn't believe he had the gall to ring me after last night. I needed to end the call, but for some reason the sound of desperation in his voice made me wonder what he could possibly be thinking. What would he say now after the way he treated me last night? I stood hesitantly with the phone against my ear, poised to drop it onto the cradle at any moment. "I don't want to talk to you."

"I can imagine Meggie. I can imagine. But you have to forgive me. You have to understand. You must realize that I got carried away when I saw you. You're the love of my life Meggie."

That comment took my breath away. It was so contradictory to his actions last night, it almost made me laugh. Ray must have heard my muffled gasp.

"Listen Meggie, listen. A man's a man, you know. You gotta expect that. I couldn't help m'self. I'd never hurt you. You know I'd never do you any harm. You have to believe me. I have to see you … now … today. You have to give me a chance to explain. When can I see you again?"

"I don't think that's possible." I turned my back to Mum so that she couldn't see the expression on my face. I could feel my body trembling. There was nothing that Ray could say that I could trust. He was a liar. "I'm hanging up the phone now. Please don't ring me anymore."

I moved to pull the phone from my ear, but the tone and pleading in his voice made me hesitate.

"Meggie, you can't do that to me … you can't do that to me. After everything girl, I won't let you do that to me."

The tone in Ray's voice changed in an instant. He was angry now. "Listen girl, you aren't going to cut me off like that. I'm not going to let you. If you don't come and see me, I'm going to come and get you —"

Shocked, I pulled the earpiece away and slammed down the receiver. Trembling, I stood staring at the phone keeping my back to Mum. She had been watching me and moved towards me.

"Megan, what's going on? Who was that? What's wrong?" she said with a concerned but stern voice.

I turned towards her slowly, not wanting to tell her anything, but knowing I had to say something. "It was Ray, one of the guys from up at Araluen. I don't want to talk to him. If he rings again, just hang up."

"Why … why? What did he say to you? He was rather rude to me. I didn't like the sound of him at all."

"I know Mum. I'm sorry. We just have to ignore him. He's not a very nice man."

"Well, I don't know what's going on, but I don't like the sound of this. I hope he doesn't ring again. I can do without this, thanks very much."

I sighed. "Hopefully he's got the message that I don't want to talk to him and that will be the last of it."

"I hope so, Megan. I really hope so." Mum didn't look convinced, but I didn't want to talk to her in depth, mainly because everything seemed in such a jumble in my head. It would be difficult to know where to begin.

"Thanks for brekkie Mum. I'm going to get dressed and get on with my job applications," I said, hoping to change the subject.

As I turned to go back to my room, the phone started ringing again. Worried that it might be Ray, I rushed to answer it. I picked up the receiver and paused momentarily before saying, "Hello?"

"Meggie ..." It was Ray again. I slammed down the phone and stood staring at it with my stomach churning. My heart was beating fast and my knees felt weak.

What the hell ... what's going to happen now? How do I stop him ringing me?

As I was about to turn away again, the phone started. I looked at Mum as I picked it up. She was frowning at me. "Hello?"

"Don't hang up ..." It was Ray again. I hung up again, putting the receiver down slowly, holding Mum's gaze as I did.

"Mum, I think we might need to leave the phone off the hook for a while."

"What on earth's going on?"

"Mum, he's not a nice person. I actually think he's a bit mad in the head. We need to leave the phone off the hook for a while. He's nuts. He's a nuisance."

"Well, I don't like this at all."

"I'm sorry Mum. I'm sure he'll give up," I said biting my lip as I said it.

Ray, the monster. What on earth had I ever seen in him?

Turning to go to my bedroom, I decided on the spur of the moment, "Mum, I might go out for a bit." I needed some fresh air.

There was only one person in the whole world at the moment that I wanted to talk to, one person that would listen to me without judging me. I would be able to pour my heart out to her and tell her all about my crazy last few days. It was time to visit Jane.

◊ ◊ ◊

It was comforting tucking my legs up and settling down to a good talk with a cup of coffee in my hands. Jane sat opposite me, so she could read my lips. I wouldn't have known that she even struggled with deafness if Andrea hadn't told me. Jane was good at hiding it, relying on lipreading most of the time. Still, it was important that I faced her when we were talking and I had to make sure I raised my voice enough for her benefit.

She was eager to hear my news and had that twinkle in her eye, waiting with bated breath to hear my tales of woe. We had a few hours to ourselves and we had a lot of ground to cover.

"Now, where to begin? When did I see you last? Yes, that's right. When we got back from Adelaide. Kevin was planning to put me in charge of Calvary then."

"Yes, that's right. You were worried about it, but he seemed convinced it was the right thing to do."

Tears welled up in my eyes at her words. "Oh Jane, I really made a mess of things. I never should have taken that role. I didn't have enough experience. I wasn't ready for so much responsibility."

"Really? I thought you were doing well. What happened?"

"A man, that's what happened. A man I thought I liked who has turned out to be, well, an animal."

Jane's eyes widened and her mouth twisted into a half smile. "Whoa! This sounds interesting. What happened?" Jane was a great listener, taking in every detail as I poured out the whole sordid mess. I paused only to answer her probing questions as she clarified my feelings and motives at different points in the tale.

By the time I got to the events of last night, Jane was sitting forward on the edge of her seat.

"Oh Megan, that's awful," she said with one hand affectionately on my knee. The other hand was on her throat as she imagined me creeping out of the room, frightened of disturbing the sleeping monster. "How terrified you must have been!" A tear had formed in the corner of her eye.

"But Jane, the worst is he's been ringing and ringing this morning. I told Mum to leave the phone off the hook. I have to admit I'm really scared now. I don't know what he might do. And poor Mum, now I've got her mixed up in it too."

"Does she know what happened?"

"Not really. She knows I left Calvary because I did something wrong, but I never told her the details. I'm too ashamed. One day I'll tell her maybe, but not now."

"She'll probably find out, you know. Do you think she needs some sort of explanation as to why he's ringing all the time?"

My shoulders drooped and I sighed deeply, another burden now pressing on my already overburdened body. "Probably. You're probably right. Hey Jane, do you have any smokes?"

Jane was surprised at my question, but answered, "You know me, Megan." I did know Jane. She was one of the youth group members who enjoyed smoking, but had chosen to keep her habit a secret. She only smoked in private or with others she felt would not judge her. "You're not smoking too, are you? Not you?"

I sighed again and nodded my head. "I am, believe it or not. Only now and again, though. Not all the time. It seems to help relieve some of this terrible stress I've brought on myself."

"Megan! No! I never would have believed it. Not you. You were so on fire for God, so committed."

"Jane, I know. I still believe being a Christian is the best way, but somewhere along the way I've lost track of who I am and what I wanted to be. I'm really confused." The tears welled up, so I looked away. A few tumbled down my cheeks so I wiped them with the back of my hand, sniffing hard to make sure no more followed. I didn't want to start crying again. That wouldn't help anything. "I don't know what to do about this Ray situation. Jane, I'm desperate."

Jane leaned back on the couch and dragged on her cigarette, thinking. "I do have an idea …"

"What Jane? Any idea would be better than none." I sat forward looking at her, hopeful.

"Well … I've been thinking lately. I've actually been quite homesick. I miss my Mum. I've been thinking of going back home to live in Sydney. Why don't you think about coming with me? I'm sure you'd be able to get a job, no worries."

Her idea had taken me off guard. It was radical, but was also better than any other idea I'd had lately. "Wouldn't that be like running away though?"

"Would it? Or maybe it would be a fresh start. A lot has gone on here the last year, when you think about it. I think I'm ready for a change." I knew Jane meant all the dramas with Kevin and Andrea. It was certainly an idea that deserved some consideration.

"Well, if you're serious, Jane, I might give that some thought. There is nothing to hold me here now. Living somewhere new might be the best thing." We chatted on while we finished our smokes.

"I'd better go, Jane. I need some time to think about this some more. If we do this, when would you want to go?"

"Well, anytime really. I'd just have to make a few arrangements, but I'm between jobs myself at the moment and I haven't really settled back in here since coming back from Adelaide. I feel a bit out of place. So there's nothing stopping me from going in the next week or two."

"Wow. That *is* quick. Okay. Let's talk again in a couple of days."

I stood up to leave and Jane gave me a big hug. As usual,

talking to her had been excellent therapy. The weight I was carrying seemed lightened. We agreed to meet together again in two days' time.

Chapter Twenty-Nine

Reversing up our long driveway could be difficult, so I parked the car out the front on the footpath. The front door was closed.

Strange. I wonder if Mum's gone out.

Peering through the frosted glass, I could see some movement. I knocked, but Mum didn't move to open the door. I knocked again.

"Who is it?" She called.

"Mum, it's me. Open the door."

Mum partially opened the door, peering out nervously. "Are you alone?"

"Yes Mum, it's just me. Open the door. What's wrong?" Only then did Mum open the door all the way and let me in. Her behavior was unnerving.

"Come inside, Megan. I'm about to call the police."

"What! Why? What's happened?"

Mum was quick to close the door behind me. "That man has been ringing on and off all day, wanting to speak to you. I told him you weren't here but he didn't believe me. Megan, he's been threatening me. He says the most horrible things. That he's going to come around here and cut me with a knife. He says *horrible* things, frightening things."

"Oh Mum! Why didn't you keep the phone off the hook?"

"Because I needed to use the phone!" Mum was cross and she had a right to be. "You're going to tell me what on earth's going on. Where did you go just now? Did you go and see that man?"

"No! Mum I didn't go and see him. I went to see Jane. We were just talking."

Mum seemed a tad relieved.

"You have to tell me what's going on. That man's nasty. Evil. You need to sit down and tell me about him. Why is he ringing you? What's this all about?"

"Okay, okay, I will. Just let me get a drink of water."

Mum followed me into the kitchen and I noticed the phone was on the hook as I walked past. I was tempted to lift it off, but resisted. I started talking as I grabbed a glass and turned on the tap. "His name is Ray, Ray Klein. Kevin let him stay at Araluen. He came there while I was at Bible College last year. I used to chat with him in the mess hall and got to know him a bit. He was trying to give up drinking. I used to talk to him and tried to encourage him. He comes from such a different background. I found him interesting."

"Mmmm, yes …" Mum could see where this was going and I sensed her stiffen in disapproval, but she said nothing further and let me continue as we moved back into the lounge room.

"Anyway, Kevin gave Ray the option of going to Calvary or leaving. He chose to leave a couple of weeks ago. I was concerned about him, was wondering how he was coping. I wanted to encourage him so I went to visit him last week." I stopped talking briefly as we sat down on the lounge chairs. I wanted to be facing Mum before I continued. This was the time to be honest with her, but I felt so ashamed of my behavior and embarrassed at how stupid I'd been. I couldn't tell her *everything*.

"Anyway Mum I didn't realize that he could be violent. He was never like that up there. He worked around the grounds and helped out. He seemed nice enough."

"Humph!" was all Mum offered. "Why is he ringing you? Why does he want to see you today?"

"He knows I don't want to see him anymore. I think he wants more out of the relationship. I've realized that isn't a good idea."

"Well, you're absolutely right. It's *not* a good idea. In fact that would be a very stupid idea! This's got out of hand. What were you thinking being involved with a man like that?"

"Mum, I didn't know he was like that. He was never like that up there. I ... I think he must be drinking again."

The phone rang. We both jumped and looked at each other, both reluctant to answer it. Mum didn't budge, so I moved towards the phone, slowly, hoping it would stop ringing before I got there. It didn't.

"Hello?" No one responded. I stood listening with the receiver to my ear. Someone was breathing heavily into the phone. "Hello? Who is this? Is that you again Ray?"

"Megan ... so you *are* there? Don't you hang up on me! Don't you hang up ... or I'll come around there and blow your fucking brains out. That bitch was lying to me, I knew she was. She'll pay for that." The hostility in his tone took my breath away. He was on the other end of a telephone line, but the blast of his fury had my whole body trembling, as if he was standing right next to me. I didn't speak, frozen.

"No no, Meggie. I don't mean that. Please listen to me. I have to see you. I have to talk to you. I'm scared that I'm going to lose you. It's making me crazy." This dramatic change in his tone was just as frightening. He had switched from uncontrolled rage to despair, in a single heartbeat. It was pathetic.

He's crazy!

"Meggie, I'm going out of my mind. I need to see you. Tell me how to get to where you are and I'll come straight away."

"Ray, how can you even ask that after last night!"

"Meggie c'mon! You know I'd never hurt you. I just wanted to be with you. I couldn't resist you. I didn't want you to leave. You're everything to me. I've been out of my mind since I woke up this morning and you were gone."

"You frightened my Mum. I can't believe you'd even ring me after what you did. I don't want to see you again ... ever."

"I wouldn't hurt her. C'mon Meggie, you know I'd never hurt you ... or her. Never! I'm beside m'self with worry. I just said things 'cos I'm desperate. I gotta see you. It'll all be alright if I can just see you."

I didn't know what to do next. Ray was pleading with me. It was so confusing. Gone was the monster of last night, and the beast on the phone a few moments ago. Now I was listening to a man seemingly devoid of pride, desperate to find forgiveness and to make amends. If I hadn't felt so frightened, I might have even pitied him.

How do I make him leave us alone? Then, in an instant, the idea crystalized in my head. I knew exactly what I needed to do. "Ray, I'm leaving. I'm going away from here. I'm leaving tonight."

"No you're bloody not! Don't even think about doing such a thing!" The beast had returned, the angry violent man.

"Ray, you can't stop me. There's no point harassing me or my Mum any more. I'm not going to tell her where I'm going. And Ray —"

"I can't do it without you Meggie. I can't make it without you. Don't leave me," Ray was pleading again. A twinge of pity stalled me momentarily. Somehow it had managed to surface despite my burning anger and paralyzing fear.

"Ray, you really need some help. Don't call me anymore. I won't be here." I hung up the phone, still trembling. Then I lifted it off the hook and put it down beside the phone. Calm had settled over me. I had made a decision. There was no turning back, I knew what I was going to do and I had to do it ... now.

Mum was hovering, watching my every move. She looked both concerned and frightened.

I walked over to her and gave her a hug. "It'll be alright, Mum. I'm sorry I brought you into this. I'm really, really sorry." I pulled back and looked into her eyes as I held her shoulders. "He's mad, Mum. I know he's threatening and he sounds pretty scary, but I really don't think he'll do anything, not really." I hoped I sounded convincing.

I let go and moved towards my room. "But I'm going to get out of here. I'm leaving. Jane has offered to go to Sydney with me. We can leave tonight ... drive down in my car. I think it's the best thing to do. With me gone, he won't bother you anymore." I paused in the hallway and turned to face her again. "Mum, you can call the police if you want. It's up to you. But I think he'll leave you alone now that he knows I'm leaving. But I'd leave the phone off the hook for the time being anyway. Just put it on the hook when you need to use it. Okay?"

"Well Megan, as crazy as it all seems, I actually think it would be a good idea for you to get as far away from that man as possible. And Megan ..." I stopped to look at her again. "Stay away from people like that, for goodness sake. You have to have more sense ..."

I sighed, "I know Mum. I know. I've learned a lot from all this. I meant well, but I've done some pretty stupid stuff." I hugged her again then turned to get my things to put them in the car. It wasn't going to be hard to pack, as most of my stuff was still in the car. I'd barely been home and hadn't really unpacked yet.

Despite the horror of Ray's threatening phone call and the sickening feeling of knowing that Mum was now involved, the sense of excitement at setting off in a new direction brought a breath of fresh air. My head was clear. I could think. The thought of leaving all this behind and starting anew relieved some of the burden I had been carrying around on my shoulders for so long. I had some hope again. I had made a decision that I hoped would lead to happier times.

"A fresh start", Jane had called it. That's what I need … a fresh start.

It was dark when I pulled up outside Jane's house. I looked at my watch. It was nearly 10:30. I sat in the car and took a few deep breaths, wondering how Jane was going to react to my proposal to leave tonight, to leave now. Mum's concerned face as she had waved goodbye, haunted me.

I hope she doesn't hear anything more from that idiot. But I feared she might.

She had been living alone since Robert had married and moved to Ipswich earlier in the year. I was glad Michael had agreed to come down for the weekend, so she wouldn't be alone.

Sitting here now in the car with the silence of the evening ringing in my ears, it all seemed rather melodramatic.

Here I am running away in the middle of the night from a madman.

Then I remembered the sound of Ray's voice threatening to come around with a gun and shoot me. A shiver went up my spine.

I need to get out of this city now. I pulled open the car door.

◊ ◊ ◊

The flat was quiet and dark. I knocked. No one came. I knocked again, more firmly. Still no one came. I began to wonder whether Jane might be out. I was about to knock for a third time when the door pulled open. Jane, pulling her dressing gown around her, was surprised to see me.

"Megan, hi. What're you doing? Is everything alright?"

I couldn't speak. At that moment the fear and trauma of the last two days welled up and washed over me like a wave. Worried that if I opened my mouth to speak, I might break down and cry, I said nothing. Jane, seeing my distress, grabbed my arm and pulled me inside, closing the door behind us.

"Megan what's wrong? What's happened? Is it that man? Has he done something to you again? Tell me!"

We stood inside the door and I continued to stare at her trying to regain my composure so that I could speak.

"Calm down Megan. It's okay. You're safe here. Take a breath. Come inside." Jane led me over to the lounge chair. "Do you want a coffee or something?"

I nodded, wiping away some stray tears. I took a few deep breaths before sitting on the couch where I lay my head back in an effort to stop any further tears and to calm myself while Jane put the kettle on.

She came back and sat down beside me while she waited for the water to boil.

"You look as white as a ghost. What happened?"

"Oh Jane, it's awful. Ray's been ringing all day trying to talk to me. He's been threatening Mum. I ended up talking to him and he said he would come around with a gun and shoot me. He's a madman and I'm the stupidest girl in the world! But I'm really scared."

"Really? Megan, this is awful. How terrifying. This is bad."

"I know Jane. It's bad. But I've made up my mind what I'm going to do. I have to do something. I have to do something straight away." I looked at her. "I've made up my mind. I have to get away … as soon as possible … tonight."

"Tonight?" Jane was taken aback and sat back in the chair. "Really?"

"Yes, I have to get out of Brisbane. I have to get away from that man … as far away as possible … as *soon* as possible."

"Wow …"

"Jane, you said you wanted to go home … to Sydney. Well, I know it's all rather dramatic, but I wondered if you'd come with me … tonight. You don't have to. I'd understand if you didn't want to. But I have to leave now. I'm going whether you come with me or not."

"Tonight? Does it have to be tonight?"

"Yes Jane. I'm terrified of that man. I want to get away … as far away as possible. What you said this afternoon … a fresh start. That's what I need."

"Megan, let me think for a minute. This is a bit sudden, not what I imagined we might do." She got up and moved over to the kitchenette to make our coffees as the jug was bubbling. We didn't speak. I was grateful for the mug when she handed it to me. I took a sip, still in silence, the hot drink soothing.

I lay back into the couch again and asked, "What do you think? Is it possible?"

"Um, I'm thinking. Let me think. It wouldn't give me a chance to say goodbye to anyone. But I guess I could write to people. I'm only staying here temporarily, so Jess won't care. It's been a bit cramped anyway."

Jane chewed her lip as she sipped her coffee, thinking. "It'd be rude to leave without letting her know, though."

"Where is she?"

Jane looked at her watch. "She went to a youth meeting.

Actually she should be home by now. Perhaps they went out for supper after the meeting." Jane took another sip of her coffee.

Then she looked up at me, smiling. "You know what, Megan, I'll do it. I'll come with you. I'd like to see Jess before we go, though." She sat back in the chair and sighed, "You know Megan, this might sound a bit crazy, but I kind of feel like this is what God wants me to do."

"Really? To come with me?"

"Yeah, I know it sounds weird but Andrea needed me and I was able to just up and go and be with her during that terrible time. You need me now and I'm able to just up and go and be with you. I think that's what I'm meant to do at the moment. At this point in time, anyway. It's my purpose." Her eyes were warm and caring as she looked at me. "It's my job to help you now after all you've done for me. I don't think I would've stayed here if you hadn't been so kind to me."

I leaned forward and held her hand. "Oh Jane, I really appreciate it." It was uplifting to think that she would actually do this for me, turn her life upside down at the drop of a hat, in the middle of the night. *What a great friend.*

"Well, you listened to my woes enough times … helped me through stuff."

"What about Chris?"

Jane shrugged, resigned. "I've given up waiting. I don't think he's ever going to be interested in me. I think it's time for me to move on too."

"Probably for the best. We're not very good at hooking up with the right men are we?" I laughed, glad to find some humor amidst all the sickly drama.

Jane laughed with me. "Unfortunately you're right! Okay. I'll need to get dressed and get packing." She jumped up and got busy. I followed her around, offering to help.

Despite the late hour and our crazy circumstances, we were

both charged with a new energy, a new vigor. We were taking off in the middle of the night, leaving Brisbane to find refuge in Sydney. We were escaping the violent threats of a madman, driven by the urgency of my plight. Ray Klein was never going to touch me again and would never have another opportunity to hurt me.

We were about to embark on a new adventure and it was the first time I had felt excited for a very long time.

A fresh start.

Chapter Thirty

We had been driving for several hours but, amazingly, I hadn't found it hard to stay awake. I looked over at Jane; she was still asleep with her head stuffed in a pillow against the window.

Her long dark hair was tangled, but she looked peaceful.

I found night driving enjoyable and relaxing. Something about being able to see the headlights of the oncoming traffic way ahead was reassuring, especially when overtaking.

It was the perfect opportunity to think, driving along in the dark, with a sleeping passenger. Since embarking on this endeavor to drive to Sydney, my head had seemed clearer. I took a few deep breaths and checked the speedo. The needle was hovering around 60 mph, right on the speed limit.

As the road sped beneath us, my mind reflected over the last few years.

Becoming a Christian had helped me to set some boundaries in my life. When I considered the way I had been living before I became a Christian, I had to admit things had improved.

It had been surprising finding out how much fun you could have without alcohol. Being in the youth group had been like having an extended family with lots of brothers and sisters. There was always so much going on with activities every weekend, church on Sunday and other meetings during the week.

Being part of the youth group has been fun.

We were all working together to build something special, a church like no other before it. It was to be a place where God was free to move by his spirit; not some stuffy boring sort of church. The sense of shared purpose within the youth group had been empowering and motivated me to make sacrifices. We had all worked really hard, together. The mate-ship and camaraderie had been a joy and when I looked back, in many ways, it had been one of the happiest times of my life.

My thoughts were interrupted by a car's headlights shining in the rear vision mirror, blinding me momentarily. He stayed on my tail. I tried to stop looking in the mirror as the lights hurt my eyes. It was a relief when he pulled out to overtake me.

Checking the speedo again, I returned to my thoughts.

But that idyllic youth-group lifestyle had been shattered by the revelation of Kevin and Andrea's relationship, especially after they had blatantly lied to me. Now, looking back, I realized that Geoff had made a good point. *'It all starts at the top'.* When I thought about it, it seemed clear that my difficulties in holding true to a Christian lifestyle had been unraveling since Kevin and Andrea's exposure. It had been then that cracks had appeared in my own resolve to lead the Christian life. I seemed to have lost some of my willpower to conquer my own weaknesses, smoking being a classic example!

I'd been so angry when I'd found out about their deception.

What had happened to my anger? Is it still there, buried?

Somehow my anger seemed to have been ingested, swallowed up.

Was it because Kevin took me into his confidence?

Sharing his secret thoughts and personal pain had somehow drawn me into a powerful, though private, alliance. An alliance from which I had to admit I had benefited. I knew that I had Kevin's ear, anytime. I just had to call. He was an influential man with many resources at his fingertips. He had promoted me in the church hierarchy, which had gained me much recognition. Despite my feelings of insecurity and inadequacy in taking on Calvary, I had enjoyed the sense of achievement, of being given so much responsibility so young. Kevin's confidence in me had been an elixir, an addictive tonic that fed my ego.

But look where I ended up … crippled by my own failure.

I had watched Kevin continue on, building his church, establishing new projects across Australia and even venturing to establish things overseas recently. He was unstoppable and fanatically devoted to serving God. I had been swept up in his enthusiasm. It was as though I'd been taken along by a freight train.

But it had all crumbled around me. Kevin's confidence in me hadn't been enough to make me succeed. Yet, even now, I had to believe that following Christianity must be the answer to life. Somewhere amidst all this turmoil there had to be a way to make sense of life and our reason for being on this planet. It seemed the only plausible explanation – to believe God loved me and had a purpose for my life. It gave me hope, despite all I'd seen and experienced. Being a Christian gave me direction, a reason to live. It motivated and inspired me, challenged me.

Kevin and Andrea seemed to have both found forgiveness. It gave me confidence I could find forgiveness. My indiscretion seemed minuscule compared to theirs. Of course, that didn't make it right and I knew I shouldn't use them as my yardstick.

I sighed deeply again. There was one fundamental difference between what I had done and what they had done. My public confession, though conducted with such excruciating pain and humiliation, had given me one clear advantage. I was not a hypocrite. I had not gone on in my leadership role, pretending. Driving along now, away to new horizons, this simple distinction seemed crucial.

I reached across the dashboard feeling for the packet of Minties. Extra energy was needed to help wrestle these deep thoughts. The first slight glow of dawn was beginning to show on the horizon.

Life seemed like a huge set of stairs, I had climbed up several tiers since becoming a Christian, towards a higher aspiration. But in recent days it seemed I had slipped back. I needed courage to start climbing again.

One thing was clear, I had mistakenly put Kevin and Andrea, on a pedestal and admired them more than they deserved, even tried to fashion my life after them. It was a mistake that I would never make again.

They are only human, after all.

Watching the sunrise, looking out the window and scanning the horizon as we drove along, comforted my bruised and shattered heart.

A new day, a new dawn, a new life. At least I can walk away with a clear conscience. I'm not a hypocrite.

The sun rising, with its rays creeping over the mountains, seemed symbolic, a sanction that indicated I was on the right track. The weight I had been carrying around on my shoulders was lightening gradually. I took a deep breath, glad to be getting further and further away from Araluen, Calvary, NSC, Kevin Williams *and* Ray Klein.

This time the changes in my life must be robust, permanent …

forever.

◊ ◊ ◊

"How are you feeling?" I asked Jane, wanting to make sure she wasn't getting drowsy. She had taken over driving after breakfast. "I'm happy to drive whenever you want."

"No, I'm fine thanks. Really I am. I'm enjoying the drive. How far to the next town? I could do with a coffee."

I pulled out the map. "Taree is the next major regional town, but there are lots of petrol stations along the way. I'm sure we could get a cuppa there and maybe something to eat."

"Good idea. I'll stop at the next one we see."

"Okay. Hey Jane, I had a lot of time to think last night."

"Okay? Talk, but speak up. You have such a soft voice, Megan, I struggle to hear you sometimes, especially when I can't see your lips."

I swiveled on the bench seat so that I was partially facing her and tried to project my voice in her direction. "Sorry Jane. I forget about that."

"Of all my friends Megan, I think you have the quietest voice. I don't want to miss anything."

"Okay. It seems all so hard … being a Christian."

Jane, amused, threw back her head as she laughed. "I know what you mean! I don't think I do such a good job at all most of the time. Have to keep trying, though."

"I still think about Ray … crazy I know. There was just something about him … something enticing, exciting. I don't really understand it. That's nuts, isn't it?"

Jane twisted her mouth as she pondered her answer. "Hmmm. I don't know, Megan. I'm sure you're only feeling that now because you feel safe again. You wouldn't have said that last night."

"You're right." I sighed, remembering the extreme

oscillations in Ray's behavior only the day before. It seemed like a lifetime ago. It had been terrifying. "He's a bastard. What am I thinking?" Jane watched me as I talked; trying to make sure she caught everything I said. It unnerved me a little, as I felt she needed to keep her eyes on the road.

"You were attracted to him. I guess on some level you still have to get over that."

"I guess."

"It was pretty tough what they made you do … at Calvary. They never made Kevin do that … or Andrea."

Her words brought back the vision of me in the middle of the lounge room at Calvary. The ache in my chest was so sudden and acute that I gripped it with my hand.

"Are you alright?" Jane said, seeing my sudden movement.

"I think I just want to forget about that night." I looked at Jane. "In fact, I think I'd like to forget about Calvary altogether."

"Really, you don't think you would do something like that again?"

"I don't think full-time ministry is for me. It wasn't like I thought."

"How so?"

"Hmmm —" Her question made me realize I hadn't thought it through. "Well, I don't know. I guess the wounds are still fresh and I'm not in a place to make those sorts of decisions at the moment. But I do wonder — if you don't serve God in the ministry — what's the purpose of life?"

"Oh Megan, there are lots of ways to serve God. You don't have to be in full-time ministry."

"Really?"

"No. I think I'm serving him by helping you now. There are lots of ways, lots of things you can do. I think it's a way of life."

I sighed deeply and scanned the side of the road, searching

for a milestone to see how far it was to Taree. It all seemed very confusing.

"Well, I don't have to make that decision now, not today." I turned my head away, watching the road. Jane peered at me, straining to hear. Alarmed, I noticed we were drifting off the road and heading straight for a guide post.

"Look out!" I yelled, pointing to the post.

Jane jumped in fright and reefed the steering wheel to the right to avoid it. We narrowly missed it but she had over-corrected and we were now heading towards the opposite side of the road. Panicked, she pulled the steering wheel to the left again. We were out of control, fishtailing down the highway as she fought to regain control of the vehicle, steering left, and right and then left again.

The car complained and unable to keep up with her ever-changing commands, went into a slide. Fortunately there was no oncoming traffic, but there was nothing to stop the terrifying slide until the two right wheels slipped over an embankment. The speed and momentum of the car and the sudden drop to the right caused the chassis to tip over onto its side and then it rolled all the way over onto the roof and came to a stop. We were upside down in a ditch, the Minties on the dash scattered around us.

"Fuck! Fuck! We have to get out of here!" I yelled, imagining the car would burst into flames at any second. "She'll blow up!"

As I had not been wearing my seatbelt, I was now sitting on the roof of the car. Thankfully my window was open, so I was able to squeeze through it and get out of the car. Lying on the grass outside my window, I turned to see if Jane was free. She had managed to undo her seatbelt and was struggling to climb out her window, which wasn't fully open. One leg was jammed under the steering wheel as she fought to pull it free.

"Jane get out. Get out!" I yelled and jumped up and ran

around the car to help her. By the time I got to her door she, too, was laying on the grass nursing her shin.

"C'mon!" I yelled and helped her to her feet. We ran away from the car and up the embankment to a safe distance before turning to look back expecting to see a fire roaring. We stood and watched, waiting for the inevitable explosion. Nothing happened. The car lay there still, silent except for one of the wheels spinning.

"Oh my God. Oh my Lord!" I yelled, my hand on my throat. "Are you alright?" I turned to Jane, looking her over from head to toe for any sign of blood. There was none.

"I'm alright. I'm alright," she said. "Just my knee and shin are sore. I think I bruised them trying to get out." We looked at each other and checked ourselves. Neither of us had a scratch. Jane sat down on the grass. I turned again to look at my car, upside down in a ditch.

"Oh Megan, I'm so sorry. Look at your car." She was on the verge of tears. We sat together surveying the scene, trying to come to terms with what had just happened. We were both in shock.

I sat on that hill and looked at my car and then I looked at Jane. Then I looked at my car again and something strange happened. I felt it in my belly first, but it worked its way up to my chest and I could contain it no longer - I burst out laughing.

How ridiculous. After all I've been through; running away from Ray Klein in the middle of the night and here I am sitting beside the Pacific Highway with my car upside down in a ditch! It was unbelievable.

For some strange reason it suddenly seemed the most hilarious predicament I could ever imagine. My body was trembling again, not in fear or shock this time, but with laughter. I tried to hold it back, but I couldn't. My whole body was shaking. I laughed until tears streamed down my face.

Jane looked at me as though I was mad. I tried to straighten my face and look serious, but that only made it worse. I couldn't hold the laughter in. I was like a school girl with the giggles, the laughter wanted to come out all of its own accord. Jane watched me with disbelief, her mouth wide open.

But laughter is infectious and I could see a smile playing on her mouth as she watched me, incredulous. And then Jane was laughing too. We kept looking at the upside down car and each other and shaking our heads. It took a few minutes for the hysteria to finally pass when we were able to calm down enough to talk again.

"What do we do now?" I said looking at Jane, fighting to keep a straight face.

"Well, it hasn't burst into flames. Do you think it still will?"

We both looked at the car, then stood up. The engine had cut out in the crash. There was no fuel leaking out of the tank. It looked harmless enough.

"Stupid movies. Just goes to show, they make all that stuff up!" I said.

"We need to get our handbags out at least, don't you think?" Jane said.

"Yes we do."

"And a cigarette wouldn't go astray."

"Good point."

Neither of us moved, still afraid it might burst into flames. Nothing happened. After a few moments of staring at the car, I slid and stumbled down the bank and looked in the window. Our things had been flung around the cabin and were all sitting on the roof inside the car amongst the scattered Minties. Crawling back through the window cautiously, I grabbed what I could, including a few Minties.

"Do you think we should get our bags out of the back as well?" I yelled at Jane as she sat on the grass beside the car.

"I guess so. I don't know. What do you think? Can you?"

"I don't know," I said, peering into the back. It looked more difficult. Still worried about a fire, I retreated. Jane and I sat as we sorted through our handbags, checking we had the crucial things – wallets, money, etc.

"What're we going to do now?" I asked.

"I don't know. Do you think it's wrecked?"

"Looks like it to me. Oh my car, my poor car." The reality that I may well have just lost my most prized possession hit me. It didn't seem so funny anymore. The laughter spent, I now felt a sense of loss and foreboding.

"I'm so sorry Megan." Jane's composure was crumbling as she put her hand on my arm. Her mouth quivered as she worked to hold back her tears.

"It's done Jane. Don't worry about it. We just need to decide what to do now." I scratched my head and thought. "We'll have to hitch a lift back to that last little town. What was it called? Kew, I think. It wasn't far back. C'mon, let's try and hitch a ride."

As we walked over to the highway I hooked my arm in hers. "It really is funny, though, when you think about it, isn't it?" The occasional giggle still threatened to escape from time to time when I looked at the car and considered our overall predicament. "It looks rather undignified, upside down like that. It's just the most ridiculous thing to happen to us. I'm glad we aren't hurt."

Jane pulled in close to me and said, "I'm glad you're taking it so well. It would have been better to have hit that guide post, you know. You gave me such a fright when you yelled out."

"You're probably right. But it's done now. Let's see if we can get some help."

Chapter Thirty-One

"Thank you so much," I said through the car window. "We really appreciate your help."

"No worries. Good luck with it. I'm sure the towie will be able to get your car out. See ya." Grateful for the lift, we waved to the man and his wife as they pulled away. We turned to find someone to talk to at the garage. A yellow tow truck was parked on one side and a large NRMA service sign was encouraging.

I pointed to it. "That looks hopeful."

"I hope so," Jane replied, chewing her lip. I knew she still felt responsible for getting us into this predicament.

The reception was deserted, so we rang the bell while we looked around for someone who might be in charge. Soon a man in greasy overalls appeared at the door from the workshop, wiping his hands on a rag.

"Good morning ladies, or is it afternoon?" he said, smiling, glancing at the clock on the back wall. "What can I do for you?"

"Um ... my car crashed ... down the road ... um ... about 20 minutes. It's upside down in a ditch. Can you help us at all? I don't really know what to do."

"Really? Upside down in a ditch? Anyone hurt? What happened?" He looked genuinely concerned.

"We're fine. We just swerved to miss a guide post and things got a bit out of control." I could feel Jane shifting on her feet as I talked.

"Well, I'm glad you're alright. Where're you headin'?"

"We're on our way to Sydney … or we were. Not sure what we're going to do now … without a car."

"Oh I see. Well let's get her out of that ditch and into the workshop and we can have a look at her." He reached for a clipboard and pulled on the pen tucked behind his ear. "Just need to get a few details."

We helped him fill in a form.

"I'll get Joe onto it now. Probably only room for one of you in the cab with him."

I looked at Jane and she shrugged.

I turned to the man. "What will happen?"

"Um, Joe'll bring it in here and unload it and we'll take a look, see what damage has been done. We'll chat then. Should be able to give you an idea whether we can fix it or not." He squinted at me as he talked. "You could be holed up here for a few days ya know … depending, if we can fix it that is."

I sighed and shrugged. "Well, I guess we just have to find out what the damage is. I think it's pretty wrecked though. Is there somewhere my friend can wait?"

"Sure. There's the Western Inn across the road. Got a restaurant and bar. Not a bad little joint."

We looked in the direction he pointed. Jane agreed to wait at the motel.

◊ ◊ ◊

Jane was reading a book when I found her in the lounge room attached to the bar. She marked her page and closed the book as she saw me approaching.

"Hi," I said.

"Hi, how'd it go? Did they get it out?"

"Yep, they're unloading it in the workshop now. I'll go over in a couple of hours and see how it's going."

"Okay."

"This looks pretty nice," I said, looking around. "Maybe we should check in here for the night. I don't know what's going to happen, but I think we're going to be here at least tonight. Might have to try and book on a bus or something tomorrow if it's bad news about the car. Sure looks pretty banged up. The roof is smooshed."

"Really? Oh Megan." Jane's face was stricken. "Yeah, we should check in here. It looks nice enough," she said.

We walked around looking for a reception area and eventually asked the barman for directions.

◊ ◊ ◊

It was a relief to unlock the door to our room once we had checked in. It had been a long few days and, like a wave washing over me, fatigue seemed to catch me when we opened the door. We threw ourselves on the beds, exhausted.

Looking up at the ceiling, I said, "Thank God for Bankcard! What would we have done without it?"

"I know! You're right. It would have been a bit of a disaster."

"We can go over and get our bags out of the car later," I said, not wanting to move. Thinking about the car upside down in the ditch got me giggling again.

"Megan stop it! It isn't funny."

"I know ... but it is. My crazy life. Hey, Jane?"

"Yeah?"

"I'm glad you're with me."

"I don't know how you can say that ... but, thanks."

Neither of us spoke further. I don't know how long we slept.

◊ ◊ ◊

Jane was reading her book again in the lounge bar when I got back from the garage.

"Hi Jane. It's great news. 'Engine mountings' they said. There's no damage to the motor but the momentum of the roll made the engine slip off its mountings. They'll fix it in the morning and we can be on our way again! I can't believe it. It doesn't look the same though. There's quite a bit of damage to the body of the car. Everything works. You can open all the doors though they make a funny noise and are harder to shut … but they work. It's mainly the roof that's dinted."

"But that doesn't matter, does it? That's just cosmetic. Can he really get it going so we can drive it again, already? We can be back on the road tomorrow?"

"Yep. Can't believe it myself. It could've been so much worse."

Jane nodded slowly, pensively, in reply.

"And I wouldn't have been able to do it without this," I said, grinning, waving my Bankcard.

I slipped in next to her at the table and we chatted about what we would do when we got to Sydney.

We were so engrossed in our conversation, we hadn't noticed how full the bar had become around us. I think we only noticed because the noise level had risen and Jane was suddenly struggling to hear me. It was becoming impossible for us to continue talking.

"Hi girls. How ya goin'?" A rugged young man stopped by

our table. We were both so unprepared for such an approach that we sat there dumbfounded and looked at each other. He didn't wait for a reply. "Where're ya from?"

"Um, Brisbane, we're from Brisbane … on our way to Sydney." I finally managed to get something out.

"Well well, city girls. You picked a good night. Band's about to start up." He waved his beer, indicating the other side of the room. To my delight, a band was setting up on a small stage. I sat back in my chair and looked around, suddenly aware of the atmosphere. The bar was filling up before my eyes with young people. The barman and barmaid were now run off their feet trying to serve everyone.

As more people pushed their way in through the door, I could see our table and chairs were becoming an envied possession. We had a pretty good view of the band from where we were sitting.

I looked at Jane. "Something's going on here. I thought this was a quiet country town. Look at all these people!"

"I know," she said frowning.

The young man had moved on. Perhaps we had appeared rude, but it hadn't been our intention. We weren't prepared to be sitting in the middle of a lively country pub. Suddenly, I wanted a drink, an alcoholic drink.

"You wanna drink?" I asked Jane.

"Drink? You mean a *real* drink?" Jane said curling her mouth in a cheeky half smile.

"Yes! I mean a *real* drink. What do ya say?"

"Um, I guess so. I can see you want to. Um … okay, I'll have a Brandy and Dry."

"Excellent, coming right up," I said, rising to move to the bar.

Jane put her hand on my arm and stopped me. "But Megan, I don't like it here. I can't hear with all this noise. It's too hard for me." I sat back down a little disappointed. "No, no. You go and get the drinks, but I want you to know I'll only have one. Anyway, get a drink. I can see you want to."

"Okay." I moved over to the bar. Jane was right. I wanted a drink and I wanted to enjoy this atmosphere. As I moved to the bar to jostle for some service, I scanned the room wondering where all these people had come from.

"Hi," I said to the guy standing next to me who was waiting patiently for some service.

"Hi!" he said, grinning back.

"I'm new here, just passing through. Where do you come from? Around here?"

"Yep, working on a property about 50 miles that away," he said indicating with the tilt of his head. "Come into town for a bit of fun."

"But it's Wednesday. Is this normal?"

"'Pends on when they can get the band here. These guys are passing through, so it works tonight. We don't want to miss out."

"Oh!" was all I could think to say before our conversation was interrupted by the barman taking orders.

I looked around the room again, waiting for my turn. A sea of animated faces engaged in lively conversation buzzed around me.

Yes, youth group was fun, but coming to a place like this looked like it could be fun too.

The youth group had been a great experience, but perhaps it was time for a change. Standing in this room, feeling the excitement, being with other young people, seemed such a contrast to my life at Araluen and Calvary. It was like looking into another world; one that had been here all along, but I hadn't been part of it.

I've been missing out.

I took a deep breath, wanting to imbibe the atmosphere, to inhale it — the sound, the laughter, the music.

We would be back on the road tomorrow, on our way to Sydney. Living in Sydney would bring new opportunities with new horizons. I could feel my mind opening to new possibilities. Perhaps it was time to change some of the boundaries I had set in my life as a Christian.

For the first time in weeks, I felt a warm glow and a sense of excitement. I felt hope for my life and for the future, like a new dawn on the horizon.

I took our drinks back to our table. Jane seemed withdrawn but accepted her drink with a smile. It was too difficult to talk, so we enjoyed sipping our drinks as we watched the interactions going on around us. I couldn't wipe the smile off my face.

I knew both of us were looking forward to getting back on the road the next day. What new experiences awaited us in Sydney? Even crashing the car seemed part of a new adventure, propelling me on to a new life. I relaxed, yielding to a sense of hope at last.

Chapter Thirty-Two

I realized I was the first one home when I opened the door. The house was quiet. Joan and Charlie would be along soon. I reached into my bag to find my address book, my hands trembling. Checking the time, I estimated I had about thirty minutes before one or other of them would pull into the driveway.

Opening the book at "K", I picked up the telephone receiver in the lounge room. But I put it down again immediately and moved over to the blinds to open them. I needed to be sure I could see if anyone pulled up outside.

Moving back to the phone, I picked up the receiver, feeling nerves tumbling in my stomach. I dialed the number of Ray's boarding house. My heart quickened when it started ringing. *Why am I doing this?*

Eventually someone picked up the phone at the other end. "Hello?" It was the voice of an elderly women.

"Hello. I was wanting to speak to Ray Klein, please."

"Ray who?"

"Ray Klein. He lives in room number eleven." Who knows

if he would even be there. He would likely be at the pub, but that didn't stop the flutter of anticipation that came with the slightest chance that I might be able to talk to him again.

"Hello?" It was Ray.

"Hi, Ray. It's me."

"Meggie? Meggie, it's you?"

"Yes."

"Oh darlin' —"

"How are you?

"Good, good. Ya'self?"

"I'm okay. I got a job working for an IT company. I love it."

"Oh honey, that's great news."

"Yeah. I've landed on my feet for once. Say, did you get a job? Are you going away to that camp?"

"Huh? Nah, nah. That all fell through. I'm tryin' to get a job drivin' a truck but haven't landed anything yet. Somethin'll turn up. Where are you?"

"I'm in Sydney. I've told you before."

"C'mon baby. I want to see you. Why can't I see you?"

"Ray —"

"Nah, it's alright. It's good to hear your voice, Meggie." He was silent.

I waited, soaking up his adulation. *Is this why I had to ring him?* It was crazy ... pointless. Yet here I was again, drawn to him.

He breathed heavily into the phone. "Meggie, it's too hard without you. I need you." He words seemed thick with pain. "Come back to me ... please."

Why did I want to hear that? Why was I torturing him and myself? He was the forbidden, and yet here I was talking to him. For what? I could not go back to him. He was mad, violent. Yet he still had some power to draw me. Was I addicted to his need for me? No matter which way I looked at, it was crazy.

But it somehow seemed safe to talk to him. He was in Brisbane; I was in Sydney. He didn't have my phone number. But even knowing there was no future for us, I had to have my little dose of him periodically, when an opportunity presented.

It was ridiculous.

"Meggie, come back to me."

"I can't Ray."

"Then why are you calling me?" His tone was changing, a touch of aggression hinted.

"I don't know really —"

A car had pulled into the driveway. Charlie was home. I had to get off the phone ... and fast.

"Ray, I have to go. I can't talk anymore. I like to hear your voice." I chewed my bottom lip. "I miss you too ... but I have to go. I have go NOW. Bye. I'll call again when I can."

"Meggie —"

I put down the phone before Charlie had his key in the front door.

"Hi," he said as he came in and put his keys on the sideboard.

"Hi," I replied, knowing my cheeks were likely flushed. "Did you have a good day?"

"The usual. Joan should be here shortly." He moved over to the aquarium to feed the fish.

"You going down to the pub?"

He looked at me with eyebrows raised as if to say "Of course". He turned back to the fish. "Don's coming over on the weekend."

"Is he?" I was surprised. "That'll be nice." I hadn't seen Don since I started living at his parent's house. Joan had been unhesitating when I'd called her with my sad tale. She agreed to take me in until I could find somewhere to live. But once I'd found a job, they'd agreed I could stay on. I think they liked me being here. Who knows, perhaps they secretly hoped I might get back together with Don. I wondered about that myself sometimes. It had been a long time since we had seen each other.

Now it seemed I might find out … this weekend.

◊ ◊ ◊

I was a little nervous waiting for Don to arrive. I tried not to show it as I helped Joan prepare the salads to go with the barbecue steak, and or course the essential … deep fried potato chips.

Joan chatted as she worked, mainly talking to herself, checking and re-checking, making sure that she had thought of everything. She was leaning over the sink when she suddenly stopped mumbling and turned to look at me.

I stopped chopping the lettuce and looked back, smiling.

"You okay?" she said.

"Sure."

"You know, we don't expect anything."

I frowned a little.

"We don't expect anything … I mean … like you and Don getting back together."

"Ooooh." My eyes softened as I broadened my smile. "I did wonder about that."

"You know I always felt you made the right decision, leaving him."

"I know." I said, feeling uncomfortable, wanting to turn back to the lettuce.

"As you know, I love Don dearly but even I, his own mother, can see he isn't good husband material."

I nodded but cast my eyes downward.

"I just wanted to make sure you knew how I felt. Nothing's changed. I'm sad you got mixed up in that awful crowd with that awful Kevin Williams. From thing's you've said it sounds suspiciously like it was some sort of a cult."

"Ah, I don't know about that. It wasn't all bad."

Joan shook her head looking back into the sink. "They certainly seemed very extreme … all those rules. That's what I like about the Army. They're straight shooters. They mainly want to help people." She turned back to me. "I feel safe there."

I smiled reassuringly. "Well, that's great Joan. I'm sure you will be happy being part of the Salvation Army. But I don't think it's for me."

She nodded slowly, accepting my words thoughtfully. "I'm sure you'll find your way —"

Colin, Don's brother, walked into the kitchen interrupting. "Hello, hello. Smells good in here."

I returned to my lettuce chopping as Joan chatted with her eldest son, glad the awkward conversation had come to an end. But it was a relief to know that she wasn't trying to get Don and me back together. However, that didn't ease my nerves. Seeing Don again after all this time was going to be a bit strange. I was excited about it, but apprehensive too. We had shared many experiences together, some good, some bad. He had been my first boyfriend and though I'd come to see that he probably wasn't the best husband choice, I did have fond memories.

Mum had always been horrified at my choice to be with Don. It made me smile to think of it now. Though Mum had never said anything to me about it, I knew she had been relieved when we broke up those few years ago. But I had always felt Mum just didn't know him. Strange that even Don's own mother felt the same way. Joan had been devastated when Don had got involved in drugs and even though she believed (or hoped) Don was out of that scene now, she remained deeply concerned about his daily heavy drinking and general lack of ambition.

I looked over at Joan briefly as she checked the chips in the deep fryer again, my respect deepening. It was impossible not to trust her. Her frank honesty, even about her own son, was compelling. There seemed so much to learn from her.

As I tossed the lettuce into the salad bowl, I felt comforted. Our friendship had gone way beyond anything to do with her son.

Yes, Joan's home was the perfect haven while I licked my wounds and tried to make sense of my confusing life.

Chapter Thirty-Three

2 Years Later, February 1981

"Are you sure you want to do this … go back?" said Jane, dragging on her cigarette as she talked.

"Yes!" I said. "I'm about to get on a flight, Jane. I'm not going to change my mind now. It's all so clear to me. I can't play around anymore. I want to go home and put things right — once and for all." I patted my tummy demonstratively, saying, "I've got someone else to think about now."

"I guess so. I know you want to be closer to your Mum, but Megan, I'm going to miss you," she said, eyeing me over her coffee as she took a sip.

Her words hit home. I was going to miss her too. I could feel my eyes stinging with tears, but I held them back. "I'll miss you too, Jane."

We both sat back in our chairs and neither of us spoke for a time. Parting from this faithful friend was painful. We were both feeling it. I couldn't help recalling when Jane had agreed to flee Brisbane in the middle of the night. Not many friends would have been so amenable to making such a radical decision on the spur of the moment.

I cupped my hand over my mouth, grinning, "Remember my car upside down in that ditch!" I could feel that old familiar giggle rising.

Jane responded with her cheeky half smile as she drew again on her cigarette, "Oh Megan, I still can't believe you found ... still find ... it so funny. So you managed to sell your car?"

"Yeah, it wasn't worth repairing. The guy who bought it wanted it for parts. The engine was still fine ... just a few dints on the roof."

"And your job?"

"Yeah, YNC have organized a job for me in their Brisbane office. They've been really good to me."

"Obviously you impressed them, Megan, or they wouldn't have taken the trouble to look after you like that."

I sighed deeply. "Yes, they have been good, very good, to me. They even got me studying again. You know I started that Marketing Certificate? Well, I actually topped the class in one of my subjects – Managing the Sales Force. The lecturer rang me up to congratulate me! I was blown away."

"Megan, that's wonderful. I'm impressed."

"Joan's been wonderful too. I don't think I'd be where I am now without her."

"She's a good woman. She's been like another mum to you."

"She has. She's done so well in her own career too. She's an inspiration in more ways than one."

"God was good to organize that one for you, that's for sure."

"Yeah, Joan and Charlie have been good to me."

"You saw Don again?"

I nodded.

"And?"

"It wasn't the same. I've moved on. He's got another lady in his life now."

"Amazing that you built such a friendship with his parents."

"I know. It's a bit weird. But it worked. They're like my second family."

Jane nodded, drawing on her cigarette again. "Now Megan, I probably don't need to say this but … you won't be trying to contact that awful man, Ray, again now will you?"

"God no! That bastard. I'd be mad to go anywhere near him. Besides, he's probably in jail by now. He's a mistake *never* to be repeated! I wouldn't even go near anyone like that again."

"Not even call him on the phone?"

My eyebrows pulled together as I wondered, perplexed, why Jane might have brought this up. "Jane, I got over that idiot not long after I got here. He hasn't even crossed my mind … for ages."

"Good. As I thought, but I'm still relieved to hear it."

I sighed. "In some ways its a shame to walk away from my life here, but I have other priorities … things I have to do now."

"Have you told your Mum?"

I nodded as I remembered that painful phone call. "Poor Mum, she must despair of me at times. She's disappointed, but of course she's willing to help me. I told her I was coming home to get sorted, but I don't think she believed me. Can't blame her for that. She's always there for me."

"But Megan, you must do something when you get back … something for me. It's really important," Jane said, leaning forward, commanding my attention.

"Oh, what?"

"You must go to a doctor and get another test … a urine or blood test. I can't believe that doctor didn't do any formal tests."

"She examined me physically," I said, surprised. "She said I was twelve weeks on."

"I know, but I talked to my Mum about it and she said it's weird the doctor didn't get a sample of urine to test. That's what they normally do ... always do. Mum said it was most unusual."

"Mmmmm." I twiddled my watch as I contemplated her words. "Maybe you're right. I should, just to make sure I guess — to be one hundred percent."

"Yes, you should. How have you been feeling?"

"Pretty good, actually. I don't feel sick at all if that's what you mean."

"Any other symptoms?"

"Ha, never thought about them as 'symptoms'. My breasts have been a bit sore. Oh Jane, the whole thing has been so confronting ... a big wake up call. It's brought me back down to earth and made me realize the things I do have consequences — big consequences sometimes. I feel like now is make-or-break time for me."

Jane nodded as I talked. "It's hard to imagine but I think I understand," she said.

Her response made me consider the choices she had made in her life so far. "Well, it's not a problem that's likely to happen to you is it?"

"You know me Megan, I'm waiting for the ring on the finger." Jane laughed as she wriggled her ring finger at me.

"You're a wise girl. I wish I could have been so good. But I can't change things now. It's too late," I said, resting my hand again subconsciously on my tummy.

"You could've changed things."

"Mmm, yes. I guess I had that choice. The doctor seemed adamant. She was actually a bit cranky when I went back to see her and told her I didn't want to go through with an abortion."

"Really? That's strange."

"Yeah, I know. It was a bit odd. I don't know why she would care so much." I shrugged as I remembered the ill-tempered woman. "I'll find a new doctor in Brisbane, I guess."

"And church? Will you go back to NSC?"

"Absolutely, of course, I want to put my life right. It's time to get serious and stop playing around. Enough of the fun. Time to get on with real living, serious living. I can't imagine going to any other church."

Jane sighed. "And I suppose you don't want one of these," she said, offering me a cigarette, while pulling another one out to light up.

"No way. That's definitely behind me now. I've given up for good, stopped cold turkey. Been two weeks now."

"Good on you," she said, looking genuinely impressed. "You don't look as though you've put on any weight either. Most people do when they stop smoking."

"Well, I'm trying jolly hard to make sure I don't. I worked so hard to get all that weight off after living at Araluen. I'm not going to throw that all away!"

"I suppose I'll give it up one day," she said waving her cigarette. "But I know it helps me keep my weight off and you know what a battle that's been."

"You look great Jane — a different person. Are you still going to Weight Watchers?"

Jane nodded, her lips grim. "I'm too scared to stop. I feel in control of my life at last. You know I'm a life member of Weight Watchers now."

"Really?"

"Yep, because I lost so much —"

She was interrupted by the paging system as they announced the boarding call for my flight. I looked at Jane.

"This is it."

We both stood up and I grabbed my cabin bag and slung it over my shoulder. Jane moved to hug me, but the bag got in the way. It was awkward.

"Well darling, I don't know when I'll see you again. I guess I might come to Brisbane to visit … one day," she said.

"You'll write?"

"Of course. Let me know what happens when you get the test results."

"Okay, I'll ring you. You really think I should check, don't you?"

"I do Megan. I do."

"I guess it is wise to erase all doubts."

Jane stood as I moved towards the boarding gate. I turned to wave. Leaving like this, jumping on a plane, seemed so final. I didn't know when I would see her again. I wouldn't be able to jump in my car and drive over to visit her anytime I liked anymore. On impulse, I dropped my bag and ran back. This time I managed to give her a proper hug.

"Oh Jane, you've been such a great friend. I'm going to miss you. Thanks for always being there for me."

She didn't say anything, but hugged me back. We stood like that for what seemed a long time. All I could think about was how she had never judged me and had always been there to listen to my ups and downs. When I pulled away, I could see the tears in her eyes. Jane said, "You'll be fine. You'll be fine — but make sure you write to me."

"I will. I'm sure we'll see each other again. I just hope it isn't too long." I turned to go and picked up my bag again. "Bye!" I yelled over my shoulder as I walked away. A few stray tears rolled down my cheeks.

I looked back one last time and Jane was still standing, waving, yelling, "Bye … bye."

I couldn't look back again. It was too painful so I picked up pace and headed to the boarding gate. Most of the passengers had already passed through. I had to run to catch up to them on the tarmac.

Another chapter closes in the life of Megan White, I thought as I climbed the stairs to board the plane.

◊ ◊ ◊

I grappled with mixed emotions as I sat on the plane waiting for takeoff; my first ever jet plane flight. The engines roared beside me and I could feel the vibrations, gentle but exhilarating, as I sat with my head leaning against the fuselage. I stared out the window, trying to hide the occasional tear from the passenger sitting next to me. I didn't even want to look at them in case they tried to strike up a conversation. I didn't want to talk to anyone. Too much was swimming around in my head.

I put my hand on my tummy, wondering about the unborn child; my child. It was so final, hearing that you are pregnant. There is no negotiating, no pondering or weighing up a decision. It was an ultimatum. Of course, abortion had been a possibility, but I had discarded that option almost immediately.

It was as though I had struck a huge roadblock, like a brick wall towering in front of me. There was nowhere to run, nowhere to hide. I had to stare the consequences of my actions in the face and deal with them.

Finding out that I was pregnant had also made me confront my relationship with Daniel Gibson.

Did I really like Daniel? Why had I been dating him?

I realized now, looking back, that hooking up with him had been more of a convenience, something that had been easy. Hanging around with young professionals at YNC had been fun. I smiled as I remembered Libby, the librarian, and the mischief we had got up to in and out of the office. Hooking up with Daniel happened without me thinking about it. But it had become clear when I found out I was pregnant, that he wasn't someone I had any intention of being with in the long term.

Great 'Christian' I turned out to be!

Shame shot through my heart like a red-hot nail. I took a few deep breaths, trying to draw on an inner strength. I was determined to look forwards, not backwards.

What do I have to change in my life to make sure I can take care of this baby?

Being pregnant had given me a quiet resolve, a determination to return to the Christian way of life and to strive again for the ideal that had proven elusive so far. There was no more time for playing around, no more casual impulsive relationships. This was a definitive moment in my life and I was determined it would motivate me in the right direction. I had to get control of my sexual desires!

As the plane began to taxi across the tarmac to the runway, I had the distinct sense that I was moving to the next platform in my Christian walk, despite my track record so far.

Yes, I have made some mistakes while living in Sydney, but I've made some good ground too. It's time to take things to the next level. I wish I hadn't been so stupid — not going on the pill! I had taken such a risk.

I banged my head on the fuselage as I remembered the constant internal battle of the last few months - whether or not to go on the pill. I wanted to go on the pill as adequate protection against pregnancy, but I didn't want to go on the pill since I felt it gave me permission to act in an inappropriate way, to give in to my sexual impulses. It was typical of the constant internal push and pull, trying to figure out how to live my life through the Christian ideal.

So stupid! Such a risk to take!

There was no point looking back now and beating myself up because it was impossible to undo the decision. I had to look forward. There was no avoiding my weakness. There was no getting away from the reality of my constant mismanagement of personal relationships.

I have to change.

I lay my head back in the seat as I felt the plane acceleration begin for takeoff. Looking out the window, the land beneath was racing past. Then I felt the gravity force as my body was pressed into the seat. We were airborne. I stared at the shrinking houses and trees, diminishing as the plane gained altitude.

Another tear rolled down my cheek as I remembered Jane standing at the airport waving goodbye. How striking she looked now, tall and slim with her beautiful long black hair. It was such a contrast to the plump, shy and insecure girl I had been introduced to at youth camp so long ago. I might never have got to know her if Andrea hadn't asked me to take her under my wing.

As the plane pulled away from Sydney, I was being pulled away from my friend and the new life I had managed to carve out for myself after all the drama of two years earlier.

I sighed deeply.

At least I have a job waiting for me in Brisbane.

It was a cheering thought. YNC had given me a warm farewell. They had been genuinely sorry to see me leave and that made me feel proud. My boss had organized a new role for me in the Brisbane office, created it specifically for me - Technical Sales Support. Being the National Manager of a software company, he was able to do things like that. It was an opportunity even if I didn't know how long I would be able to work.

Some good, some bad ... but it doesn't matter. I have to put things right. There is no point looking back.

I settled back in the seat determined to enjoy the flight despite the challenges ahead.

It was time to move forward no matter what.

Chapter Thirty-Four

"Hi, my name's Megan White. I'm calling to get the results of a blood test."

"Sure, do you mind holding while I check to see if it has come back yet? What was your name again?"

"Megan, Megan White."

I sat down on one of the dining room chairs as I waited. Mum was due home shortly, so I was glad to have a little time to myself to sort this out. I had promised Jane I would get undeniable proof of my pregnancy. This was the last step.

The doctor I'd seen hadn't hesitated in taking a blood test when I told her I hadn't had a period for over 12 weeks. She had not even considered examining me. She had simply asked a few questions and asked for my arm. Watching her gently pry the needle into my vein had reminded me of my early days in Sydney taking drugs. I had to push those thoughts out of my head. Those days were behind me now.

The receptionist came back to the phone and said, "Yes, Mrs White, the result of your blood test has come back."

"Okay, what does it say?"

"Um, sorry Mrs White, only the doctor can give you the results of the test. I'll see if I can put you through."

"Okay thanks." I tried not to sound frustrated but it was an effort. I felt sure the woman must be able to look at the test herself.

Why couldn't she simply say 'positive' or 'negative'. It seemed straight forward enough and I wanted to know *now*.

"Are you there, Mrs White?"

"Yes. I'm here," I said, biting my tongue to resist correcting the 'Mrs'.

"I'm afraid the doctor is with a patient at the moment. Would you like to hold?"

"Actually, I don't want to hold. I want to know the results. Can't you tell me? Can't you just tell me the result?"

"I'm sorry. Mrs White. Only the —"

"Sorry, what was your name?"

"Me? I'm Sally."

"Hi Sally. Listen, it's a pregnancy test. I want to know if it's positive or not. Can't you tell by looking at it? I really need to know … *now*."

"Oh I see," Sally said, still sounding uncertain.

"C'mon, please. I already know that I'm pregnant and have just taken the test to make one hundred percent sure."

"Just a minute." I could hear Sally shuffling some papers on her desk and the muffled sound of her talking. "Are you there?"

"Yes."

"I'm not supposed to do this, but since you're so insistent, I will tell you. The test was negative."

It was as though a jolt of lightning hit me. "What did you say?" I asked incredulous.

"Mrs White, it's negative. I'm terribly sorry but the test is negative. You aren't pregnant."

"Oh, are you sure? Are you absolutely sure?"

"Look, you asked me to tell you the results. I'm sorry for your disappointment. I can put you through to the doctor if you like."

"No, no, no. I'm shocked, that's all. I was so certain. I'd been told ..." There didn't seem much point talking any further. "Listen, Sally. Thanks a mil. I appreciate your time."

"Would you like to make another appointment?"

"Um, no, that's fine. Thanks again. Bye."

"Bye Mrs. White and ... good luck."

I returned the receiver to the cradle and sat, dumbfounded.

I'm not pregnant!

My mind was spinning, trying to digest the information. I had resigned my job, flown to Brisbane, and uprooted my life to face my responsibility and now I'd suddenly found out that I had been utterly and completely misled.

I'm not pregnant! I even told my mother for God's sake!

I paced the dining room floor.

What have I done? Where am I now? What do I do now?

It was such a shock. Then I remembered my interaction with the doctor when she had first examined me. She had been angry when I had told her that I had no intention of following through with an abortion. It had been rather puzzling. She had treated me as though I was a foolish girl, given me no respect for my intention to face my responsibilities.

That bitch. She must have been in cahoots with some abortion clinic. Maybe she was trying to gain some financial reward. How shocking to take advantage of me like that!

Now I was angry, humiliated ... furious! I could feel that my face was flushed.

What the hell is going to happen next in this crazy life of mine!

I fumbled through my handbag for my address book and looked up Jane's phone number.

◊ ◊ ◊

I held my breath impatiently as I waited, listening to the phone ringing at Jane's house. "Pick up. Pick up, please," I pleaded into the earpiece. No one answered.

Finally, just as I was about to give up, someone answered the phone. It was Jane, breathless. She must have raced to the phone.

"Hello?" she said.

"Jane I'm so glad you picked up. It's me, Megan."

"Oh Megan, hi. It's so good to hear from you. How are you?"

"I don't know how I am to be honest. I needed to talk to you. I got the blood test."

"Oh yes. Good and how'd it go?"

"Negative Jane. It was negative. I'm not pregnant." There was silence at the other end of the phone.

"Phew ..." was all Jane could say eventually. We both stood holding the phone to our ears trying to make sense of this shocking news. "Oh, Megan. I don't know what to say ... It's good news really but, oh God, a shock too."

"Exactly how I feel. I'm not pregnant. Overall, despite the feelings I have right now, I'm incredibly relieved. *I'm not pregnant!*"

"I know. It's good. But ... you told your mum. Who else knows?"

"Well, I haven't told anyone else except you and Mum. But Mum told the family. My brothers think I'm pregnant. Of course they all think it a terrible shame. It's a blow to the family image — me being pregnant with an illegitimate. But I know they would be there for me. But now they don't have to. Fuck!"

Jane was quiet again, taking it in.

"Jane, I can't believe that doctor! What a bitch! Do you think she might have deliberately misled me?"

"I don't know. I don't know. I just know Mum thought it really unusual that they didn't take a test immediately."

"Yeah, and the doctor I saw here didn't hesitate. She didn't even try to give me any sort of physical examination. She just pulled out a needle and took some blood."

"Hmmm, all very strange. But, what are you going to do now? You could come back to Sydney."

"I know Jane. It's crazy isn't it? I've turned my life upside down and now I find out I didn't need to. But seriously, I think this jolt has been a good thing for me. I've realized that it doesn't matter where you are in the world, your problems follow you. It always seems greener on the other side ... until you get there."

"True, true. I wish it wasn't true, but I agree with you ... the grass isn't greener on the other side, it just looks that way because you want it to."

"I'm twenty-four. It's time to settle down and sort things out and stop mucking around. This whole experience has been a huge wake-up call."

"I can imagine. But you could still come back."

"Yeah, I know. But Brisbane is my home. I'm gonna stick it out here and try to make things work." I paused and then groaned, thinking about having to tell Mum that I wasn't pregnant. "Poor Mum. I do feel for her. But I guess overall she'll be relieved too."

"She will and I'm sure she'll forgive you. At least she was willing to be there for you."

"Yeah, she was, even though I know she was deeply disappointed about it all."

"She's a good Mum."

"She is. Oh Jane, what a mess I always seem to get myself into!"

Jane laughed gently, comfortingly. "Don't worry Megan.

We're all good at getting into pickles. The point is what you do about it. I know you'll sort this out."

"Yes, Jane, I will. I don't want any more of this sort of pain and agony in my life. It's time to play by the rules ... time to get back to church, time to get my life right once and for all."

"Have you been yet?"

"Not yet. I've set up a meeting with Kevin though. It's tomorrow. I thought I'd go and see him and tell him I'm back."

"Good idea. I'm sure he'll be pleased."

"Maybe. I don't know about that."

"Oh Megan, of course he will. I know he has a very high regard for you."

"Don't know why he would. I've made such a mess of things along the way."

"Oh, it wasn't that bad. Nothing you can't ... or haven't recovered from."

"Maybe, but I can do a lot better yet. How have you been going?"

"Me? Pretty much the same ... you know me."

"How's your weight?"

"Good. It goes up a bit sometimes but I go back on Weight Watchers and lose it again. I'll never go back to the way I was."

"That's great news!"

It was such a relief to be able to talk about more mundane things for a change. We chatted for a while.

"I better get off the phone. It'll be costing a fortune," I said at last.

"True. Okay, well, I appreciate you letting me know about the blood test Megan."

"I really needed someone to talk to about it. It's all so crazy."

"It's such a relief though. You can get on with your life

now."

"Yeah, you're right. It was such a shock. I have to turn around so much of my thinking and planning … again."

"Promise me one thing …"

"What's that?"

"Don't do that again. Go on the pill or … something."

"Ha ha. Don't worry Jane, it won't be happening again. I can promise you that. I'm getting my life right, no more playing around."

"I hope you do. Thanks again for calling. Bye."

"Bye." I put the phone down gently, feeling calmer.

It was a relief knowing that I wasn't pregnant. I just had the embarrassing job of explaining what had happened to Mum.

Poor Mum.

Chapter Thirty-Five

The church offices had changed a lot since the last time I was here. They looked much more professional, polished. The modern furniture in the foyer area matched the reception desk and looked new. The receptionist was answering the phone every few minutes, needing to constantly refer to a long list of staff members. I don't know how many times I looked up, hearing a door open, only to be disappointed that it wasn't Kevin. It was a busy place.

I looked at my watch. It was ten past four.

Ten minutes late.

I felt a little nervous about seeing Kevin. I wasn't sure what sort of reception I would get. It had been two years since I'd taken off in the middle of the night, fleeing from Ray Klein. It all seemed so stupid now when I looked back on it – getting involved with such an unsavory person. Actually, I had blocked most of it out, but sitting here in the NSC offices was bringing back memories involuntarily.

I picked up a magazine and thumbed through it, trying to focus my mind elsewhere. Surprised to see some familiar faces in the pages, I flicked back to the front cover: 'The Grapevine'.

Wow, the church has its own magazine now.

I think I may have been actually dozing when Kevin finally appeared and called out my name, "Megan, Megan. So good to see you. Come in. Sorry to keep you waiting. Come in."

I jumped up and nearly bumped into Kevin as I did. I took his offered hand and he shook mine firmly, squeezing until it hurt. His presence, as usual, was overpowering and intimidating. I didn't speak, but followed him into his office.

He closed the door behind me and invited me to sit in the lounge area he had on one side of the room. There was a circle of comfortable chairs surrounding a coffee table.

"Would you like a coffee?"

"Um yeah, I guess. That'd be great."

"Just a minute." He moved over to a door, which I assumed led into an adjacent office and spoke to someone on the other side. I couldn't hear what he said, but I gathered he was requesting coffee. It felt strange to be the one being treated to a coffee rather than being the one making the coffee. I tried to relax as I waited for him to come back and sit down.

"Well well, Megan. I have to say you are looking fantastic. I was so surprised and pleased to hear from you. How are you? What's going on? How long are you here for?" Kevin was smiling and seemed genuinely pleased to see me. The creases on his face had deepened since I'd last seen him and perhaps there were a few more grey hairs scattered through his thick mop of black hair. Although I found his presence a little intimidating, I tried to breathe normally and talk calmly.

"I'm pretty well actually. I've been on a bit of a health kick and got fit. I've been running."

"I can see. I can see. Good for you."

"Yeah, it's been fun. Well, I flew back from Sydney a few days ago. I decided to come home."

"Did you?" Kevin's eyes lit up with this news and his

eyebrows hovered expectantly, waiting for me to go on.

"Yeah. I wanted to come home. I've come back wanting to get involved. I want to get committed again. I've had enough of playing around the edges."

"Really? Megan, I can't tell you how excited I am to hear that. So you've come back to Brisbane for good?"

"Yep, for good. It's home and I want to be here now. It's the best place."

"And what do you plan to do? Do you want a job? I'm --"

"No no. I'm not looking for a job. I've already got something lined up. The firm I was working for in Sydney has created an opportunity for me in their office here."

"Well, I can imagine they would want to keep you, a talented girl like you."

There was a knock on the door and we both looked up to see his secretary juggling a tray as she negotiated her way through the door. I didn't recognize her, but couldn't help noticing she was a good deal older than Andrea had been. Kevin didn't get up, but turned back to me and asked, "So what is this job you'll be doing?"

Surprised at his interest, I answered, "Well, I'm working for a software company. I'll be supporting the sales teams in a technical capacity. I've found I'm pretty good with computers."

"Really? Sounds wonderful and very challenging."

Kevin's secretary worked around us to put the coffees on the table. It was a bit awkward for her to squeeze through the furniture, but she laid everything down as unobtrusively as possible. I smiled at her as she worked but Kevin made no move to introduce us. I couldn't help thinking what a different situation this was to when Andrea had worked in this role. Those days were gone now.

I waited until the secretary left the room before continuing. "But Kevin, what I really wanted to talk to you about was …

well ... I want to get involved again. I know I've been away for a while, but I want to immerse myself in church life. I couldn't stand to just be a pew warmer on Sundays. I want to do something. So I thought it a good idea to have a chat with you and let you know."

"Well, this is good news," Kevin said smiling, putting his arms behind his head and kicking his feet out in front as he lay back in his chair.

"Megan, I can't tell you how good it is to have you back. And you want to get involved again. You've made my day. Let me think —"

I leaned forward to pick up my coffee and waited quietly, feeling a little uncomfortable. I wondered whether he would bring up my indiscretion and my relationship with Ray Klein. I had broken the fundamental rule in counselling — getting romantically involved. My mind raced as I stirred my coffee. But how could Kevin accuse me? I knew too much about him and his own inner demons.

He leaned forward to put some sugar in his coffee and stirred the mug, pensive. Finally he said, "How's this for an idea?" He sipped his coffee, leaning back again. "You know that John, John Fieldman, took over the youth group after Andrea?"

"Yes. He was doing a great job. I'd like to work with him again. That'd be excellent."

"Well no, actually, John's moved on. He is now an associate pastor, working for me in the big church."

"Oh," I said, a little deflated.

"But the new youth leader, Tom ... well, to tell you the truth, he's struggling a bit. Do you know him? Tom's John's brother."

"Tom? No, I don't think so."

"Mmmmm, perhaps that's where you could help. Perhaps you could take over the youth group. Well, Tom would stay on as youth leader but you could act as a senior youth leader and provide advice and support. What do you think about that?"

I was shocked and unprepared. I had never considered that Kevin would offer me a role with so much responsibility — after all I'd done and been through. I looked down at my coffee, taking another sip, trying to regain my thoughts.

I wanted to say, *Are you serious? You'd give me that much responsibility again after all that happened?* Instead, I said, "Okay, but how do you think Tom will feel about this?"

"Tom? Oh I'm sure he'd appreciate any help he can get. Perhaps the two of you could get the youth group firing again. It hasn't been quite what it used to be lately." He put his coffee down and leaned forward, his eyes probing mine. "And Megan, you know how much I love the youth group. It's like the soul of the church. It's very important to me, always has been. Always will be."

"Well okay, if you think I can do it, make a difference that is. I'd be happy to give it a go."

"Of course you'll make a difference. It's done then. I'll let Tom know in the next day or so and you can get started."

I sat for a moment staring at Kevin. As usual, he'd made the decision without hesitating, enthusiastically. It was impossible not to propelled along by his energy. "Well, okay. I guess I'll get together with Tom next week sometime. I'll have to find out what's been going on. I'm pretty out of touch."

Kevin nodded, grinning and sipping his coffee. Now that the decision was made, it seemed that his mind was elsewhere.

Feeling uncomfortable, I finished my coffee and fumbled around for my handbag. I felt that I had taken up enough of his time, which was always in high demand. My question answered, it was time to leave. My movement seemed to startle Kevin out of his reverie.

"I guess I better get going."

Kevin was surprised. "No, no. You don't have to rush off. You're my last meeting for the day. No need to go yet." His eyes fixed on me with an intensity that seemed to penetrate my soul, stopping me in my tracks. "You know, Megan, I always enjoyed our chats. I've missed them. There aren't many people I can be myself with, you know. It's a rarity these days."

I put my handbag down again, immobilized by his declaration of absolute trust in me. I didn't know what to say next, so I sat quietly, wishing I hadn't finished my cup of coffee. Kevin was about to talk again when his phone rang, cutting across the atmosphere in the room. It made me jump.

"Excuse me a minute. I'm sorry Megan." Kevin moved to answer the phone. He talked quietly with his back to me and then I heard him say, "Please wait a minute." He turned to me and said apologetically, "I'm so sorry Megan, I have to take this. It's urgent. Let's talk again soon." He turned his head away again and continued his conversation into the phone.

Just like that, our discussion ended. I picked up my bag and left as quietly as possible.

It had gone much better than I anticipated.

◊ ◊ ◊

I could hear the music as I got out of the car. Goose bumps broke out on my arms. The sound triggered memories of my early days in the youth group.

Oh, to be able to reclaim some of that sense of purpose, of destiny, of being part of something so much bigger than my own life.

I locked the car. Smiling, I made my way to the auditorium, feeling the anticipation and excitement glowing like a hot coal in my stomach.

Expecting to be greeted when I came in the door, I stood

alone at the back of room, watching. The band was playing, which was helping to create an atmosphere in the room but the young people gathered seemed not to pay them much attention. Young men and women were standing around talking and laughing. A couple of the guys were playing a chase and tag game amongst the seats. There were fewer people than I expected.

No one noticed as I made my way down the aisle and took a seat towards the back.

Finally someone took the microphone on the small dais. I guessed it was Tom. He looked a little like his brother John, but I judged he was not as tall, nor as handsome. I'd always admired John. It was going to be interesting, getting to know his brother Tom.

He flicked his fingers on the microphone to make sure it was on. Then putting it to his lips, he said, "C'mon guys. It's time to get started. C'mon everyone, take a seat."

No one moved or seemed to notice that he had spoken.

Tom said it again, louder this time, "C'mon everyone, time to start the meeting. Find a seat."

Again, no one responded. Tom turned to the musicians who were still enjoying jamming together and got them to stop playing. That seemed to work. Everyone stopped talking and looked up to see Tom at the microphone. That got them moving and jumping over the seats as they scrambled to find a place.

I couldn't help but feel disappointed that no one had noticed me, a newcomer. The culture in the old youth group had always been to be on the lookout for newcomers. We considered it vital to make people feel welcome, especially if they were new.

Kevin had been right. The youth group wasn't what it used to be. It needed a lot of work.

Chapter Thirty-Six

"You've done well," I said to Tom, looking around his modest office. We were sitting opposite his small desk. He had to be careful with his chair as a filing cabinet had been squeezed in behind him. Stuffed with papers, one of the drawers was partially open. Tom was at risk of banging his head on the corner of the protruding drawer, but he didn't seem to notice.

He smirked and shrugged his shoulders. "I don't know about that."

"Full-time youth pastor, that's a pretty cool job and you've got your own office."

Tom shrugged again, but I could see red creeping up his neck. We sat for a moment in awkward silence. I couldn't help wondering how much influence John had on Tom's appointment.

It seemed we were both waiting for the other to take the lead. Tom fiddled with a pen, twirling it around his fingers.

"Did Kevin talk to you? Did he let you know I was coming to visit?"

Tom scratched the back of his neck with his hand, nervously. "Yeah, he said something. He said you'd be around and could give me a hand."

I nodded, watching. "How's it been going?"

"Good, good," was all he offered.

"What're your plans?"

He laughed a little and turned to a large organizer on the wall to his left. The Saturday column had been marked with 'Youth Meeting'. "We've got our regular meeting on Saturdays. It's pretty well attended."

I squinted at the chart, expecting to see more entries.

"When's your next Youth Committee meeting?"

Tom moved in his chair uncomfortably. "Um, there isn't one scheduled at the moment. We haven't got any decisions to make. I don't like taking up people's time unnecessarily."

"Oh, okay." I watched Tom, trying to read him, but it was difficult. He wasn't giving much away. "Well, how about we schedule one? We can get some new ideas going. I'd like to hear what everyone's involved in, get more of a feel for what's happening."

Tom frowned, nodding his head as he continued to twirl his pen artfully through his fingers. "I guess we can set that up. Could be a bit of fun."

"Who's on the committee?"

"Um, well …"

"You do have a committee, don't you?"

"Yeah, yeah, we do. It hasn't changed since John moved on. I'm not sure that you'd know them though."

"Yeah, you're right. I probably wouldn't know them. Best to meet them face-to-face. Okay, so when will we have a meeting then? This week? Which night is best for you?"

Tom blinked his eyes. "This week?"

"Why not? Might as well get into it."

Tom yielded and opened his diary and flicked through the

pages. "Okay, okay, let's do it. How about next Monday at seven? We can meet in the kitchen at the back of the church hall. How about that?" Tom slammed his diary shut.

"Sounds excellent, Tom. That'd be great. I can meet everyone then. I've got a few ideas we can talk about."

I wasn't sure, but it seemed for an instant a shadow passed across his face before he smiled and stood up, crashing his chair into the filing cabinet. "Next Monday, then." Tom was ready to end this meeting.

"Alright Tom. Look forward to it." I paused a moment, eyeing him before standing as well. I offered him my hand. He took it, but his hand was limp, the shake unenthusiastic. I squeezed tightly in return and grinned without saying anything further.

As I turned to leave I couldn't help feeling excited. Tom needed help, lots of help and I had lots of ideas going around in my head. I was needed and felt confident that I could actually make a difference. The youth group was going to get moving again even if I had to drag Tom along behind. With Kevin's support, I felt I had the upper hand and I intended to play it.

◊ ◊ ◊

"Megan, it's so good to hear from you. It seems like ages. What's happening?" It was wonderful to hear Jane's voice again. Cradling the phone with my chin, I sat down on one of the dining room chairs, looking forward to a good chat.

"Oh, so much is happening, I don't know where to begin." I sipped on my cup of coffee as I thought about where to start.

"Have you been to church?"

"Yep I have, but there's more than that … so much more. I don't know where to begin. Jane, I'm really getting it right this time. Although it was awful at the time, thinking I was pregnant has actually been a good thing for me in the long run. It's got me back on track."

"Really Megan. Well I'm glad you aren't pregnant and hopefully there's no chance that's going to happen again?"

Chuckling at her concern, I said, "Jane, no way. I told you I'm doing it right this time. My eyes are on God. I only have eyes for him. I'm not even thinking about a relationship."

"Good. So tell me about church. How is everyone?" We chatted happily, exchanging names and news. "But Jane, guess what the best bit is?"

"What?"

"I'm involved in the youth group! I went to see Kevin and, can you believe it, he asked me to take over the youth group?"

"Really … you're the youth leader?"

"Well, not exactly. John Fieldman's brother Tom is the youth leader. Did you know him?"

"Um, Tom? No, I don't think so."

"No, me neither. He must have joined after we left. Anyway, John is an assistant pastor in the big church now. So Tom took over the youth group. The youth group wasn't going so well, so Kevin asked me to help out. They were basically meeting on Saturday's at the hall. They've got a nice bunch of kids but they weren't really doing anything. Tom doesn't seem to have much of an idea what do to. He doesn't understand that the kids need to be busy; that he needs to find ways for them to feel involved and important. They were just having a good time."

"That's not such a bad thing …"

"No of course they need to have a good time too. But they also need to be reaching out and spreading the good word, you know; doing stuff. Anyway, we got the Youth Committee together. I think it was a pretty good team when John was the leader. You know, it's weird, but Tom hadn't ever even got them together. Maybe he thought he had to come up with all the ideas himself, silly boy. Anyway, we had a meeting and I shared some of my ideas. The committee was ecstatic. We've got a great social program worked out for the next three months. All sorts of stuff, like we used to do, not just having a youth meeting, which is like church all over again. But the best bit …"

"Yes, I'm waiting, what?"

"We've started up street-witnessing again. We're going to run some training and get a team together and go back out on the streets."

"Well Megan, I can tell you're excited. But street-witnessing was never my thing, you know."

"I know Jane. You were never really into it. It can be a bit scary going up to strangers to talk to them, but it's wonderful to get the youth out there reaching out. There are so many kids out on the street who need help. We can make a difference."

"Yeah, I know. That's great Megan. It is good to hear you so excited about something again."

"I can't sleep, I'm so excited. We've also started up the youth host and hostess team again. It's only a small team but they have to prowl the hall on Sundays to find other young people. They're looking for people coming for the first time. We want to make them feel welcome and invite them along to youth activities. You know how boring church can be at times, especially if you're new —"

"Megan take a breath! I can see that it's all happening up there for you. Man, you're making me feel a bit jealous, like I want to come back too."

"Oh Jane, that would be great. Would you? Would you really come back?"

"Hold on, hold on. You know I love being back in Sydney and being around my family. I guess I am a bit tempted but I know I'd miss my family again. I'd miss Mum too much. But it's great hearing all about it. You do sound happy."

"I am, Jane. I feel like my life is important again. I'm not just pleasing myself and doing whatever I feel like. I'm doing something good."

Jane sighed heavily into the phone. "Good for you. Megan, I'm going to have to go. Mum's waiting to use the phone."

"Oh really? Okay then. I've given you all the good stuff now anyway. I do miss you and would love it if you came back, but I understand. You love your family and you know, you love Sydney too and the way of life there. Have you found somewhere to go to church?"

"No, I'm still looking around. It's hard to find one to match NSC."

"I can imagine. Have you heard from Andrea?"

"Yeah. You know she's in India now, working as a missionary?"

"Yeah. I did hear that, amazing."

"Anyway — have to go. Take care darling. We'll talk again soon."

"Okay. Your turn to ring next time."

"Okay, bye."

"Bye." I hung up the phone a little disappointed it had come to such an abrupt end. But nothing could dampen my spirits these days. Life was looking good.

Chapter Thirty-Seven

Jumping out of the car in a rush hadn't been such a good idea. My ankle twisted as I put my foot down; probably because I was trying to yank my folder and papers off the seat at the same time I opened the door to get out. "Damn!" I quickly looked up to make sure no one heard me swearing.

It was getting a bit difficult at times, juggling all my commitments with the youth group and my new job. I couldn't avoid this meeting. It was critical to get the youth host and hostess team mobilized. Getting them together helped to give them a sense of identity, of being part of a team. It all helped to build enthusiasm.

I was a little out of breath as I rushed into the room. The meeting was already underway.

"So sorry everyone. I got held up at work and couldn't get away," I said, interrupting as I dropped my bag and looked for a seat. The mood seemed a little tense as I sat down.

Tom was sitting forward on his seat twiddling his pen, as usual. He said, "Go on, Jason. You were saying?"

Jason shifted in his seat. He looked at me before starting

again. I hadn't known him for very long, but he had been keen to get involved in the team. He swept his hair out of his eyes as he answered. "Hi Megan. Don't get me wrong, I love what's going on around here. Things are really happening. They're moving and it's great to be a part of it, but --" He paused mid-sentence, waiting for my reaction.

"Well? What's the problem?" I asked. "C'mon Jason. It's okay. If something isn't working, we need to talk about it."

"Well, to be honest, it's the reports. I feel like I'm doing stuff just because I have to write it down on a report. The report seems to be taking over, that's all."

I nodded, thinking, listening, trying to take it in.

"It's a joke really. I mean, this isn't a job. It's not a company. We're a church for goodness sake." Tom jumped in, quick to express his support for Jason's position.

I looked at him a little surprised. "The reports are meant to motivate you to get out there and talk to people. I know it can be hard sometimes to be the one to make the first move. The idea of reporting on what contacts you make is to help give you that little push. Make you go the extra mile." I looked around the group. Most of them had their eyes on the ground. "So you don't think it's working? You don't think the reports are motivating you?"

"Well they are, I guess, in a way," Jason responded slowly. "But Megan, it seems a bit over the top. It seems like it's become all about the reports. I feel guilty about filling out my report, not about who I have or haven't talked to."

"Let's vote to scrap the reports," Tom said.

I jumped in, "Well, I don't know. Let's not rush into this. Apart from the reports, how else is it going? Are you meeting new people?"

Everyone was quiet, looking from me to Tom. No one was smiling.

"Louise, how did you go on Sunday? I saw you talking to

some people. Did you meet anyone new?"

Louise's black curls bobbled as she pulled her head up a little startled. Perhaps she wasn't expecting to be drawn directly into the debate.

"Aaah, I did meet some new people. That is, I didn't know them. But they weren't new to NSC. That happens a lot. You think you're greeting someone new but then they tell you they've been coming for ages. It's a bit embarrassing. You feel like a jackass, actually." Her cheeks glowed red and she shrugged her shoulders looking around the room for some support.

There seemed to be general agreement as others nodded, confirming they had encountered similar problems. Louise had broken the ice. Suddenly everyone started talking at the same time, mostly complaining.

I sat back in my chair feeling a little exasperated. *Why is everyone being so negative?* I looked at Tom. *Was that a smile on his lips?* This wasn't going so well. *Was Tom working against me … deliberately?*

I let the group chat amongst themselves briefly while I collected my thoughts. Finally I decided enough was enough, so I yelled over the top of them to get their attention. "Okay, okay everyone. I hear what you're saying." The room quietened and everyone looked at me. "Does everyone agree that it's worthwhile having a youth host and hostess team?"

"Of course!" Jason was the first to respond and everyone agreed.

"Well that's good! We are in agreement about that. For me, I think it's extremely important for young people that come to NSC to make contact with other young people. Even if they have been coming for a while, why aren't they coming to youth events? Maybe they don't know about them? Maybe they haven't made any friends?" I paused, looking around the group making eye contact with each of them momentarily.

Everyone was nodding in agreement. I had their full attention, so I went on, "Maybe we need to work on some lines. Let's think up some things you can say if someone says they've been coming for a while, but you've never met them before. It's a big place. It's going to happen. Who's got an idea? What would work?"

Louise was quick off the mark. "How about this? How about we ask them where they sit, show them where the youth sit and maybe invite them to come and sit with the youth, or something like that."

"Not bad," said Patty. "Louise, that's a really good idea. I might try that next time. It's true. Where you sit does make a big difference in a big church like this."

Finally everyone was talking and involved. The atmosphere in the room had changed and we were working together … at last. In the end the team was encouraging each other with little help from me.

As the meeting drew to its close, I got up to put on the jug to boil some water. Time for supper.

When I moved over to the kitchenette, Jason brought up the sensitive topic again. "So what about the reports? Do we still have to do them?"

I'm not sure whether he addressed his question directly to Tom because I was partially removed from the group or because he felt he would get the response he wanted. Either way, Tom took the opportunity and jumped in before me. "Nah, forget the reports. Let's just get on with talking to people."

I could feel the prickles on the back on my neck as a flush exploded involuntarily across my face. Opening cupboard doors in search of coffee and sugar was a good camouflage. It kept my back to the group. I didn't know what to do, how to handle Tom's behavior. Whether the reporting regime was right or wrong seemed irrelevant. What was important was the realization that Tom and I were not working together as a team. At least I had a few cupboard doors to slam to relieve some of the tension.

This is getting so frustrating.

I ignored the conversation, mainly because I didn't know how to handle the situation. I needed time to think. Maybe the reports weren't the best approach, but I still felt they provided some motivation.

There was only one course of action I could think of to take and that would have to wait. Tom mightn't like me very much, but directly opposing me in front of the team was taking things too far. It was time to get the big guns involved. I needed to talk to Kevin.

◊ ◊ ◊

Making a private call at work always made me feel uncomfortable. My boss had left his desk momentarily, so I seized the opportunity to make the call. Standing as inconspicuously as possible, I felt a bit of a jerk as I stood at his desk ringing NSC's phone number. I'm sure cupping my hand around the mouthpiece was a waste of time, as everyone could see I was making a personal call. I shielded my mouth anyway, hopefully creating an illusion of privacy.

"Can I speak to Kevin Williams please?"

The woman who answered was polite but curt, "Who's calling please?"

"Megan, Megan White."

"One moment, please."

It seemed an age before she came back on the line. "Are you there?"

"Yes," I said.

"He won't be a moment. Please hold."

"But —" She was gone and I had to stay on the line, even

though I could see my boss coming back to his desk. He smiled at me which made me feel a little better. Finally Kevin came on the line.

"Hello?"

"Hi Kevin. It's me, Megan."

"I know. How's it going?"

"Good and bad. Kevin, I really need to talk to you. I need to make an appointment and come and see you. It's about Tom. Most things are going great, but there are some things that aren't going so well and it's getting a bit harder. I need some advice."

"Oh I see …" I could hear him flicking through his diary. "It's crazy at the moment. I'll be away. We're building the new church, starting up a Bible College in the South Pacific. You know, we're doing so much. There is less and less time for appointments these days. Let me think …" I closed my eyes hoping that he would hurry up. "What about … no, that doesn't work. Um … what can I do? Hmm, what about Friday night?" he asked.

"Friday? We have street witnessing. I'll be out with the team."

"Mmmm Megan. This is very tough. There is a lot going on. Can you get away for a while on Friday? I'll be in town myself that night, anyway. Megan, that's the only opportunity I can see … unless it can wait."

"No, it can't wait, not really. Okay, I guess so. It'll have to do … if that's the only opportunity. I suppose I could get the team started and get away for an hour or so and then get back in time for supper with them. I could probably get away about eight."

"Eight? Okay, yes, that might work. Good then, Friday night. I'll work something out. Ring me Friday and I should know more. I'll know when and where I can meet you. Got to go now, sorry Megan. Someone's waiting. Bye."

Kevin hung up before I could say anything further. It seemed an odd time to meet but I shrugged my shoulders, knowing Kevin's diary was chaotic. He worked through the night most of the time. I chuckled as I remembered how he told the church recently of his decision to wean himself off sleeping. Each night he was sleeping less and less. There was no doubt Kevin was dedicated to building the church in Australia. He gave it absolutely everything he had.

Chapter Thirty-Eight

I kept checking my watch nervously. It was exciting knowing that I would be able to talk to Kevin shortly, but I was also feeling a little anxious about leaving the team unsupervised. It was 7:40. We had arrived later than usual due to confusion around who was traveling in whose car. The teams were paired up and you could feel the anticipation in the air, an excited buzz, as they prepared to move away from our rendezvous point at the fountain in King George Square. Soon they would be looking for young people who might be willing to talk to them.

I went over how the team had been paired off in my mind. It was important to make sure more confident team members were with those more apprehensive. Depending on their confidence, they might just hand out tracts and flyers advertising NSC youth events. The bolder members would strike up conversations with passers-by and invite them to church.

You never knew what would happen. Every night was different. Putting ourselves out like this was both frightening and exhilarating. We had to push ourselves outside our comfort zones in order to reach out to those around us. We were on a mission, a God-directed assignment and the shared vision bound us together like no other church activity. We were on the front line.

I checked my watch again and searched the Square for Tom. Spying him, I moved towards him and caught his arm. He turned, startled.

"Sorry Tom. I just need a minute." I turned to the young man he was talking to saying, "Hi Brian. Sorry, but I need Tom for a minute."

Brian smiled and shrugged. "Okay Megan. No worries."

I pulled Tom away a little so that we had some privacy. For some reason, I felt it would be better if the team didn't know what I was up to.

Tom looked at me like I was acting crazy. "What's up?"

"Um, I've got something urgent I need to attend to for a bit. I'm going to have to leave the Square … just for a little while. You'll be cool to look after things?"

Tom, caught off guard, looked perplexed. "Yeah, sure, I guess." He scratched his head and looked around the Square. "Everyone's pretty much gone out now anyway."

"Yeah, they're all getting into it. I know it's not the best, but it's really important I go and this is the best time to leave. I'll be back before they're due back. Okay?"

Tom's brow was still furrowed, but he nodded. "Yeah, okay I guess. No worries."

I turned and walked away without looking back, trying not to draw any further attention to myself. I checked my watch again, 7:52.

Hell, I need to get moving.

Tom didn't know I was going to meet Kevin.

Why didn't I tell him?

As innocent as it was, for some reason I'd chosen not to

share the exact reason for my departure.

Best he doesn't know. He might ask why and then I'd feel uncomfortable. After all, I am going to talk to Kevin about him.

Kevin had attended a function at the Sheraton Hotel and had organized to meet me in the foyer at 8:00. It was about a ten minute walk to the hotel from King George Square. I accelerated my pace, still feeling uncomfortable about leaving the team. I tried to focus on how I was going to broach the topic of Tom's lack of support. *What exactly am I going to say to Kevin?*

◊ ◊ ◊

I ran up the stairs at Central Station following the signs to the hotel. Then, standing on the escalator which took you into the hotel foyer, I heard notes from a piano floating on the air. The escalator nudged me off as I reached the top. As I took that last step, it was as though I had been transported into another world. A pang of guilt stabbed as I looked around.

What am I doing here?

The foyer was reasonably crowded. Laughter rose and mingled with the piano notes. The atmosphere was charged with Friday-night workers ramping up for a good night out at the end of the week. I paused before moving into the room. Looking down at my t-shirt, casual jeans and gym boots, I could feel a flush creeping up my neck.

What am I doing here?

The contrast between the atmosphere in this foyer and the comradeship and the shared purpose of my team in the Square was acute. Another stab of guilt caught me. I turned on my heel to go back down the escalator. Nearly tripping, I realized I was still standing at the up-escalator. I moved towards the down escalator.

"Megan, Megan. There you are. I've been waiting." Kevin

was heading towards me, calling out. He must have been looking out for me. He saw my hesitation.

He grabbed my arm and directed me firmly. "C'mon. It's too crowded here … and noisy. Let's go somewhere quiet so we can talk. We don't have a lot of time."

"Oh … okay." I let him lead me away, but peered over my shoulder as we moved. The scene was enticing. A woman in a red after-five dress was being handed an elaborate looking cocktail, complete with pineapple and mini umbrella. She was smiling through bright red lipstick.

I'd be smiling too if someone gave me a drink like that.

The sound of the pianist, the laughter and the chatter muted as we moved around the corner to the elevator access point. I sighed, relieved to be removed from a scene that seemed so incongruent with the intention of my evening and my planned meeting with Kevin. Thrown, my mind raced.

What did I want to talk to Kevin about?

To regain my focus, I recalled the scene at the Square which I had just left. I pictured the street witnessing team sitting around the fountain. Gradually my heartbeat stilled a little, my flush ebbed and my breathing returned to almost normal.

"Are you okay?" Kevin said, looking at me quizzically.

"Yeah, I'm fine. I'm fine. Just seemed weird being in there," I said, pointing my finger around the corner.

Kevin laughed. "A bit of an unorthodox place to meet I have to agree. But you wanted to see me and this was our only opportunity. C'mon. Let's go somewhere we can talk." He led me into one of the elevators and selected the 5th floor.

As the doors slid shut a frightening thought suddenly dawned on me. I looked at the floor to hide my expression.

Was it possible? Could it be?

Now I had to be honest. That little voice that I had so carefully suppressed since making these arrangements was now booming in my head. Until now I'd managed to ignore it, pretend it wasn't there.

What are Kevin's intentions here?

"Kevin, I need to go to the bathroom. Is there one around here?"

I needed some space to think, to collect my thoughts. It was now painfully clear that I could well be in a very vulnerable position. I didn't want to believe it. Perhaps I was imagining it. Either way, I needed to be better prepared.

"Sure. Just a minute and I'll show you. Down here."

The doors opened on level 5 and he reached into his pocket and pulled out a hotel room key. "Along here, Megan. There's a bathroom there."

He put the key into the door marked 512. As we walked in he pointed to the bathroom on the left. "In there. I'll put the water on for a coffee."

"Thanks." I shut the bathroom door behind me.

What the hell am I doing here? I'm in a hotel room with Kevin Williams!

I gripped the basin with both hands and stared at myself in the mirror. The nagging doubt that had troubled me since making these arrangements was no longer submersed. It was at the front of my mind. I hadn't let myself consider it remotely possible. I didn't want to believe that in bringing me to this place, Kevin Williams might have some intention other than helping solve my youth group problem. I had not allowed the thought to crystallize until now. But it had been there, lurking in the backwater.

You knew this could happen. That's why you came. You wanted to see, to find out … if things had changed. You wanted to find out what was going on in Kevin William's head.

I cupped my face in my hands, staring at my reflection, pulling at my cheeks until my eyes were bulging.

I'm in a hotel room with Kevin Williams. Maybe I'm imagining things. It could be innocent. Maybe …

I plonked myself on the toilet seat in an effort to silence the internal dialogue.

Nothing's going to happen. You're going out there to talk about Tom. If anything wrong does happen you will leave — but then you will know. You'll know whether Kevin has really ever changed.

Breathing heavily, evenly, deliberately, I worked to calm myself. "Are you okay in there, Megan?" Kevin called through the door.

"Yeah, won't be a minute." I stood up and flushed the toilet, resigned to go through with this.

You took the risk coming here.

I opened the bathroom door and walked into the room, feigning a confidence I didn't feel. Pausing momentarily to search for a place to sit, I moved without hesitating further. There was only one chair in the room. I sat down. Kevin, who had been leaning by the window, moved over and sat on the edge of the bed.

Suppressing my inner voice again, I said, "So, Kevin. Thanks for agreeing to see me. I'm sorry for inconveniencing you and taking some of your free time, but —"

"Megan, that's no problem at all. I'm glad we could organize it. What did you want to talk about?"

It's going well. I was imagining it. Nothing's going to happen. Phew!

"Well, I really need to talk to you about Tom."

Kevin, frowning, interrupted me before I could go on. "Before you start, Megan, I need to tell you that I think you're doing such a great job with the youth. I'm getting great feedback. Things are happening again like they used to. I knew you could do it. I can't tell you how thrilled I am to see it happening."

Blushing, I smiled. "Really? Gee thanks, Kevin. I'm having a go but —"

"You've got the kids out on the street again, reaching out. I can sense the excitement back in the air! I must get along to a youth meeting again. I love the youth. If I had my way, I'd spend all my time with them. They're the salt of the church. You know, they're our future. I can't tell you how important they are to me … to the church and the work of God here. And Megan, you're at the center of it."

It was happening again. This was old familiar territory. Kevin had that way of building me up, encouraging me. He could make me believe things about myself I never would have considered possible.

I sat back in the seat, eyeing him. This reminded me of times at Calvary, memories I'd worked hard to suppress, memories of feeling puffed up, puffed up like a balloon, stretched thin with an artificial confidence. Kevin was a master of flattery.

I shifted uneasily in my seat. Despite my flashback, I had to admit, I was enjoying his admiration. His compliments were gratifying.

"You know, you remind me a lot of Andrea. You share a great deal in common with her." He was watching me carefully, probing.

Unsure how to respond, I looked directly at him. It was hard to believe that he thought I was like Andrea. In spite of all that had happened, I still held her in high regard in so many ways. Those early days in the youth group had been idyllic. Despite the pain and confusion that followed, I still held fond memories of Andrea's leadership. My life had been invigorated, changed forever. I could not imagine myself filling Andrea's shoes nor being able to match her charisma, her leadership, her dedication.

"I don't know about that. But I'm having a go. But what I need —" I stopped mid-sentence. Glancing around the room a little nervously, my eyes had come to rest on a large bouquet of red roses on the sideboard.

Kevin, following my glance stood up a little awkwardly. "Ha ha. Yes, Megan. I forgot about them. These are for you, to show my appreciation for all you've done with the youth group."

I stared at the flowers, my mind racing with my heart again, suspicions threatening panic. Feeling my mouth open, I tried to think of something to say. I needed a diversion.

Before I could speak, Kevin continued, "Andrea liked roses. They were her favorite. I used to get her flowers from time to time, you know … to show my appreciation."

I didn't want to talk about Andrea; not here, not now.

"Wow. That's nice, Kevin. But what I really need to talk to you about is Tom. I don't know if I can keep things going --"

"Hang on. I boiled the water. Do you want a coffee?"

I looked at my watch, 8:45. "Um, Kevin, I don't have much time …"

"Oh, the youth'll be fine. Stop worrying. We need to take this opportunity while we can." He was making coffee, ignoring my concern.

Walk out now. Walk out now.

But I'm not sure. Maybe I'm imagining things, misreading things. I looked at the roses again.

While Kevin poured the water, I moved to the edge of my seat. Like a mouse that hears an unfamiliar sound, waiting, nose twitching, ready to run, I was ready to flee. I wanted to believe the best, believe that Kevin had changed. I wanted to believe in his power and intimacy with God. I wanted to believe the ideal that he preached, the ideal I aspired so much to follow, the ideal I always returned to when life got difficult.

But it seemed as each moment passed as I sat in this hotel room, hope in that ideal was dwindling … yet again.

My inner voice was yelling. *Leave now!*

No, I have to be sure.

Sure of what?

Sure of his intentions.

Kevin stirred the coffee. I couldn't think of what to say, so my eyes followed him as he brought the mugs over to the little coffee table.

"Thanks." I continued to sit in silence, unsure what to do next. My real reason for being here seemed to have slipped out of my mind.

Kevin sat down on the bed. Silence weighed heavily in the room.

"It's good to see you, Megan."

I looked up, sipping my coffee, eyeing him trying to find some words to fill the void. Kevin had kicked off his shoes and pushed himself further onto the bed and was now leaning against the pillows, legs stretched out in front. "It's been a rough day today. There's so much going on." He sighed, digging one hand into his shoulder muscles, working to release some tension. "You wouldn't be able to give me a massage would you?"

My cup poised at my lips, I stared at him, my eyes knife blades penetrating his soul.

There is no doubt now. Leave.

Kevin kept talking. "Andrea used to do that for me sometimes. It would help relieve some of the tension. My muscles get like knots in my shoulders sometimes. It's so painful." He kept working the muscle casually, as though he was talking about the weather.

I did not want to believe what I was seeing and hearing. The cup still at my mouth I continued to sip at my drink in an effort to mask my shock ... my horror ... my disappointment.

Time was suspended. I'd been working so hard, driving myself, extending myself, for what, for whom? Neither of us spoke. All I could hear was the blood pumping through my ears.

Placing my cup on the table I forced myself to stand.

"Kevin, I need to get going. It's getting late. The kids'll be getting back in the Square. I need to go."

Kevin was off the bed in an instant. "No no, I'm sure they'll be fine. You don't have to rush."

My heart skipped a beat.

Will he make me stay here? Surely not.

I backed away from him. "Thanks for making the time. I really appreciate it, but I've got to go. Sorry. It's getting late." Tapping my watch as I spoke, I inched closer to my only escape route, the door.

"Don't go. I don't know when we will get another opportunity."

At the door, I wrenched it open. It was heavy and slow moving. "See ya!"

"Do you want me to —"

Scraping my shoulder on the door as I squeezed through, I waved without waiting to hear what he was going to say. The door slammed heavily behind me. Worried that he would open it again and follow me out, I ran down the hallway. I wanted to get as far away as possible, as quickly as possible.

Chapter Thirty-Nine

I couldn't think. I didn't want to think.

Kevin had hit on me! Kevin Williams was still playing up, still the hypocrite. After all this time, leading and growing this huge church!

I welcomed the cool air as I strode down Ann Street back to the Square. It helped to soothe my flushed face. It was calming to be on the streets of Brisbane again in the open air. The streets were quieter now late night shopping had come to an end.

I tried to filter through my feelings and un-jumble the thoughts speeding through my mind. A memory flickered, flashes of words long buried, broadcast in my mind. It was a conversation I'd had with the wife of one of the men working at Araluen. It came bubbling up, out of my subconscious.

What was her name? Christine, that's right. Her name was Christine.

A vivid recollection of the conversation played out in my mind suddenly. We were walking down the driveway at Araluen on our way to the mess hall. Christine had told me

Kevin had said things to her, had made her feel uncomfortable. She was very suspicious of him. Looking back now, shocked, I realized I hadn't believed her. In fact, I had only half listened to her complaint.

What had she said?

"He freaked me out, Megan. He scared me. There is no doubt in my mind what he was looking for and it wasn't a friendly chat. The way he looked at me ..." She had shivered as she talked. "I've been avoiding him ever since."

I remember she and her husband had left Araluen, returning to New Zealand not long after. I hadn't given it another thought until now.

My head hung and my chin dropped to my chest. Shocked by my memory, I stopped walking. Grasping my chest as a sharp pain caught me unprepared, visions of Stella flashed through my mind.

My good friends, my old friends, Cat and Stella. I hadn't believed them either.

Trying to soothe the pain, I rubbed my chest with one hand. These old memories haunted me, but it was as though a veil had been lifted and I could see things clearly — things I hadn't wanted to see before.

But would anyone believe me?

There had been no witnesses tonight. I couldn't prove anything. Everyone wanted to believe Kevin. They wouldn't want to believe me. Most likely they would be suspicious of me and my intentions. I guess I couldn't blame them for that. My own track record hadn't been the best.

Thinking of the team waiting in the Square, I managed to put one foot in front of the other and push my body into motion. These thoughts had to wait until later. There was a job to do now.

The team was gathering as I approached the fountain. Everyone was busy chatting and comparing stories, sharing their evening's adventures. We would wait until everyone had returned and then head out for supper together. It was a great routine as it gave them a chance to debrief as well as an opportunity to strengthen team bonds.

Tom and I exchanged nods from a distance. All was well. It was a relief to have something to focus my mind, to still the confusion of thoughts competing for my attention.

I feigned interest as the team gathered, yet managed to avoid any direct conversations. Coldness, like a shadow, had settled on my heart and soul. I needed time alone to sift through my confused thoughts. But even as I stood in the Square, in the midst of the team, one emotion prevailed above all others. It couldn't be stilled. As I walked around checking on each team member and acting out the role of leader as I usually did, clarity came about one aspect of my experience with Kevin.

In spite of my shock at his behavior, I had to be honest with myself. I felt special, singled out. Knowing that Kevin was interested in me, though his attention was unsought and unwanted, somehow made me feel empowered, complimented even. His words of praise and admiration still reverberated. I couldn't deny that I had enjoyed hearing such acclaim from such a powerful man. My head was swollen and my confidence inflated.

Am I mad?

It was a relief to pull up at home at the end of the evening. Sitting in the car with the ignition turned off, my ears rang in the silence.

Kevin Williams had tried to get me into bed with him tonight!

I replayed the evening from the moment I had entered the foyer at the hotel, to the point where Kevin had asked me to give him a massage. I had to dispel all possible doubts, to reassure myself I hadn't imagined it.

Grabbing my shoulder bag, I finally got out of the car. The night chill seeped through my clothes. The suburban street was silent and the house in darkness.

Who can I talk to? I need someone I can trust. It was too late in the evening to call Jane.

Tiptoeing up the back stairs, I was taken by surprise to find Michael in the kitchen boiling the water for some coffee.

"G'day. Wasn't expecting to see you."

"Hi Megan. Yeah, we came down to visit Mum. It's easier to stay the night. Lorraine and the kids are asleep downstairs. I've been reading, but needed a cuppa."

"Oh good. I'll have one too. It's been a big night." Sighing, I dropped my bag on the laminated table in the middle of the room and perched on a kitchen stool.

"Sounds a bit ominous. What's going on?"

"Well, you know I'm involved with the youth?"

"Mum said something."

"Yeah, well it's Friday night. We go street-witnessing."

"Oh yeah. How'd it go?"

"Pretty good, I guess. The usual."

"So what's so big about the night then?"

Eyeing him carefully before answering, I leaned over the table resting my chin in my hands.

"You okay?" he asked.

"Well Mick, it's big. I don't know. I'm not sure you really want to hear."

Michael looked at me quizzically, "Say what?"

I sighed deeply. I needed to share the events of the evening with someone. I needed to share the pain and confusion, the burden I was feeling. Michael was here. I trusted him.

He bustled around the kitchen pulling out some mugs, getting the coffee ready. "I'm not sure what you mean, but

Meggie, you can try me, eh?"

Was he the right person to share this with? Was it a coincidence that he was there right now, a ready audience?

Michael was a good brother, like a father in lots of ways. He had tried to support me at Araluen and had a willing ear to listen to my woes. I remembered one time at Araluen when I had fallen from the flying fox. You were supposed to let go when you were over the dam water, but I had lost my grip with wet hands. I'd landed on my elbow on the dirt. What a painful night that had been. I remembered Michael bathing my arm with warm water in the middle of the night, comforting me ... like a dad might have.

Watching him get the coffee ready, I pondered my next move.

His dedication had always impressed me. He still worked at Araluen in the kitchen, but I knew he would be leaving there soon. He had decided to become a full-time pastor. He and Lorraine were waiting for the right opportunity to emerge, a door to open.

The coffee made, Michael, sensing my hesitation, moved beside me and put his arm across my shoulder, tenderly. "Hey Meggie, what is it? What's up?" His concern was touching and encouraging. I sighed again.

"Well ..."

Here goes.

He listened in silence with his eyes downcast, sipping his coffee, as I told him of my rendezvous with Kevin earlier that evening. I could see his brow furrow deeper and deeper and his eyelids blinked with greater and greater frequency as the tale unfolded. But he sat in silence. It was difficult to gauge his reaction.

As the story tumbled out onto the table, I felt some instant relief; the weight pressing on my chest lightened, the problem shared.

As I neared the climax, I stood up and started circling the table in my agitation. It was harder to keep my voice hushed so as not to disturb the sleeping family. Anger was emerging as I recalled the scene in the hotel room — me perched on the only chair and Kevin lying on the bed, shoes off, with his back against the bed head.

"Michael, he wanted me to give him a massage! He actually took me to a hotel room and asked me to give him a massage! Mick, it's crazy, but Kevin is not in the right place. He shouldn't have done that. It's *wrong*! I thought all that stuff was over, but it obviously isn't. He was trying to get me into bed!"

Michael still hadn't said a word, still continued to sip his coffee staring at the table, though his frown had deepened and his face darkened. Finally he looked up and I searched his eyes, looking for his reaction – any reaction rather than this silence.

"Well Megan, I admit it probably wasn't the wisest thing for him to do, to meet you in such a place. But I can't believe that he had the wrong intentions towards you. It doesn't make any sense, no sense at all. It's not possible. Kevin wouldn't do something like that. I know him. I know him really well and I know that he's a straight shooter." He took another swig of his coffee, staring at the table, thinking, his eyelids working overtime, blinking incessantly.

Then he looked up at me before continuing. "I'm convinced that Kevin would never do something like that. There's too much at stake. He's dedicated his life to serving God and building NSC. I can't imagine that he would do anything to compromise the work he has done. It doesn't make any sense."

I nearly fell off the kitchen stool, astonished at his words. I managed to maneuver myself to perch on it again while gripping the edge of the table. Words escaped me.

He looked at the clock above my head, "Heck, it's really late and I think we're getting a bit loud. Don't want to wake the baby, nor Lainy … or Mum for that matter. We've got a big day tomorrow. Hey Megs, you need to get a good night's sleep too. You have to put this out of your mind and get on with it. You're worrying about nothing. I'm positive. Nothing happened, did it?"

I stared at him, unbelieving. Putting his coffee mug on the table, he moved towards me and took my head in his hands, kissing my forehead. It was a loving gesture and I'm sure he meant well, but I felt nothing but exasperation. I watched as he rinsed his mug in the sink and whispered good night before stealing down the stairs as quietly as possible.

He didn't believe me. No one will ever believe me.

Now further confused rather than relieved, I stumbled down the hallway in the dark to my room. There I lay on the bed, staring at the ceiling.

*There is no point telling anyone because they won't believe me. They don't **want** to believe me.*

My eyes wide, my mind wired, sleep was nowhere to be found. The room started to move and swerve. I felt dizzy. I had the most ridiculous sensation that I was on a merry-go-round, going round and round.

I remembered sitting in Andrea's office confronting her about Stella's accusations. I had chosen to believe Andrea, not Stella.

*Why? Because I **wanted** to believe Andrea. Poor Stella.*

I remembered sitting in the classroom at Bible College hearing the news of Kevin and Andrea's relationship two years later. And yet I had never shared Stella's accusations with anyone. Neither had I shared Andrea and Kevin's subsequent denial to those accusations. Those secrets had remained buried.

I'm such a sucker. I'm such a bloody sucker! Why did I protect them?

I'd worked so hard to look beyond Kevin and Andrea and their mistakes. I'd looked to God, the supreme being. I'd tried to focus on him and to use Jesus as my measuring stick rather than the people around me.

But the reality was that, regardless of where my attention was focused, Kevin had been my role model.

It was Kevin that had made NSC what it is today. He was the driving force. It had been both Kevin's and Andrea's sermons that rolled around in my head and inspired so many of the choices in my life.

When faced with my own crisis, thinking that I was pregnant and out of wedlock, it was to Kevin that I had turned. Even then I had wanted to be a part of NSC again.

What a disappointment. What had I been thinking? Why had I been so gullible? Why had I thought that NSC and Kevin Williams could change me?

Kevin obviously hadn't been able to change himself.

I rolled over and closed my eyes, trying to push the thoughts away and still my mind. Sometime, eventually, blackness and sleep crept over me and brought some blessed relief to the never-ending turmoil. There was no way to find an answer no matter which way I tried to look at things.

Chapter Forty

I was unusually late as I strolled towards the church. The service had already started and I could hear John's voice drifting out the windows and doors as he exhorted the congregation to worship. The sound didn't draw me like it usually did. I felt disconnected, removed, an observer. It had been like that since Friday night.

I smiled to myself as one of the youth hostesses jumped to her feet to greet me as I came in the door.

"Hi Patty. Good to see you." I gave her a brief hug and moved on without stopping to chat. The youth were gathered in their usual rows of seats to the right of the platform, but I wasn't drawn to sit with them today. Instead I found a spare seat up the back. We always joked that people who sat in the back seat were rebellious by nature. No doubt we had been right.

My usual excitement at being in church was numbed. There was only a cold ache inside my chest and my head felt light and empty. Thoughts had been swimming around in my mind uncontrolled for days. They seemed unable to find a landing place. It was as though my anchor had been pulled up and I was in a rowboat, without oars, drifting on the surface of the water, subject to the winds and weather.

The congregation was on its feet responding to the music and worship. It seemed a happy place, but as I sat on my seat watching those around me, I wondered how many individuals were really happy. You could never tell what was going on inside people's minds and hearts. But still, they were here. They believed in this place and they believed in Kevin Williams. They wanted to be a part of this work of God.

I sat forward on my seat looking for Kevin but it was too difficult to see through the crowd and I had no desire to stand.

Why is God letting this happen? He must know what is going on inside Kevin's head.

It didn't add up. The contradictions were too frightening. Unanswerable questions swarmed my mind again. At times I felt I was on the threshold of going crazy, stark raving mad.

How do I know that God is real?

Kevin's behavior towards me had been a blatant contradiction to what he preached every day. I sat back in my seat and closed my eyes.

Vivid recollections of Bible College reared up; the sense of excitement and expectation we had all felt when Kevin took a class. We had loved his sessions above all. I could see him now, prowling the front of the lecture room, enigmatic; holding his Bible in one hand as though it was a precious jewel, quoting verse after verse by heart. His piercing, probing eyes, glittered with passion; his love of the Bible and it's teaching contagious, inspiring.

He had encouraged us to explore the answers to difficult questions and wanted deep debate amongst the students. We had wrestled with such questions as: Does God pre-know what choices we will make? Do we really have a free choice or is our life predestined to follow a certain path? What happened to people who never got an opportunity to hear about Jesus? Did they go to hell? If God loves everyone equally, why did he single out the children of Israel – the Jews?

There were many such questions, unanswerable questions.

Sitting here now, I wondered why I had stopped asking them. I had never found any satisfactory answers. Perhaps I'd put them aside because it was easier. It was less complicated to give up wondering about the plethora of confusing contradictions. Whatever the reason, I realized now that at some point I'd stopped thinking about them.

The singing reached a crescendo around me, pulling me back to the present. I opened my eyes. Many of the church members were dancing to the music, if you call jumping up and down on the spot dancing. It wasn't very elegant, but created enthusiasm and a sense of unity. The rows of people swelled in response to the music in a sporadic rhythm.

There was no joy in me today.

As the chorus ended, John moved to a quieter song. The tempo changed. The congregation, well trained, stilled. Normally I would have responded with them. This was the time to focus on God in a personal way, looking inwardly or upwardly. Many of those standing around me swayed gently, almost imperceptibly, subconsciously. The music was soothing, healing.

But it failed to soothe and heal me today. The tirade of thoughts continued to tumble and mill around in my mind.

Had I found the answer to life here?

I thought I had. Good things had come … and bad things.

My mind drifted again to that night, years ago now, when Stella and Cat had come to church. It had been weeks of work and persuasion to get them to agree to come. How ironic it seemed now when Stella, shocked and bewildered, had identified Andrea as "that secretary having an affair with her minister". I had wanted to run to the platform, take the microphone and declare the deception. I had been outraged. It had only been Stella's firm hand on my arm that had restrained me. I wondered now why Stella had stopped me. Had she acted out of wisdom, a sense of knowing that a force like Kevin Williams would be difficult to stop?

Where is my rage now?

The quiet around me drew me back to the present. The singing had stopped. A rumble rolled across the congregation as each person took their seat, fumbling with their things and jostling for room. Alone in my row of seats at the very back, I didn't have to move at all. There was plenty of space.

John had called Kevin to the platform and was handing him the microphone. The service was moving into its next phase. I could see people reaching for their Bibles and a woman in front of me was scratching around in her handbag for a pen.

I chuckled out loud. I couldn't imagine anything that Kevin might say today that I would be remotely interested in writing down. An older gentleman two rows ahead gave me a sideways glance, disapproving. I shrugged and smiled.

Should I race up and grab the microphone and tell everyone that Kevin is a hypocrite?

But even as the words went through my mind, I knew that I would not do that. No one would believe me anyway. Hell, they'd probably *blame* me somehow. That's pretty much what they had done to Andrea ... blamed her, sent her away in disgrace. And here was Kevin still in charge, still spearheading the move of God, as though nothing had ever happened.

I scanned the congregation, guessing there must be around two thousand people. They were all quiet now, listening with expectation. Only the occasional cough or restless child could be heard from time to time.

They all love Kevin. They all want to hear what he has to say. They want to model their lives on the message he is about to bring.

Realizing that Kevin was talking, I tried to tune my ears to hear what he was saying. I could hear his voice but I was unable to take in his words. They drifted by.

I spied Michael and Lorraine not far away. My niece, Claire, was jumping up and down on her mother's lap. Lorraine was having difficulty keeping her quiet.

Michael hadn't believed me.

It didn't seem to matter anymore. I sat back in my seat, lost in my own thoughts yet again.

People believed what they wanted to believe. I'd believed what I wanted to believe. I'd wanted to believe in Kevin and Andrea. I'd admired them and wanted to be like them. How painful it had been to learn that it had all been a ruse; that they had been unable to live the ideals they so forcefully preached.

And yet I'd forgiven them, given them another chance. Had it been worth it?

There was no doubt looking back that I was in a better place today than I had been when I first came to NSC. Believing had worked, for a while anyway. It had improved many aspects of my life, helped me develop some self-control, got me out of the drug scene.

I didn't know what I believed anymore.

Finally Kevin's words managed to pierce my thoughts. I could hear what he was saying. It was a familiar message from the Old Testament. He was telling the story of David who fell in love with another man's wife – Bathsheba. I'd heard him bring this sermon before, but today I was looking at Kevin with different eyes.

The platform had turned into a theater, a theater with one actor — Kevin Williams. It was one of the things I loved about listening to Kevin, his ability to bring characters and stories in the Bible to life. He helped you imagine them as people, living today. He was mimicking David now, helping you to imagine the agony and guilt David experienced in falling in love with another man's wife.

But today I was having trouble entering fully into Kevin's theatrics.

I knew where this story would go. Kevin would take the congregation to a point where they would marvel at God's forgiveness. He would lead them to appreciate the depths of David's sin; how he stooped so low as to orchestrate the death of Bathsheba's husband so he could have her all to himself. Yet through all this, David managed to find peace and forgiveness and the mercy of God.

Kevin would show the congregation how they could be forgiven too, no matter what their sin. No sin is too great to find God's forgiveness.

I sat forward in the chair. I didn't want to hear the end to this story, not today. It suddenly seemed eerily contrived.

Standing up abruptly, my seat flung shut. It made a loud bang and those sitting near me shifted uncomfortably in their chairs, some stealing furtive glances. I didn't care. In fact, I wanted them to look at me. Edging my way to the end of the row, I moved into the aisle.

It was time for a change; time to leave this hypocrisy behind, once and for all.

Reaching the door, I was tempted to look back. I hoped that Kevin was watching me leave, but I knew it would be unlikely. He was in the grip of his performance. I marched confidently out the door.

It was time to find meaning elsewhere in this crazy life. It was time to filter through what I had learned here, to keep the good and leave the bad. This group of people had the right to choose whatever they wanted to believe and so did I.

As I weaved through the streets of West End to find my car,

another thought troubled me. I'd held secrets for such a long time, protected Kevin and Andrea.

Why had I protected their hypocrisy? Why had I kept their secrets? Why had I felt so privileged by Kevin's confidence in me?

Suddenly it struck me like a bolt of lightning.

I had kept their secrets because I wanted to believe in the Christian ideal. I had wanted a better life for myself and believed that Christianity would help me find it. Being a Christian had made me feel special, that I had a unique purpose in life, a reason for existing. The Christian ideal was quite seductive in that way.

I had wanted to embrace the dream Kevin and Andrea espoused even though they were unable to live it themselves. I had protected them to protect my own beliefs.

Crazy! What now? Should I expose him?

I'd found my car and was about to put the key in the lock.

I need more time to think.

At the last minute, I took a detour and walked down to the riverbank, which was only a block from the church. I sat down on the grass. It was a beautiful day. Some boys were out rowing on the river. I could hear the coxswain calling the rhythm across the water.

I remembered coming home from my rendezvous with Kevin last Friday night. I had told Michael what had happened as I tried to come to grips with what it all meant.

Michael hadn't believed me.

As I soaked up the warm sun, it became clear that there wasn't any point telling other people the truth about Kevin. I realized that if I tried to tell someone a truth that threatened to ruin their hope and shatter their faith, they wouldn't believe me. They wouldn't want to hear it. They wouldn't want to lose their lifeline.

I could see now that I had been one of those people. I hadn't heard the truth. I hadn't believed the truth. I'd held on to my lifeline through thick and thin. But now I knew irrevocably that Kevin Williams was a liar and a sham.

I wasn't going to pretend or delude myself anymore.

I lay back on the grass closing my eyes to the sun. I took a few deep breaths, listening to the birds in the nearby trees. My mind stopped going round and round in circles. I wasn't perfect and neither was Kevin, nor Andrea. We were all struggling to get on with our lives the best way we could. I sighed deeply. A peace settled over me.

There was nothing else to think about. It was time to start enjoying life. Time to just get on with it.

Life is a perplexing mystery and that's just the way it is.

It was time to move on to new horizons and leave NSC and the Christian ideal behind, for good.

Epilogue

I wish I could have come to the conclusions Megan made in this story much sooner in reality. The last chapter is a condensed version of what really happened within me over the next ten-year period. Unfortunately, the push and pull of my belief system oscillated for some time before I finally decided to walk away from the church and Christianity. It took me many years, also, to break the spell that seemed to hold me captive, in some obscure manner, to Kevin Williams.

But writing this story helped me further decipher truth and I have come to a deeper understanding of the powers of denial when we embrace our beliefs too passionately. Such passion dis-empowers rational reasoning and critical thinking.

The two characters, Kevin and Andrea, in this book continue their church careers and both hold, to this day, senior roles in large Evangelical churches. I believe they did manage, in the end, to reconcile their behaviors with their beliefs. I wish them well on their journey, but have found it a relief to share the secrets I held for so long, in sometimes rather perplexing circumstances. I've learned that there are times to hold a confidence and there are times when secrets should be shared. This was my time to share them.

I hope you have enjoyed the journey with me and, on some level, been helped to understand yourself and your own belief system better. Take the good, leave the bad and above all, believe in yourself.

One Last Thing

Sign up
If you like my work, sign up at to receive an e-Book free at margottesch.com.au/free-ebook-izzy *Izzy* — a sample of my current major work.

Leave a Review
If you enjoyed this book, I'd be really grateful if you would post a short review on Amazon. Your support makes a difference. I read all the reviews personally, so I can respond to feedback from my readers and write even better books.

Follow my blog
You can read more of my writing by following my blog. I blog about addiction, philosophy and life living on our cattle property at Spring Creek, Australia. Check it out at: margottesch.com.au

Thanks for your support!

Mind Minders ... coming soon

When faced with a crisis, it's the conversations in our head that can make or break us.

Jay has found her real mother, Alice, and, seeing herself in the mirror for the first time in years, is deeply shocked. Her body is deteriorating rapidly due to her drug addiction. Jay faces a further crisis when her speed-addicted partner, Eric, makes a sale to a mother whose toddler is screaming for her mother not to take the drug. With her heart torn with such shame, how can Jay meet her birthmother and find out the mystery of her beginnings with her head held high?

What is happening in Jay's mind as she wrestles with this conflict? The challenging side of her brain is desperate to drive the transformation, but the protective side of her brain is equally enthusiastic to maintain the status quo. Who will win? *Mind Minders* takes a confronting look inside Jay's mind. It exposes the complexities and facets of her nature, but most of all, *Mind Minders* reveals the dynamic power humans always have ... to change.

This manuscript was short-listed (one of three) for the Horizon Publishing Group's Outstanding Literary Awards in 2014.

About the Author

MARGÔT TESCH is an emerging author. *Beyond Belief* is her first major work and she took this opportunity to tell her own story. Her next work, *Mind Minders*, is literary fiction and tackles the difficult topic of addiction in an inspiring work with a unique approach to story-telling. She is currently working on another major project inspired by the idea of mirror neurons. Coming soon.

Margôt is passionate about philosophy and fascinated by religion and the role it plays in humanity … both for good and bad.

Her goal in writing is to challenge her readers, to encourage them to see themselves and the world from new perspectives.

You can read more of Margôt's work at:
http://margottesch.com.au.

www.ingramcontent.com/pod-product-compliance
Lightning Source LLC
Chambersburg PA
CBHW071153300426
44113CB00009B/1193